HAVE YE NO HOMES TO GO TO?

THE HISTORY OF THE IRISH PUB

KEVIN MARTIN taught English and communications and cultural studies for twenty-five years. He is married with two children and lives near Westport, County Mayo. He loves pubs, travel and reading. This is his first book.

For my wife, Maria

HAVE YE NO HOMES TO GO TO?

THE HISTORY OF THE IRISH PUB

Kevin Martin

The Collins Press

FIRST PUBLISHED IN 2016 BY
The Collins Press
West Link Park
Doughcloyne
Wilton
Cork
T12 N5EF
Ireland

© Kevin Martin 2016

Kevin Martin has asserted his moral right to be identified as the
author of this work in accordance with the Irish Copyright and
Related Rights Act 2000.

A CIP record for this book is available from the British Library.

Paperback ISBN: 978-1-84889-275-0
PDF eBook ISBN: 978-1-84889-581-2
EPUB eBook ISBN: 978-1-84889-582-9
Kindle ISBN: 978-1-84889-583-6

Design and typesetting by Patricia Hope
Typeset in Sabon
Printed in Sweden by ScandBook AB

P. 250: 'An Irish Pub Song' is by The Rumjacks, songwriter
Francis McLaughlin, from the album *Gangs of New Holland*.

⚜ CONTENTS ⚜

Introduction:

The Dublin Literary Pub Crawl

For better or worse, the pub has long been a focal point in Irish society. It is synonymous with the country; the proliferation of Irish pubs worldwide is a reflection of its iconic status. Some of the most famous pubs in the country are tourist attractions. A few privileged premises in Dublin also carry the lucrative mantle of 'literary pub'. In *Dublin Pub Life and Lore,* Kevin C. Kearns defines a literary pub as one 'where a significant number of writers and intellectuals congregate on a regular basis to discuss matters of literature as well as every other matter under the sun'. In *An Age of Innocence,* Brian Fallon points out that even though the literary pubs of Dublin only had a lifespan of roughly forty years, from the mid 1930s to the mid 1970s, 'they are as interwoven into the cultural, intellectual and social life of the period as Vienna's coffee-houses are with its golden age, or the classic cafes and bars of Paris are with its great period from the years just before the first World War to the decade after the second'.

The Dublin Literary Pub Crawl is a guided walk through some of the hostelries most associated with Irish men of letters, but is also a walk through Ireland's history, proving (if proof were needed) how inextricably linked the Irish pub is with Irish life. It starts in The Duke, a pub just off Grafton Street, the city's premier shopping street. James Joyce was partial to a drink here, according to Colm Quilligan, the co-founder of the tour. In a darkened upstairs room he begins the nightly tour by telling some Joycean anecdotes. Nora Barnacle, Joyce's eventual wife, was the only one who 'stuck to him'. Joyce, Colm said, had the apparent ability to detect his wife's flatulence: 'I think I would know Nora's farts anywhere. I think I could pick hers out in a roomful of farting women.' After a rendition of 'The Waxies' Dargle', a popular Dublin folk song often sung in pubs, Colm tells the story of The Duke.

Opened in 1882, it became one of the city's busiest pubs when Charles Bianconi, sometimes described as the founder of public transport in Ireland, opened his coach-travel business across the road, taking travellers to every town south of Carlow. Initially trading as The National Hotel and Tavern, it was a popular haunt for those awaiting their transport, who would play bagatelle and billiards. Winners were awarded tokens, exchangeable for drink. The pub was given a makeover in the 1890s and the Victorian façade has since remained largely untouched. From the early twentieth century it became a popular meeting place for writers and political activists, numbering James Joyce, James Stephens, Oliver St John Gogarty and Arthur Griffith among its guests. In the 1940s and 1950s it was frequented by the poet Patrick Kavanagh, his arch-enemy the writer Brendan Behan, and the renowned satirist Flann O'Brien (also known as Myles Na gCopaleen and Brian O'Nolan). It was also a haunt of Michael Collins, leader of the Irish War of Independence (1919–21), who was engaged to Kitty Kiernan, a niece of the then owner. According to Colm, Collins occasionally used the snug to plan actions during the War of Independence. The pub has been owned by Tom Gilligan since 1988 – his name is on the front but, as is common in Ireland, should you ask for Gilligan's you may be met by a blank stare.

The tour moves on to O'Neill's in Suffolk Street, a pub with one of the most impressive snugs in the city. Snugs are a defining feature of many Irish pubs. Their name describes their character: small and separate, a place away from the rest of the pub. These self-contained units, usually to the side of the bar at the main entrances, were traditionally the preserve of women who were not accepted, or did not feel comfortable, in the main bar. They were also frequented by members of the clergy, police, members of the upper classes and the occasional lovers. While many snugs were torn out of pubs across Ireland in the name of modernisation, there are plenty of stunning examples remaining, particularly in Dublin and the other main cities. Typically, snugs have a wooden door with leaded glass above eye level so the occupants cannot be seen from outside. In some of the more salubrious establishments, like Ryan's of Parkgate Street in Dublin, the top section of the door is mirrored to ensure further privacy. In many cases, snugs could even be locked from the inside to keep out unwelcome intruders. Historically, the seating tended to be rudimentary – frequently little more than wooden benches. There was normally a bell to get the attention of the barman, and a hatch through which the drink was served. Over time, snugs became a normalised part of the pub and were frequented by people of all classes. In Britain, it was common for the prices to be higher in the snug, but this did not tend to be the case in Ireland.

O'Neill's is built on the exact location of the Vikings' administrative headquarters in Ireland, the *Thingmote* (from the Norse *thing*, meaning 'people', and *mote*, meaning 'mound'). Here, they sat on top of a 40-foot-high mound and promulgated laws for their newly acquired territory, held sporting contests and may have hosted ritual sacrifices. The *Thingmote* was levelled in 1681 on the orders of the Chief Justice, and the soil was used to raise the level of nearby Nassau Street to prevent flooding. In 1172, the same site was used by King Henry II to meet a group of Irish chiefs in an attempt to bring political stability to the country. The building housing the present-day O'Neill's was the residence of the Earl of Kildare in the early eighteenth century. The section of the pub now running into Church Lane was the location of a printing press in the late eighteenth century. In 1783, *The Press*, a republican newspaper established by Arthur O'Connor – one of the leading supporters of the nationalist Wolfe Tone and his United Irishmen – was printed here. William Butler printed the *Volunteers' Journal*, a paper censured in the British House of Commons for its nationalist views, in the same office in 1792. From 1755, the Coleman family used a part of the building to run a grocery, also selling wine and spirits. It was subsequently leased by the Hogan brothers, and bought by the O'Neill family in 1927. The inside, a labyrinthine warren of nooks and crannies, has long been a popular drinking place for students of nearby Trinity College.

The Old Stand pub, named after a demolished part of the former national rugby ground on Lansdowne Road, is the next venue on the itinerary. Michael Collins also used the snug here to plan activities with members of the Irish Republican Army. Directly across the street is a building that once housed the Burton restaurant. It was to the Burton that Leopold Bloom – the central character in James Joyce's *Ulysses* – first went on 16 June 1904 (now known as Bloomsday), but he was so sickened by the smell of boiling meat and 'men's beery piss' as they sat slopping in their stews and pints that he continued on to the nearby Davy Byrne's. Joyce called Byrne's a 'moral pub' because the proprietor was a teetotaller. Bloom famously stopped here for a Gorgonzola sandwich and a glass of wine:

> Mr Bloom ate his strips of sandwich, fresh clean bread, with relish of disgust pungent mustard, the feety savour of green cheese. Sips of his wine soothed his palate. Not logwood that. Tastes fuller this weather with the chill off. Nice quiet bar. Nice piece of wood in that counter. Nicely planed. Like the way it curves there.

Bloomsday, an annual celebration of the work of James Joyce, takes place every 16 June. On that day in 1904, Leopold Bloom set forth on his fictional adventures around Dublin. Writers Patrick Kavanagh and Flann O'Brien claimed to be the first to hold a celebration of Bloomsday on its fiftieth anniversary in 1954. They went to visit the Martello tower in Sandymount where Joyce lived for a short period, before retiring to Davy Byrne's pub to toast the writer's achievements and read some passages from *Ulysses*. Today it is a much more elaborate affair, with liver and kidneys for breakfast, and readings and re-enactments taking place across the city. However, the cheese and wine is still available in Davy Byrne's.

McDaid's on Harry Street – not on the tour this night – is most associated with 'peasant poet' Patrick Kavanagh and his nemesis, writer Brendan Behan. When Kavanagh joined the staff of *Envoy*, a literary and arts journal established by John Ryan in 1949, his monthly 'Diary' provided a platform from which he could snipe at all those elements of Irish society he so disdained. His many targets included the Catholic Church, the Abbey Theatre, Radio Éireann – the state broadcasting company – and the resident drinkers of the Pearl Bar.

It became the *de facto* office of *Envoy*. John Ryan described McDaid's to Kevin C. Kearns as a most unlikely literary hub: 'McDaid's was a dowdy little pub. Oh, the plainest possible pub. That was one of the things in it I liked. And 90 per cent of the people in it were working class.' Paddy O'Brien, barman and 'stage manager' at McDaid's for thirty-five years, concurred: 'McDaid's was nothing at all. It was a dreadful place. Just an ordinary pub with little snugs and partitions and sawdust and spittoons and you'd have elderly men in little groups spitting and all this sort of filth. And TB was rampant but you had to wash out those spittoons.'

O'Brien encouraged John McDaid to strip out the nooks and crannies and make it into the sparse space it is today. He tried to buy McDaid's when it went up for sale in 1972 but was outbid by a wealthy Englishwoman who had her mind set on owning a literary pub in Dublin. He moved on to Grogan's of South William Street, which came to have a literary and Bohemian atmosphere of its own. Now the work of local artists can be viewed on the walls and bought there.

In *Dead as Doornails*, a memoir of Dublin intellectual life in the 1950s, Anthony Cronin describes McDaid's as more than a literary pub. Its strength, he writes, 'was always in variety; of talent, class, caste and estate. The divisions between writer and non-writer, Bohemian and artist, informer and revolutionary, were never rigorously enforced. The atmosphere could have been described as bohemian-revolutionary.' The democratic nature of the literary pub is also mentioned by Tom Corkery in *Tom Corkery's Dublin*:

> The poet could and did share the same as the peasant and no man had need of looking up to, down or askance at his fellow man. Patrick Kavanagh could be heard discoursing in McDaid's of Harry Street on such esoteric topics as professional boxing, the beauty of Ginger Rogers, or the dire state of Gaelic football in Ulster. Flann O'Brien could be heard in Neary's or the Scotch House on any subject known to man and Brendan Behan could be seen and heard everywhere.

The building now occupied by McDaid's once housed a chapel for the Moravian Church, considered the oldest of all Protestant denominations. Established in the now Czech Republic in 1457, it developed a tradition of standing corpses upright, and it is said this is why there is a high ceiling in the pub and tall, Gothic-style windows with ornate stained glass. Previously the building housed the City Morgue.

Ireland: A Terrible Beauty is perhaps the most iconic photo essay about Ireland. Written by Leon Uris, with photographs by his wife Jill, it purports to tell 'the story of Ireland, the Irish and today's troubles'. Published in 1976 at the height of political unrest, it focused heavily on Northern Ireland. In the short section on Dublin, there is a photograph taken outside McDaid's. Uris mentioned the pub's literary significance and described in a fictional anecdote how it fell on hard times and was put up for sale:

> A Dubliner entered for a last sentimental cup. Strewn about the place were those 'literary' lights who had called it a second home. In various states of decomposition, one was out cold on his face in the bar, another was glassy-eyed with runny nose to match, and yet another, a poet, mumbled his last published work incoherently; the one he had written twenty years ago. Surveying the human wreckage and thinking of the upcoming auctioneer's hammer, the observer opined, 'it appears the ship is deserting the sinking rats'.

Patrick Kavanagh's biographer Antoinette Quinn describes his mien on entering McDaid's: 'When he arrived unaccompanied, he would peer around the door for a couple of seconds, deciding which party to join, then stride in and make for his chosen group, attracting their attention with some general observation made in booming tones or launching into an anecdote.' Kavanagh was loud, argumentative and unconcerned with issues of personal hygiene, according to Quinn. On one occasion when an apprentice barman spilt drink over the unpublished work of a young poet, Kavanagh told him he was 'a useless barman but a fine judge of poetry'. In April 1966 the acclaimed American journalist Jimmy Breslin wrote a profile of Kavanagh for the *New York Herald-Tribune*. He met him in McDaid's, where he was 'hunched over in his rumpled overcoat with his arms folded'. His tie was loose, with the long end thrown over his shoulder, his shoelaces were untied and he was wearing two pairs of spectacles, both 'cockeyed and steamed up'. Breslin found him 'rude and rough and delightful and profane' but was quick to acknowledge, 'in Ireland where the poet is important, Paddy Kavanagh is considered the best today'.

Kavanagh became a sought-out cultural commodity, and McDaid's was besieged by literary tourists. Americans, in particular, came to stare at him and attempt conversation but were frequently given short shrift. Kavanagh ultimately fell out with John McDaid, over a financial misunderstanding. Paddy O'Brien, the barman, was aware Kavanagh's cheques were frequently no more than promissory notes and was wise enough not to attempt to cash them until he heard there was money to meet them. This arrangement continued for a number of years, but came to an abrupt end when John McDaid attempted to cash a bundle of cheques he found behind the till. When they bounced, he called Kavanagh to account. In a fraught meeting, their relationship sundered and McDaid's was forever more without the Monaghan poet.

Honor Tracy, author of *Mind You, I've Said Nothing: Forays in the Irish Republic*, came to Dublin with her partner in the 1950s to meet 'Dublin intellectuals'. They went to

The Palace Bar and reference being joined by 'one of Dublin's major poets, with a thirsty look on his face'. He was glad to depend on their kindness that evening because 'the confidence he felt in certain racehorses turned out to have been misplaced'. It is likely this was Kavanagh, knowing his penchant for betting with his own and others' money. According to Tracy, the poet started a diatribe 'against Ireland and all her works, her passion for mediocrity, her crucifixion of genius'. He lamented the passing of his best years among 'marshmen and Firbolgs' and threatened 'to shake the dust of her off his feet and to seek a living hence-forward in strange places among foreign men'. He did go to England once, but hated it and returned to Dublin, where he stayed for the rest of his life.

In his biography of Brendan Behan, Ulick O'Connor describes the attraction of the Dublin pub:

> Talk is the attraction . . . often brilliant, witty, savage, cruising down corridors of the mind, swelled by the euphoria which the chemistry of personality arouses in the Irish imagination. The weakness of the pub is that it can become an emporium of paralysis for a race whose Latin religion has led them to regard work as a necessary evil, and who are already heavily committed to side-stepping the tyranny of fact.

Some of these men of letters had genuine problems with alcohol, but many went to the pub to escape the lonely literary life. Brendan Behan – the self-styled 'drinker with a writing problem' – was a chronic alcoholic and dead at forty-one. When asked why he went to the pub so often, he replied, 'It is because I am a lonely old bastard.' As Brian Fallon observed:

> Drink was the accepted, quasi-official national outlet, the safety valve of society, as sex and the milder forms of drugs are in our own day . . . an almost essential element in intellectual chat and social interchange . . . not an end in itself . . . the habitual drunkard was regarded as a nuisance and a barrier to good talk . . . he soon faced social and intellectual ostracism.

Terence Browne writes of Patrick Kavanagh, Brendan Behan and Flann O'Brien in *Ireland: A Social and Cultural History* that Dublin pubs in the 1950s were a poor compensation for lack of 'public appreciation of their real artistic ambitions' and of any financial support for 'these unhappy writers'.

The Palace Bar is considered by many to be one of the most beautiful pubs in Dublin. Along with Ryan's of Parkgate Street, it is one of the best preserved Victorian bars in the city. When many of the pubs in Dublin were having their antique interiors stripped out, the owners of The Palace Bar and Ryan's met to discuss the future and mutually agreed not to change their premises. The back of the Palace has a high, vaulted ceiling, supported by Romanesque arches and seen to good advantage on a sunny day. There is also a small snug at the front where Michael Collins is also said to have met with some of his confederates during the War of Independence. It holds only five people and, unusually, can be booked in advance. Until 2006, *The Irish Times* was printed on Fleet Street and the Palace was traditionally a gathering place for members of the fourth estate. It was the hang-out of R. M. Smyllie, then editor of *The Irish Times* and entertainer-in-chief. The corner where Smyllie and his acolytes gathered was termed the 'intensive care unit'. He left the pub for good when cheques he cashed there were returned to him with the pub stamp on the back. The editor of the 'paper of record' was not happy that his bank manager was aware his finances were funnelled through a public house.

There is a large reproduction in the Palace of a drawing that hangs in the National Gallery of a group of literary habitués at a Christmas party in the back bar. It is by New Zealander Alan Reeves and includes Flann O'Brien, Patrick Kavanagh and the poet Austin Clarke. Kavanagh was an admirer of the Palace: 'When I first came to Dublin in 1939 I thought the Palace was the most wonderful temple of art.' Flann O'Brien was a renowned prankster, and the Palace was the scene of one of his best-known stunts. He parked a car without an engine outside the pub. He sat in it and, when challenged by a police officer, claimed he could not be prosecuted for propelling a mechanical vehicle. O'Brien did not find every pub as attractive as the Palace, however: 'No Irishman could feel at home in a pub unless he was sitting in a deep gloom on a hard seat with a very sad expression, listening to the drone of bluebottle squadrons carrying out a raid on the yellow sandwich cheese.'

Many of the pubs these men frequented are now tourist attractions. James Joyce's *Dubliners* and *Ulysses* brought Dublin pubs to the attention of literary scholars and tourists alike before the men of the 1950s did, however. Oliver St John Gogarty – whose name now adorns one of the most frenetic tourist bars in Dublin – had mocked this possibility:

I should hate to have my pubs stalked by German professors who take pub-crawling seriously. The moment our pubs become the subject of literature, that is the moment they are undone. Even we who patronise them would become self-conscious. The last thing drink should do is to make one self-conscious. We would become actors, as it were, in a play, and not patrons of our own pubs.

On the Dublin Literary Pub Crawl, groups of tourists wander from pub to pub on a nightly basis absorbing a vanished world. It is a lucrative business for the tour owners and guides. However, long before any pub in Ireland was an attraction for foreign visitors, they were part of the native culture. The central role of pubs in Irish society and identity is the substance this book.

High Kings, Saints and Alewives:
The Pub in Ireland from the 6th to the 17th Century

After a dispute had rumbled on for many years, the owners of Sean's Bar in Athlone, County Westmeath, and The Brazen Head in Dublin agreed to go on national radio to decide which of their establishments should be recognised as the oldest pub in Ireland. The late DJ Gerry Ryan hosted the debate. The owner of Sean's Bar provided evidence – verified by archaeologists and historians from the National Museum – that strongly suggested the presence of a retail premises on the site dating back to AD 900. During renovations in 1970 the walls, part of which are now on display at the National Museum, were found to be made of wattle and daub. The builders also found coins dating from the period, minted by local landlords and probably used as beer tokens. The owners highlighted written evidence of a rest stop for pilgrims on their way to nearby Clonmacnoise. The Brazen Head had no answers and graciously admitted defeat. They may have taken some small consolation when a signature etched on one of their windows was confirmed to be from 1726 and was awarded the title of the oldest piece of graffiti in the country. The writing – in a whorl on a bottle-glass pane – is so small it cannot be read with the naked eye, but with the aid of a magnifying glass it is possible to decipher the spidery writing: 'John Langan halted here 7th August 1726.' The Brazen Head dates itself to AD 1198 but it is likely that the pub appropriated the name from a nearby building called The Brazen Lady and was established in the sixteenth or early seventeenth century. The oldest documentation provided by the owners was a court certificate of ownership from 1613 proving the pub belonged to Richard and Eleanor Fagan. They also furnished a legal document from 1703, which stated 'all that large timber house called The Brazen Head containing 35 feet 6 inches in front, 49 feet in rear and 168 feet in depth with all outhouses, stables and yards' was granted to James King in a claim against the estate of the Fagan family following a period of political upheaval.

However, ancient Irish history provides evidence of pub-like facilities a good 300 years before Sean's Bar came along, and not alone were these proto-pubs good social outlets, but the food and drink were free. In ancient Ireland, a man was reckoned rich not by what he owned but by what he gave, and the right hand of the generous man was said to be longer than the left. Under Brehon Law – first codified in the sixth and seventh centuries – each local king was required to have his own *bruigu* (also sometimes spelled *brughaid*), or brewer. A *bruigu* was obliged to have 'a never-dry cauldron, a dwelling on a public road and a welcome to every face'. He had to provide hospitality to all comers in his *bruidean* (usually translated as hostel). This was like a super-gastropub, with free lodgings, entertainment, food and drink. The *bruigu* was effectively the owner-occupier of the king's public house and kept his job for life as long as he obeyed all the laws. The book of Brehon Law stated: 'He is no *bruigu* who is not possessed of hundreds. He warns off no individual of whatever shape. He refuses not any company. He keeps no account against a person, though often he comes.'

There were two categories of *bruigu*: A '*bruigu ceadach*' and a '*bruigu leitech*'. The *bruigu ceadach* had 100 animals and 100 servants. Some of the more powerful leaders had *bruigu leitech*, who owned 200 of each. The *bruidean* of the *bruigu leitech* had to be located at the crossing of six roads. High King of Ireland Conaire Mór's *bruidean* was particularly impressive. Located under the Dublin mountains, it had seven doors, and a great fire was lit each night: 'When a tree was drawn from its side, each spurt of flame issuing from each outlet was the size of an oratory on fire.' Conaire Mór and his *bruidean* were ultimately destroyed by his enemies in a fire. The King cut a dashing figure when he went to the *bruidean*, if the Saxon chief Ingcel is to be believed. He described King Conaire when he went to meet him in his poem 'Togail Bruidne Da Derga':

I saw his many-hued red cloak of lustrous silk,
With its gorgeous ornamentation of precious gold
bespangled upon its surface,
With its flowing capes dexterously embroidered.

I saw in it a great large brooch,
The long pin was of pure gold;
Bright shining like a full moon
Was its ring, all around – a crimson gemmed circlet
Of round sparkling pebbles –
Filling the fine front of his noble breast
Atwixt his well proportioned fair shoulders.
I saw his splendid linen kilt,
With its striped silken borders –
A face-reflecting mirror of various hues,
The coveted of the eyes of many –
Embracing his noble neck – enriching its beauty.
An embroidery of gold upon the lustrous silk –
Extended from his bosom to his noble knees.

Owning a *bruidean* was a high honour, but it was also potentially ruinous. In 'The Tale of Mac Dathó's Pig', a feast was due to take place at Mac Dathó's *bruidean*, one of the five great *bruidean*s of ancient Ireland. The building had 'seven entrances, seven cauldrons full of beef and salted pork, and seven hearths; and fifty paces between each pair of doorways', but eventually proved to be a millstone around his neck. Under Brehon Law, if a nobleman had no hospitality available, a Bard – one type of ancient Irish poet – could be commissioned to write a satire impugning his integrity and berating him for his meanness. *Enech ruacha,* or 'blush fines', were thus levied. Embarrassment in front of peers and subjects and loss of face were severe sanctions under Brehon Law.

Blaí Briugu, a *bruidean* owner in the Ulster Cycle of Irish mythology, had a particularly onerous position. He had an obligation to sleep with any single woman who came looking for hospitality. When a young lady called Brig Bretach visited his premises, he performed his duties, but she turned out to be married, and Blaí Briugu was murdered by her husband Celtchar for his troubles. Breas, one of the ancient kings of Ireland, lost his title because of his lack of hospitality: 'Breas did not grease their knives. In vain they came to visit Breas. Their breath did not smell of ale at the banquet.' His position became untenable after the poet Cairbhe wrote a scathing satire – believed to be the first written in ancient Irish – after a visit he made to Breas. Expecting a feast, he was put in the dungeon instead and given three small stale cakes of bread to eat. He languished there for seven years. Breas had ignored the very first rule laid down in the *Crith Gablach*, the Brehon Law text that outlined the duties of a king: 'Sunday, at ale drinking, for he is not a lawful lord who does not distribute ale every Sunday; Monday, at legislation, for the government of the tribe; Tuesday, at chess; Wednesday, seeing greyhounds coursing; Thursday, at the pleasures of love; Friday, at horse-racing; Saturday, at judgement.'

The *bruidean* had to be located at a crossroads; have four doors, one on each of the approaching routes; have torch-bearing greeters on a lawn outside so nobody would pass by unwelcomed; and stay open twenty-four hours a day. There were strict rules on provisions: the *bruigu* had to stock three uncooked red meats, butchered and ready to cook; three stewed meats, cooked and kept heated; and three types of live animals, ready to slaughter at short notice. The *bruigu* was also required to keep three sacks at hand at all times, containing malt to brew ale, wheat to make bread and salt to enhance the flavour of the food. Three different cheering sounds had to be heard in the *bruidean* simultaneously: the cheers of the ale-makers going happily about their work, the cheers of the servers bringing alcohol from the cauldron, and the cheers of young men playing chess.

If the *bruigu* fulfilled and maintained these conditions, his job attracted a number of perks. He was allowed to have as many servants as the king, was given a tract of land, held a magistrate's licence and arbitrated land disputes, hosted political meetings and elections, sat beside the king at any feast or celebration, and was entitled to the next best cut of meat after the king. No duelling could take place on his lands, and he was exempt from military service. It was a path to great wealth for a person of non-noble lineage. Only harpists and poets could rise above their station in a similar fashion.

Irish monks were skilled brewers who had originally brought their skills back from trips to the 'Fertile Crescent' of Mesopotamia – modern-day Iraq, Turkey, Iran, Syria and Kuwait. They too served alcohol with food to passing travellers, and kept their own thirsts slaked. Cistercian monks at Jerpoint Abbey in County Kilkenny, for example, were allowed to drink a gallon of ale per day, but other religious orders were not so lucky. Under Brehon Law, a commoner was allowed six pints a day, but monks had to be happy with three. St Columbanus, a sixth-century Irish missionary priest high in the firmament of Irish religious figures, had a fervent last wish: 'It is my design to die in the brew-house; let ale be placed to my mouth when I am expiring.' This did not happen, but he did have the useful ability to change water into beer. His dying wish was simple: 'When the choirs of angels come, they may say, "Be God propitious to this drinker."' He once reputedly turned enough water into beer to satisfy sixty thirsty pilgrims at a monastery in Fontaines, France. He could apparently reverse the process, too. It is claimed he once turned a cauldron of beer into water by blowing on it at a pagan festival in Bobbio, Italy, after taking exception to a group worshipping Woden, a god in Germanic mythology identified with the Roman god Mercury.

St Brigit, one of the most revered Irish saints, was a similarly gifted ale brewer, and once came to the assistance of a thirsty party of lepers. When they came looking for beer, her supplies were exhausted, but she noticed water being prepared for baths nearby. She commandeered it, blessed it and transformed it into beer. An eleventh-century poem attributed to her, 'Saint Brigit's Ale Feast', describes a true beer lover:

> I'd like to give a lake of beer to God.
> I'd love the heavenly
> Host to be tippling there
> For all eternity.
> I'd love the men of Heaven to live with me,
> To dance and sing.
> If they wanted, I'd put at their disposal
> Vats of suffering.
> I'd sit with the men, the women and God
> There by the lake of beer.
> We'd be drinking good health forever
> And every drop would be a prayer.

St Patrick, patron saint of Ireland, reputedly had his own brewer and personal confessor, Mescan. It is said that St Patrick once met a king on his travels through Connacht who appeared to him 'sadly in liquor'. St Patrick was not impressed with this lack of respect, and put a curse on the king and all his descendants. They would, according to the curse, all come to a bad end as a result of alcohol. Sadly, this prophecy is said to have come to pass. St Patrick's own beer is said to have been very sweet, having hints of bog myrtle and heather, with a low alcohol content. Monks were often expert herbalists, and Mescan was known for the addition of gentian to his ale. There is now a microbrewery of the same name in the shadow of Croagh Patrick in County Mayo, where the saint reputedly spent forty days and forty nights.

The word 'tavern' – originally from the Latin *taberna,* meaning hut – was first used when the Normans occupied parts of Ireland in the twelfth century. The Normans were wine lovers and imported the best wines from their homeland. At first, the alcohol was managed by wine merchants, or vintners, and delivered to the cellars of the castles of the Norman lords, who largely resided inside the Pale, an area surrounding greater Dublin, the boundary of which regularly shifted. Occasionally, they held wine-tasting events when new stock was imported, and over time began to sell the surplus at the point of storage. These taverns became meeting places for important members of society where alcohol and food were served and issues of the day discussed. Dublin's Winetavern Street, referred to as *vicus tabernariorum vini* in Latin – 'the street of the wine taverners' – was the main centre of distribution and retail. In 1979, while excavating the controversial Wood Quay site nearby, archaeologists found over 2,000 pewter tavern tokens dumped in a refuse pit. Used when currency was in short supply, they were rendered obsolete when the round farthing was introduced by King Edward I in 1279. Known as 'Edward the Longshanks' due to his great height and size, the King was thorough in his elimination of the tokens, and the silver farthing, originally only intended to pay taxes to the English, soon dominated.

In 1192, Dublin's Royal Charter set out a plan to protect indigenous trade and regularise customs duty, stating: 'No foreign merchant shall have a wine tavern, unless on ship board, liberty being reserved to John, that, out of every ship arriving with wines in Dublin, his bailiff in his place may select two butts of wine, one before and one behind the mast, for John's use, at 40 shillings.' The John referred to was the son of Henry II, of England. The 'foreigners' were the native Irish.

Ale continued to be brewed during Norman times, a job normally carried out at home by women known as 'alewives'. It was largely a drink of the lower classes; it was much cheaper to produce than wine, and usually sold in alehouses, which were often nothing more than a simple room attached to the residence of the manufacturer. The profit margin was slight after oats and barley were paid for. When fresh ale was ready, the woman of the house raised a stick or a flag – sometimes referred to as 'an ale wand' – over her door to alert potential customers. It was important to sell it immediately as it spoiled quickly. The local alehouse became the local meeting place, an antecedent of the local pub. Many alewives were actually widows, and it was also a common occupation for young and unmarried women. In 1455, female ale brewers were explicitly warned by decree not to adulterate the brewing process by adding straw. If a woman was found guilty of selling substandard merchandise, she was fined, and if she reoffended her operation could be closed down and she could be flogged. 'The Alewives' Invitation to Married Men and Bachelors', a popular nineteenth-century ballad, may be a clue to some of the goings-on in the alehouses:

> Therefore take my Counsel, and Alewives don't
> trust,
> For when you have wasted and spent all you have,
> Then out of Doors she will you headlong Thrust,
> Calling you Rascal and shirking Knave.
> But so long as you have money, come early or late,
> You shall have her at command, or else her maid
> Kate.

British soldier and writer Barnaby Rich was not impressed by the alehouses when he visited Dublin in 1610: 'There is no merchandise so vendable. It is the very marrow of the commonwealth in Dublin. The whole profit of the towne stands upon alehouses and the selling of ale. There are whole streets of taverns and it is a rare thing to find a street in Dublin without a tavern, as it is to find a tavern without a strumpet.' In *A New Description of Irelande*, Rich made it clear that he was a fan of neither the Irish nor alcohol. 'The Uncivility Both of Manners and Conditions Used by the Irish', an early chapter heading, gives fair warning of his coming fulminations. He was disgusted when he discovered the only commodity on sale at the festival of St James on 25 July was ale, and despised the 'multitude of rascal people . . . installing themselves in some brothel booth . . . drunk all the day after.' He abhorred drinking at holy wells. Sundays were a particular affront, when 'every filthy alehouse' was full of people 'drunkening and quaffing and sometimes defiling themselves with more abominable practices'. Rich reserved his most virulent bile for the alewives: 'the most filthy Queens in the country . . . filthy and beastly alehouse keepers . . . idle housewives that are very loathsome, filthy and abominable, both in life and manners . . . some of them known Harlots.' He also railed against the quality of their produce. He had been so long among these 'filthy alehouse[s]', he wrote, his head had started 'to grow idle'. He was not surprised because 'the very remembrance of that hog's wash is able to distemper any man's brains, and as it is neither good nor wholesome, so it is unfit for any man's drinking but for common drunkards'. Rich completed his tirade against these medieval breweries by calling them 'nurseries of drunkenness, of all manner of idleness, of whore-dom, and many other vile abominations.'

In 1612, Fynes Moryson, travel writer and explorer, was not enamoured of the Irish when he travelled around the country. He wrote: 'For howsoever while they lived in woods and cabins with their cattle, they could be content with water and milk, yet when they came to townes nothing was more frequent than to tie their cows at the doors and never part from the taverns until they had drunk them out of sack and strong water, which they call usquebaugh, and this did not only the lords, but the common people, half naked for want of clothes to cover them.' He had been to feasts where he was shocked by the behaviour of the women. He noticed an unsettling practice among them – public urination. He saw 'the wives of Irish lords void urine in full assemblies of men', a sight he had seen only once previously, in Bohemia. The Irish, according to Moryson, were afflicted by 'four vile beasts: lice, rats, priests, and wolves'. Despite his reservations about the Irish people, he believed the whiskey in Ireland to be superior to all other countries he had visited.

The *Great Parchment Book of Waterford: Liber Antiquissimus Civitatis Waterfordiae* contains records of the city from 1356 to 1649. Written in a mixture of Norman French, Latin and English, it includes a passage on the 'abhomynable trade of horedom' most associated with female servants in taverns. Certain landlords, it claimed, retained 'nawghtie corrupte women by whose procurement and meanes other honest damsels are often drawn to folly'. This was perceived to be such a problem that local legislation was enacted to ensure 'never more shall any woman, maid, wife, wench or wyddowe, be wyne taverner or wyne drawer in any place within the cittie or suburbs upon payne of five powndes in money may be levied of his goodes and cattell'. Two years later, the legislation was strengthened. If the previous 'holsome remedy' was not solution enough and any taverner failed to dismiss a servant 'suspected to play the whoore', they could be heavily fined. In 1604, a further law was enacted. Now no woman of any 'qualitie or degree' could retail drink within the city. This time the justification was not just to avoid 'whordom', but also to avoid 'conseal-ment of goods stollen' and 'for strengthning of the Cittie'. From then on, no women were allowed to work in pubs in Waterford city.

In 2003, Tom Maher, proprietor of the Moondharrig House, O'Connell Street, Waterford, died at the age of ninety-two. For seventy-seven years, he ran a 'men only' pub, and despite pressure from feminist groups, no woman was ever served at his counter. He was said to be the longest-serving publican in the country at the time of his death. When asked why he never served women, he replied that 'weak women, strong drink . . . long hours and short skirts are a bad combination'. He opened the pub whenever he felt like it and refused to work any more than forty hours a week. He closed every night at 10 p.m. Maher summed up his business ethos: 'I don't want to see my customer too early, too late or too often.' In 2003, under an amendment to employment equality legislation, it became illegal to refuse women entry to a pub.

Clean Cocks and Fresh Newspaper:
*The Development and Regulation of the Irish
Pub from the 17th to the 20th Century*

The early history of alcohol-related law in Ireland is largely one of rejection, subterfuge, confusion and contradiction. Much of it was labyrinthine and completely ignored. However, there have been points in the evolution of the law that can better help an understanding of the development of the pub in Irish society. This chapter, then, is not a complete account of all the legislation, but an analysis of the more important changes.

In 1613, the Register of Patents and Inventions recorded the first Elizabethan licences issued for Irish taverns. Seven licences were issued that year, while only one was granted in 1614. In 1616, a further seven licences were allowed. In reality, there was little control, and illegal outlets were rampant. In 1633, the Lord Deputy, Thomas Stafford, Earl of Wentworth, complained to Archbishop Laud of London about the use of the crypt in Christ Church Cathedral as a place of sale for alcohol and tobacco. The first law against the establishment of new unlicensed premises was enacted in 1635, and it was damning of those already in existence:

> Many mischiefes and inconveniences doe arise from the excessive number of alehouses, from the erection of them in woods, bogges, and other unfit places, many of them not in towne-ships, but dispersedly in dangerous places and kept by unknown persons not undertaken for, whereby many times they have become receptacles for rebels and other malefactors and harbours of gamesters and other idle, disordered and unprofitable livers, and that those who keep those alehouses for the most part are not fitted or furnished to lodge or entertain travelers in any decent manner.

The housing of 'rebels' and 'malingerers' runs through accounts of pubs in every report by British authorities for the next 260-odd years. Pubs were consistently perceived as hotbeds of political intrigue and incubators for revolutionaries and criminals. The new legislation of 1635 was ambitious. If an individual wanted to establish a public house from then on, he would have to provide 'two beds for strangers' and 'sell provisions to travellers at reasonable prices'. There could be no drunkenness, gambling or unlawful games, and it would be illegal to 'harbour improper persons'. The authorities now had a financial interest in regulating the market. In 1635, there were 1,119 taverns in Dublin alone. In Ballymote,

County Sligo, twenty-seven houses out of a total of 200 had a licence to sell alcohol, while in nearby Gurteen, six of the fifteen houses in the village were pubs. By 1667, there were 1,500 licensed premises in Dublin. The act was spectacularly unsuccessful; illegal drinking establishments continued to multiply. In 1685, the Lord's Day Act allowed policemen to enter pubs for the first time, and from then on licences were supposed to be renewed annually. It also prohibited Sunday trading during the hours of worship, a perennial subject of debate in the British Houses of Parliament over the next 250 years. From 1689, public houses were legally obliged to provide hospitality and accommodation for soldiers and their horses. In the same year, King Charles II incorporated the brewers of Dublin in an attempt to curtail home production of ale and beer: 'There are in or about our city of Dublin and the suburbs, liberties and two miles of the same, very many persons of the trade or mystery of brewers who might be better ordered and governed, and ale and beer to sell may be better and wholesome boiled and brewed, if the said persons of the said trade or mystery of brewing were incorporated.' This attempt at regulation failed miserably, too.

In 1691, William Petty, father of laissez-faire economics, published *Political Anatomy of Ireland*. He was asked by King Charles II and Oliver Cromwell to analyse the economic structures in Ireland and recommend how the country might be better organised. There were far too many public houses, he argued: 'It is manifest that two thirds of the alehouses may be spared even though the same quantity of drink should be sold.' He estimated 120,000 too many people were working in the drinks industry, and these 'spare hands' could be better employed elsewhere.

Neither brewers nor publicans declined in number. The early eighteenth century was the heyday of the notorious gin palaces. King William of Orange, after his victory at the Battle of the Boyne in 1690, banned the importation of French brandy, and promoted the use of his own favourite drink: gin. The restrictions on distillation were light, and gin shops multiplied, particularly in London and Dublin. The effect on the urban poor was horrendous. William Hogarth famously depicted *Beer Street* and *Gin Lane* in two prints designed to support the Gin Act of 1751. The beer drinkers were jolly and healthy; the gin drinkers were filthy and drunken. *Gin Lane* shows scenes of infanticide, starvation, madness, decay and suicide, while *Beer Street* depicts industry, health, bonhomie and thriving commerce. In *Gin Lane,* a mother in a drunken stupor is shown dropping her baby on its head. The Gin Acts of 1736, 1743 and 1751 increased the excise significantly, and allowed only licensed premises to sell spirits. Many of the former gin shops became public houses and began to sell ale too. Alehouses and taverns gradually came to be called public houses, a term first used in Britain to distinguish private drinking clubs from those that were open to the wider public.

The widespread practice of allowing drink 'on the slate' was addressed in the Drink on Credit to Servants Act of 1735. It also attempted to stop workers being paid by chit, which could be cashed in a pub. It, too, was totally ignored. The year 1753 saw the introduction of a ban on home distilling of spirits in an attempt to limit illegal drinking establishments. Of all the legislation enacted before Ireland became an independent state, this was perhaps the most ignored of all. It became illegal to marry in a pub at this time, too. The development of stagecoach travel was a boon to the trade, and many coaching inns where it was possible to get food and lodgings, sprang up. In 1789, the establishment of mail-coach lines and a national postal service further advanced the trade. The mid nineteenth century saw the development of the rail network, allowing greater movement of goods and people, and stimulating a further expansion of the licensed trade. Many of the inns were rudimentary, and did not always meet with visitors' expectations. Edward Wakefield, British philanthropist and statistician, travelled through Ireland in 1810 and recorded his opinions in *An Account of Ireland, Statistical and Political.* Ireland did not fare well in comparison to England. The buildings were inferior, and the innkeepers unwelcoming and rude. Ireland was not the only country with poor standards, however: 'In an Irish inn, the eye, as in France or Spain, is everywhere disgusted with filthy objects. The olfactory nerves are also affected by the noxious effluvia arising from the same cause.' If there was a waiter present, he was likely to be so ridiculous in appearance he would form an excellent subject for 'eminent caricaturists'. A typical waiter's hair hung down in a pigtail, which he never combed or washed, and 'his hands, perhaps, have not been washed for a month, though water is far from being scarce in the country'. He never saw a waiter with a clean shirt or clean shoes. Things were much different in England, where 'neat country girls' saw to the needs of the customers. Wakefield further pointed out that his descriptions were of 'the first-rate inns in Ireland', and that he could only imagine the state of lesser ones. He was particularly unimpressed by an establishment in Ballyragget in County Kilkenny, where he saw 'a wretched hovel pompously denominated on a painted board "The Hotel", the title given to all the principal inns in Ireland.' He was equally affronted by the prices: 'The landlords seem to be thoroughly acquainted with one aspect of the business, for if their gain be small they take care to make up the deficiency by heavy contributions on their customers. The charges in these houses are enormous; equal to those in the first taverns in London; and the perquisites which the waiters, chambermaids, waiters and ostlers expect . . . greater than those ever given in England.' He was happy, however, to recommend the hospitality available in the houses of some 'gentlemen' he stayed with, and noted that, 'respectable persons may travel from one end of Ireland to the other without putting their feet within the threshold of an inn'.

The early nineteenth century saw a huge increase in the number of licence holders. The brewing industry was booming, long since displacing the humble alewife. Breweries frequently supplied credit to new licencees. In 1818, the Fair Trading Vintners' Society was established in Dublin, partly to assist the huge numbers of new publicans who had entered the market and become financially distressed. In his introduction to the first handbook published by this body in 1825, secretary William Phipps noted, 'great improvements have been made of late years in the metropolis, cities and large towns in Ireland'. Pubs were cleaner, had a more respectable appearance and were commonly patronised by the 'humblest in society as well as the middle and wealthier classes'. Most public houses now had spacious and comfortable rooms for the well heeled, and 'a common tap-room, for the lower classes'. Phipps was both critical of and sympathetic to many of the publicans who had entered the trade in recent times. Many thought it was merely a matter of supplying a bottle of whiskey or a pint of beer. Nothing could have been further from the truth: 'Never did any business require more circumspection, and few, comparatively, from the many in the trade are adapted for carrying it on respectably and giving satisfaction to the frequenters of their houses.'

The wrong people entering the trade had caused widespread disruption and brought about too many closures. Phipps discussed the role of the distilleries and breweries who were too quick to 'venture their property with persons of no capital on speculation in houses'. He had seen many houses 'puffed off', and saw inexperienced vintners occupy them with dreams of making certain fortunes, but they were instead 'completely ruined in a short time'. He advised those entering the trade to avoid giving credit, be careful who they trusted, settle all accounts annually, dress conservatively, be honest at all times, be mean to nobody and keep up the dignity of the house. A stout advocate of manner and decorum, he advised the publicans to be 'complaisant to the meanest as well as the greatest' because they were as much obliged 'to use good manners, for a farthing as a pound'. He strongly recommended a personal touch: 'Endeavour to be as much in your shop or warehouse or whatever place your business properly lies as possible as you can – leave it not to servants to transact, for customers will not regard them as yourself.' He also had practical advice on dealing with customers:

> Be not too talkative, but speak as much as is necessary to recommend your goods, and always observe to keep within the rules of decency. If

customers slight your goods and undervalue them, endeavour to convince them of their mistake, if you can, but not affront them; do not be pert in your answers, but with patience hear and with meekness reply, for if you affront in a small matter it may probably hinder you from a future good customer. They may think you are dear in the articles they want, but by going to another may find it not so, and probably may return again; but if you behave rude and affronting, there is no hope either of returning, or their future custom.

A good landlord should keep two spirits in his shop: 'One for such as is used in drams, which is of a newer description and consequently cheaper, and the other of old spirits, which he would make use of for punch.' It was the latter he considered most important because 'upon it the people of the better description so much depend'. It was imperative that spirits were never adulterated, but it was acceptable to add some 'treacle, turmeric or elderberry' to achieve a light colour. This adulteration of alcohol was slow to die out. In 1864, Robert Peel MP told the House of Commons that the beer sold in Ireland was commonly adulterated with 'a great many deleterious substances . . . Cocculus Indicus, nux vomica, copperas to give it a head, vitriol to give it smartness, molasses to give it colour, and various other things'. If a publican did not get his porter and ale right from the start, his business would not prosper. It was vital, Phipps said, that the owner was 'circumspect that his cocks are clean and have fresh newspaper or wadding about them' when he was tapping his barrels. He had seen too many 'cheap defective cocks' brought over from Birmingham and Sheffield 'apparently to the eye very staunch', but they soon started to leak. He recommended that the vintner 'get his cocks from a respectable brass founder and give a fair price for them'. Bad cocks were a false economy: 'The prices of cocks for his vessels even of a good description are trifling indeed when compared with the continual loss sustained by using a bad article.' Phipps also provided advice on employees and, as Edward Wakefield had also noted, the standard of worker was sometimes lacking:

> Some waiters are very unhandy, by which the Vintner is much annoyed, and company awkwardly served; other waiters are very slovenly and dirty in their appearance, and certainly it is not so pleasing to receive liquor or any other article from their hands; other waiters are very surly, disagreeable, and unaccommodating, often remarking on the customer, and believe me a customer does not seem satisfied with remarks, he expects civil treatment and is entitled to it if he behaves with propriety.

All too frequently Phipps had seen waiters who seemed to have a good character and were 'civil, attentive and obliging' at first, but became 'saucy' after they had made some money. It was an important task for the publican to find employees without the much-despised 'sauciness'. The grounds on which an employee could be fired had to be carefully explained before commencement of employment: 'staying out when sent on messages, betraying any of his master's secrets or the smallest act of dishonesty' were all valid reasons for dismissal.

In keeping with the temperate message of the time, Phipps finished by telling his membership the biggest enemy to business success was a 'sottish landlord', an 'unfair man who drank his own profits' or allowed his servants to do so.

At the start of Phipps' handbook, the members of the newly established group are listed. A significant number are brewers and distillers, and the total number of publicans listed for Dublin is fewer than 200 – a small percentage of those in operation. Samuel Bell was the proprietor of Wicklow and Wexford Private Cars, while Frederick Dempster is listed as owning the Queen's Head Hotel and Livery Stables in Bride Street, where there was a medicinal spring adjacent to the premises 'of such peculiar quality as to cause the evacuation of worms of different descriptions from horses and other animals, which have been preserved and can be viewed'. John Gosson was a mail- and stage-coach maker from Balbriggan, while Martin Merry was a pewterer, porter and spirit machine manufacturer from Bride Street. Ann Horton of 31 Bridge Street is listed as the proprietor of The Brazen Head, 'established as an inn upwards of 200 years in the most commercial part of the city' – a more realistic claim than is currently made.

In 1833, the Licensing Act of Ireland was introduced in an effort to control public drunkenness and the continued widespread availability of cheap illegal spirits. In 1833 and 1834, 16,000 illegal poteen stills were confiscated and destroyed. Poteen was traditionally distilled in a small pot still and made from malted barley, grain, treacle, sugar beet, potatoes or whey. Despite previous Acts in 1661 and 1760, the authorities had consistently found it impossible to stamp out production. Like moonshine whiskey in the southern states of America, it was traditionally manufactured by the rural poor and was particularly associated with the west of Ireland. The 1661 Act imposed a tax on manufacturers of spirits for personal use, but proved unenforceable. The 1760 Act made it illegal to own a poteen still, but was totally ignored. The increases imposed on the price of whiskey meant poteen operated as a secondary currency in many parts of the country. Peasants and landlords were sometimes complicit in the process; poteen paid the rent. The excise men were commonly open to bribery too. The Great Famine decimated the illegal market in the 1840s.

John Edgar, Presbyterian minister, professor of theology, moderator of the Presbyterian Church of Ireland and the founder of the Ulster Temperance Society, was asked to give the House of Commons an account of the public-house licensing situation in Ireland in 1835. He first cited figures for Dublin: 868 licences in 1824, 1,074 in 1825, 1,400 in 1826 and 1,714 in 1828. In Clonmel, County Tipperary, there were 1,700 inhabitants and sixty-four spirit shops in 1811. This had increased to 129 by 1833 and to 150 by 1844 – one for every twenty-two families. Claremorris, in County Mayo, had 800 inhabitants and fifty licensed premises. This did not include shebeens, which in Claremorris were 'all about'. Edgar read a letter from the 'Lord Mayor, Sheriffs, Commons and Citizens of the city of Dublin in common council assembled', petitioning the body to close the pubs on Sunday. Mr James Silk Buckingham, author, journalist and traveller, told the committee he had recently gone on a trip around Ireland and noticed that four out of every five shops sold alcohol. In one street in Belfast, he claimed to have seen seven whiskey shops side by side. He was not surprised the Irish were so poor, and believed there was no point in putting relief plans in place unless this 'dreadful evil' was first addressed. There was also handwringing about the type of people running 'gin shops'. Sir Robert Bateson, Conservative MP from County Down, distinguished such establishments from 'beer shops'. The gin shops were 'the receptacles of every vice' and could even be established by 'vagabonds who escaped from prison'.

The Coroners Act of 1846 decreed a dead body had to be brought to the nearest public house for storage until further arrangements were made. The beer cellars were cool and slowed decomposition, and it became common for publicans to have marble tables in their cellars for autopsies. This legislation was not removed from the statute books until 1962, and the dual role of publican and undertaker is still common in Ireland. *The Freeman's Journal* of 9 April 1869 carried a story of a bus crash in Dublin. The injured were brought to Lawler's pub to be treated, instead of to the nearby Saint Mary's Asylum where nurses and doctors were in attendance. The editor complained the choice was inappropriate because the publican had no beds. Patrick Lawler saw fit to write to the paper to defend his actions:

> I beg to say that the body of Mrs Byrne was brought into my house by the direction of Dr Monks, and laid on the table of the taproom, where a large fire was burning. Blankets were at once brought down from the bed of my own family and wrapped round the body. Every possible effort was made to resuscitate her. My house was closed and business suspended

while she remained there; everything required by the
doctor and those in attendance were supplied by me.

Around 1850, the number of public houses in Dublin started
to level off. Frederick Shaw, the Recorder with the power to
bequeath licences, refused to issue any new ones, and the
value of a licence increased by 500 per cent over the next
twenty years. Many publicans became more prosperous and
climbed the social ladder. It was now prohibitively expensive
to enter the trade and it became the preserve of the more
well-to-do.

It became a legal requirement to display the proprietor's
name over the front door of the premises after legislation
passed in 1872. The legacy of this law is often cited as one
of the unique features of the Irish pub. Often, a public house
operates under a long-obsolete family name – a signature
feature in the boom of 'Irish Pubs' outside Ireland. This
change in legislation limited the previous inventive array of
names: in Dublin, The Sots Hole in Essex Street, The
Wandering Jew in Castle Street, Three Candlesticks in King
Street, House of Blazes in Aston Quay, The Blue Leg in High
Street, The Holy Lamb in Cornmarket and The Golden
Sugar Loaf in Abbey Street are all long since defunct. Some
pubs, such as The Bleeding Horse and The Brazen Head,
kept both a family name and original title.

The 1872 Act made it illegal 'to knowingly permit . . .
a premises to be the habitual resort of, or place of meeting
of, reputed prostitutes', and from this time on it was judged
a crime to be drunk in public. The Act distinguished 'simple
drunkenness' from 'aggravated drunkenness': being drunk
on any highway or in any other public place, on a licensed

premises or at a sporting event were categorised as offences of 'simple drunkenness', while refusing to leave a licensed premises when requested and being drunk when minding a child under seven or possessing a loaded firearm were considered 'aggravated drunkenness'. The 1872 Act further tightened the standards required to obtain a new public-house licence. One would only be approved if the applicant could produce a certificate awarded by the Recorder or local Magistrate attesting to his good character. Before the certificate was granted, six householders had to vouch for the applicant. Licences were renewed annually and most publicans, aware that they possessed a valuable asset, toed the line.

In 1872, Sir Dominic Corrigan, an MP for Dublin, cardiologist and personal physician to the Queen when she was in Ireland, raised the perennial issue of Sunday closing time in the House of Commons. Since the Perrin's Act of 1833, pubs in Ireland had been allowed to stay open on Sunday and, in his opinion, publicans now saw Sunday opening as an 'immemorial right'. The Act had been repealed for Scotland in 1856 and Corrigan demanded the same be done for Ireland. In 1834, only one year after the passing of the Perrin's Act, a petition from the Corporation of Dublin referred to an increase in drunkenness, and Corrigan maintained that, from that year on, a constantly increasing demand for the closing of public houses on Sunday had been spreading throughout Ireland. He explained the different nature of drinking in Ireland and England to his fellow parliamentarians: 'Beer is the general drink taken in England; beer taken in excess stupefies. Whiskey is the general drink in Ireland; whiskey maddens. The habits of drinking, too, are different. In England each man drinks his beers in such quantities as he likes. In Ireland, in country parts especially, they drink in rounds in parties of five or six; each stands his round in turn, treating the party in glasses of whiskey.' Purchasing alcohol in 'rounds' – or 'treating' – has always been a central characteristic of Irish drinking culture and is often cited as a contributing factor to excessive consumption.

Corrigan addressed the consequences, mentioning the frequently voiced fear of political unrest conceived in drinking establishments: 'Swearing into illegal societies too often follows, for the designing entrap the unwary.' He told the parliamentarians of two recent written submissions he had received, one from Cardinal Cullen and thirteen Archbishops and Bishops of the Catholic Church, another from three Bishops, sixteen Deans and twenty-one Archdeacons of the Protestant Church. The Heads of the Presbyterian Bodies and the Wesleyan Methodists had also petitioned him. The Lord Mayor of Dublin had held an 'aggregate meeting' the previous March attended by all classes and religions. Furthermore, Corrigan had canvassed the wider public for their opinion and called a meeting at the Mechanics' Institute for all working men in Dublin. The hall was filled with hundreds of people and 'only four hands were held up against total Sunday closing time'. He read a written petition, which he claimed had been agreed upon by everyone at the meeting, describing Sunday opening as a 'grievous injury' to the morals of Dubliners. He presented signed petitions from holders of important public posts and interested parties; one from a group of 253 Dublin publicans, and another from twenty-three publicans from Moate, County Westmeath. He also read a letter from Dr Conaty, Catholic Bishop of Kilmore, which claimed many of the deeds of daring and violence, 'which have disgraced our people, were concocted and matured in public houses known for their Sunday traffic'.

Corrigan then turned his attention to 'the young people' working in the public houses. He estimated 3,000 youngsters in Dublin and over 60,000 nationwide worked in public houses. These unfortunates could not get to bed on Saturday night before midnight or 1 a.m. and had to be behind their counters from 2 p.m. to 11 p.m. or midnight on Sunday night, 'exposed to the company often of the depraved and dissolute'. They had no time for recreation, religious attendance or 'moral instruction', and barely a chance to rest and eat. He read a petition he claimed to have received on behalf of these young people, stating they worked sixteen hours on weekdays and nine on Sundays. 'You will search in vain for a parallel for our position,' they supposedly wrote. Corrigan reported voluntary Sunday closing was in operation in parts of the country and some priests in Dublin had convinced the publicans in their parishes to stay shut. Dr Leahy, Archbishop of Cashel, was successful in his efforts, according to a letter he sent to Corrigan. 'Rioting and blasphemy', common before the introduction of the local decree, had ceased 'to desecrate the Sunday', and the towns were no longer disgraced, he wrote. Dr Furlong of the Diocese of Ferns had introduced a ban fifteen years earlier when 'the scenes of drunkenness and disorder were too frequent'. Such incidents had disappeared, and the calm and abstinence from all disturbance and disorder on Sunday was the result of closing the pubs, for which, he said, they had to be 'thankful to Providence'. Corrigan had no doubt the women of Ireland would also want pubs closed on Sunday if they were polled. He saw no evidence of an increase in illicit drinking in those areas where a voluntary code had been adopted. If such drinking dens were established, he was sure the police and the clergy would convince the people to desist. The debate became mired in a discussion of corruption levels in Irish society and whether it could be trusted to self-regulate. Mr Richard Dowse – the then Irish Attorney General – threw cold water on the entire debate; all of these proposals were unworkable and would cause undue expense. A second vote was taken and defeated.

By 1873, conditions had been improved for those working in mines and workshops, but they remained poor for staff in public houses. The indefatigable Dominic Corrigan again beseeched the House of Commons to instigate mandatory Sunday closing. This was not, he said, a religiously motivated argument, but rather an attempt to provide 'a rest from toil' and a day of 'rational and healthful recreation' for the workers. It would also mean they would be 'less exposed to the handling, and sight, and smell of that which was a strong temptation'. If the situation continued, 'their very fatigue increased the inducement to indulge in it'. No person under the age of twenty-one should be allowed work for longer than ten hours a day in a public house, he argued. It would also be beneficial for the publican; he would save on Sunday expenses, enjoy time with his family and would have one day for 'innocent and healthful enjoyment in common with the other classes of the community'.

Corrigan compared the use of beer in the diet of English and Irish people. The English consumed beer with their dinner, but 'very few of the artisan class in Ireland used beer at their meals, and therefore they would not be inconvenienced in this respect by the public houses being closed on Sunday'. Colonel William Stuart Knox, MP for Dungannon, viewed the situation politically: 'Fenians, Home Rulers and other rebels assembled in public houses on Sundays to plot against the country.' On the other hand, Mr William St James Wheelhouse, MP for Leeds, thought it a bad idea to prohibit public houses opening on Sunday because 'the populace will be left without access to alcohol for medicinal uses'. Once again, the debate ended with no change made to the legislation. The Sunday drinker remained safe.

In 1876, Richard Dowse spoke with characteristic directness in the House of Commons. It was once said to him that 'the best cure for Ireland would be to put it at the bottom of the sea for a short time', but if the assembled gentlemen could see their way to close the pubs on Sunday, the situation would greatly improve. He proceeded to lay petitions on his desk signed by 230,000 people asking for the public houses to be closed on Sunday. He told the House that the executive committee of the Irish Sunday Closing Association had organised a poll in the six principal towns and cities of Ireland: Dublin, Cork, Limerick, Belfast, Waterford and Londonderry. The results were decisive; in Dublin, there were 25,077 in favour of the measure and 3,104 against it; in Belfast, 23,277 for and 2,809 against; in Cork, 9,172 for and 1,499 against; in Limerick, 5,292 for and 632 against; in Londonderry, 3,082 for and 649 against; in Waterford, 3,425 for and 195 against. The aggregate vote of the licensed traders in all these towns was 830 for and 735 against. The Irish authorities had become so concerned, he said, they observed public houses on Sundays to see if there was as much drinking as reported, and were shocked to see more people go into the pubs in one town than there were adults in the local population. Dowse said he knew the opposition would say the same people were counted a number of times, but was adamant that was not the case. He gave an example from the recent assizes at Londonderry to highlight the possible dangers. There, three young men were convicted of a 'shocking outrage' upon a young woman on a Sunday evening. They had spent the Sunday afternoon drinking in several public houses. One of the young men was the son of a respectable widow. He was not 'a habitual drunkard, but he fell into the temptation of the Sunday tavern', and he and his companions were sentenced by Judge Keogh to fifteen years' penal servitude. 'Is it for the accommodation of young men of this stamp that we are asked to keep the public houses open on Sunday afternoons?' Dowse thundered. The majority of parents of young families wished to see the pubs closed on Sunday, he argued, and if the vote was given to those over sixteen years of age, he thought the young people would, too. Shebeens would not be a problem, he contended. If the police had been able to count the number of people entering public houses on Sunday, then they would easily be able to 'sniff out' any illegal drinking dens. He was aware of deputations sent by distillers and others to political representatives, but questioned their validity. He claimed certain individuals believed those behind the movement to close the public houses on Sunday were all teetotallers and 'do-gooders', but stated that was not so; in fact, not all non-drinkers were in agreement. Some of the 'good Templars and Rechabites' refused to sign the canvassing paper in favour of Sunday closing, because they regarded the demand as too small. They were 'willing to spill all the drink and swill the streets with it', but they did not see their way to join in an effort merely to limit its use. The 'Rechabites' referred to were the members of the Independent Order of Rechabites – a temperance organisation also known as the Sons and Daughters of Rechab – established in Salford, Manchester, in 1835. The 'Templars' were members of the Freemasons' group the Knight Templars who were granted properties in Ireland during the reign of Henry II.

According to Richard Smith MP, the Chief Secretary had said there would be riots in all the large towns if the pubs were closed on Sunday, but he had still something to learn of Ireland and Irishmen: 'An Irishman is always ready for a riot when he has got drink, but no man ever saw an Irishman creating a riot in order to get it.' He finished by asking the English representatives to put aside their own self-interests and do what was best for Ireland: 'It is seldom Ireland asks a favour from the House,' he said, but if they could see their way to override any vested interests, it would be a 'great measure of Justice to Ireland and her people.' English MP Sir Walter Young expressed sympathy for young men who, he had heard, left Cork city for the day to venture out to Queenstown (today's Cobh) for the good of their constitution, and were 'surely deserving of refreshment'. He believed there was no more legitimate demand than that of the 'excursionist', and some provision should be made to supply it. There were many places where excursionists went on Sunday, he said, and if pubs 'were closed altogether, a great hardship would be inflicted on the respectable tradesman who went on an excursion with his wife and children, carrying his dinner with him, and who would naturally want to get a glass of beer'. He was also concerned about those who came in to berth in fishing ports on Sunday, as he believed they might be 'a class who would resent more strongly and vehemently than any other the closing of public houses against them on Sundays'.

Mr John Murphy, MP for Cork, had heard no solid evidence of increased trouble and drunkenness on Sunday from anyone in the House over recent years, so he had taken it upon himself to seek information from the police in Cork. In 1873, 2,680 people were arrested for drunkenness, 2,531 in 1874, and 3,026 in 1875. Of these, 242 were arrested on Sunday in 1873, 204 in 1874 and 261 in 1875. The average number of arrests on Saturday was just over seven, and it was three on Sunday over the three-year period. These figures gave lie, he contended, to the argument for closing pubs on Sunday. There were fewer arrests on Sunday than on any other day of the week. Closing the public houses would not solve anything, and it certainly would not deter those who wanted to get drink, which, he was at pains to point out, were few in number and 'he should blush for his country if for one moment someone would say that the whole of Ireland was intemperate'.

Sir Michael Hicks Beach (also known as 'Black Michael'), MP for East Gloucestershire and future Father of the House of Commons, thought the surveys of the city dwellers inadequate and that the people who mattered – 'those labouring men who used the pubs' – were not canvassed. He took issue with figures he had heard bandied about. In Dublin, 28,000 householders were canvassed, but the census of 1871 showed 62,000 families in the city; not even half the population was included. In Cork, 16,000 voted, from a total of 20,000, 5,900 out of 14,000 voted in Limerick and 3,600 out of 6,200 voted in Waterford. The vast majority of public houses' customers took 'moderate and necessary refreshment', Beach said. He was not convinced by the number of clergy who signed the petitions: 864 priests could only be a small proportion of the clergy operating in Ireland. He claimed arrests were inconsequential; according to his contact with the police authorities in Dublin, 1,410 arrests were made between the hours of 2 p.m. and 9 p.m. in 1875 for drunk and disorderly behaviour. The figure of 122,000 people visiting the pubs in Dublin on Sunday may be too high, but, he argued, there was remarkably little trouble for the many thousands who did frequent the public houses on Sunday and 'a very small proportion caused themselves or anybody else any harm by so doing so'. Nor did he find the voluntary codes imposed by the clergy in some dioceses convincing. It did not necessarily follow that a compulsory law would be successful. People who normally obeyed their clergy and practised self-denial 'might fight against coercive legislation', he said, 'which might be represented to them as imposed, if not by a Saxon Parliament, perhaps at the instance of a section of their countrymen who were not in sympathy with themselves'.

A Mr Law disagreed. In Dublin, 28,000 householders were canvassed; voting papers were left at all accommodations in the city, but over 30,000 families did not bother to register a response. Lack of engagement was an issue in other towns and cities as well. When it was considered that 25,000 of 28,000 voted for the proposal, it should be as much information as anyone needed, he said. The counting of people entering the public houses annoyed him. Everyone in Ireland knew the tradition was to drift from one pub to another, 'either from want of something else to do or to gratify a vicious appetite, until at last, perhaps, they are taken in charge by the police', he said. He posed one final question. Why had the House passed a bill the previous year compelling 'places of public amusement' to close on Sunday, and it was now considering allowing public houses to remain open? If people could not go to the Brighton Aquarium on Sunday, why should they 'keep open houses which lead people, not to places of harmless amusement like the Aquarium, but to the police station, if not to gaol?' He was aware, he said, most people did not go out deliberately to get drunk. Drunkenness in Ireland often happened accidentally. People casually met their friends, went to the public house for a social drink, and started buying drinks for each other until they were 'landed, perhaps, in gaol for some unpremeditated act of violence, which would never have been done if the publican had been prevented from tempting them with his drink'. Crime, he argued, was casually produced by casual Sunday drinking. This casual drinking could result in people 'casually falling out, and casually attacking each other in a way that would be wholly unintelligible, if we had not this wretched whiskey-drinking to account for it'.

Mr William Redmond, Home Rule Party MP for Wexford, did not believe the Irish were 'habitual drunkards'. The Irish peasant did not drink at all in many parts of the country, and it was only when temptation came his way that he was likely to succumb. He did not drink every day like the English peasant, but only when he went to a market or after Mass on Sunday. Unfortunately, he admitted, this sometimes caused problems: 'They drank away their wages and their wits. It was not only what was spent on Sundays, though that made a considerable difference in the wages; there generally followed a fine at the petty sessions. The wage of the Irish labourer left little to spare to dress and rear his children; and justice to the families was enough to call for the suppression of the Sunday drinking.'

Major Purcell O'Gorman of Waterford city was the last to speak, and wished to put across the view of the type of common man he knew best – the farmer:

> There is a large number of respectable farmers in Ireland who every Sunday of their lives, after they have performed their religious duties, sit down in the public houses with their friends to have a glass of beer, or whatever it may be, and to talk about the occurrences of the week or month, and compare notes about stock, the price of corn, and one thing and another. They go to the public house, take a small quantity of liquor, and after staying an hour or two, they go home to their families and sit down with them at their meal. Now, Sir, what will the closing of public houses on Sundays do to such a man? The men I speak of are respectable farmers, responsible men, men who love their landlords, and whom their landlords love – men who have been 50 or 60 years upon their farms, against whom no complaint has ever been brought, and whose lives might have been written by Plutarch.

If this motion was passed it would cause undue hardship for these men, O'Gorman believed. They might be tempted to go to one of the local illegal drinking dens, and get in trouble with the law. They could be imprisoned for a month, with terrible consequences: 'When a man who has been so sentenced goes back to his farm, what does he find? That his horse instead of being fat is lean. We say in Ireland, "It is the master's eye that fattens the horse," and that is perfectly true. The firkins in his dairy should be full, but they are empty. What becomes of that man? Why, he abandons himself to despair. He says, "I will go into the town. I will pay my landlord no more rent, and I will spend all my money in drink".' His speech may have influenced the house. The motion was defeated once again and the pubs were allowed to stay open on Sunday.

In reality, the Irish people could get drink whenever they wanted to, in shebeens. In 1877, a Dublin Metropolitan Police officer described the situation in the tenements to the House of Commons:

> In the low squalid districts are miles of filthy streets with lanes off them where there are houses known to the police carrying on illicit trade where crowds of people congregated and got drunk – but there was no getting legal evidence of this fact. As many as 50 or 60 people, labourers, common people, upon a Sunday morning would be seen going along whistling and chatting in groups and gradually disappear into a house. But by signals and otherwise communicating rapidly from one end of the street to another it was utterly impossible for the police to reach that house in time to get evidence.

On one Sunday morning, this officer and his partner had observed 168 people entering an illicit drinking establishment, but were powerless to do anything because of the warning system used by the punters. Even when caught, the fines were disproportionate to the profits made. Police corruption was also rampant.

In 1883, a cap on the number of licences was removed, but a new public house could only be opened if the applicant and premises were deemed suitable and there was a recognised shortage of public houses in the geographical area. According to the Royal Commission on Liquor Licensing Laws, there were a staggering 21,000 pubs in Ireland in 1888 – almost three times the number today. Despite this, the calling had become nobler, particularly in urban areas. Many publicans had become wealthy and politically active. By 1890, twenty of the sixty aldermen and councillors on Dublin Corporation were publicans, and it was common for the sons of publicans to enter the priesthood or the medical profession. The Irish Licensing Act 1902 aimed to reduce significantly the number of licences granted, and prevent any further abuses of the system. From this time onwards, pub licences acquired even greater value and could be used as collateral in business transactions.

The twentieth century in Ireland would bring a constant barrage of alcohol legislation. As J. V. Woods notes in *Liquor Licensing Laws of Ireland*, 'the history of the licensed trade is one of almost continual conflict between legislators and licence holders with the result there is probably no other business which has been so much legislated for or litigated on as that of the Publican'. These complex and lengthy legal provisions bear testimony to the centrality of the pub in Irish society.

Whipping the Herring:

Temperance and the Pub in 19th-Century Irish Society

'If whiskey produces brutish rebels among men, among women it destroys all feminine modesty, producing viragos and sluts.' – *The Dublin Committee for Drunkenness 1798*

There is a fundamental problem in trying to provide a balanced account of Irish pub culture during the nineteenth century. The peasantry did not write accounts of the great nights and interesting conversations they had at the local pub or shebeen. Travelogues with descriptions of public houses are very few, and those that do exist are overwhelmingly the interpretations of the economic elite, many of them members of temperance movements, and some with an inherent anti-Irish and anti-Catholic bias. The accounts are also usually second-hand. Many believed drinking and everything associated with it was a moral failing. In 1805, the Reverend James Whitelaw wrote in his *Essay on the Population of Dublin*: 'Dram shops are the most alarming of all nuisances . . . they vend raw spirits, a poison productive of vice, riot and disease, hostile to all habits of decency, honesty and industry, and, in short, destructive to the souls and bodies of our fellow creatures. These houses, open at all hours by day and by night, are scenes of unceasing profaneness and intemperance.'

The Establishment rarely saw any positive role for the pub in society. Sir Charles Cameron, Chief Medical Officer for Dublin Corporation during the later part of the nineteenth century, was an exception. In his report *How the Poor Lived in Dublin*, he wrote: 'The workman is blamed for visiting the public house, but it is to him what the club is to the rich man. His home is rarely a comfortable one and in the winter, the bright light, the warm fire, and the gaiety of the public house are attractions which he finds difficult to resist.' His was one of very few sympathetic voices. He was tasked with managing sanitation for the city of Dublin, and was overwhelmed by the poverty; the city was widely cited as having the worst living conditions in Europe at the time. Despite this, he did his best, and his work was so appreciated that he was granted the status of Freeman of Dublin in 1911.

Newspapers only reported calamities and tragedies related to public houses. Even advertisements for them were rare, and pertained to the finer establishments. For this reason, the House of Commons records are particularly valuable. There was rarely universal agreement on any legislation applicable to alcohol in Ireland, and frequently multiple viewpoints were voiced, often predicated upon political and ideological fault lines.

In 1834, the Select Committee on Drunkenness discussed the widespread practice of paying workmen in the pub and the associated custom of 'treating'. John Edgar spoke about Belfast, where the worker had to purchase a glass of spirits to have his wages paid and where 'a number of masters pay very late on a Saturday night, so that a man's family cannot be provided with necessary things for the Sabbath'. Foremen were often allowed to drink for free in the public house where they brought their men. Some employees were deliberately paid in notes of large denomination, Edgar said. For changing the note, the 'Master of the House' expected the man to buy at least one drink. The Reverend George Whitmore Carr, a prominent temperance campaigner from New Ross, County Wexford, had seen the same 'source of evil' in Dublin: 'The public house provides change, and in winter heat and candle light, and everyone who goes there to be paid is expected to take a little in return for those accommodations; here the evil commences, but does not often end til the wretched drunk, having spent his week's wages on Sunday, returns on Monday to his hopeless family, their dread and scourge.' Carr furnished an example from a letter sent to him the previous week by a Councillor Mackey, pleading the case of a master coachbuilder whose son had got into trouble with the police for drunken brawling. The coachbuilder had a daughter married to a grocer who paid his workers with 'a docket on the shop'. One of those paid in this way was the coachbuilder's son, and in consequence he had debauched himself with alcohol. He had no furniture in his room except for a straw bed and a pot for boiling potatoes. This 'truck and docket' system had ruined many people, the coachbuilder said.

Carr turned his attention to the profusion of distilleries and spirit production, unwittingly foreshadowing a catastrophe looming on the horizon. Whenever there had been a shortage of corn in Ireland, there was less public disturbance because of limited alcohol production; so much so that, according to Mr Carr, 'it became a frequent saying in Ireland, if you wish prosperity in Ireland, pray that God may bring a famine, but you wish for her destruction, petition the Legislature to legalise distillation'.

In his 1839 paper *The Philosophy of Artificial and Compulsory Drinking Usage in Great Britain and Ireland*, John Dunlop discussed the treatment of alcohol among different trades and classes of workers, starting with the carpenters of Belfast. They 'treated' each other, he said, in turn, by buying a 'dram' for all the other workers each morning. When a carpenter started his apprenticeship, he was obliged to give the workshop a 'footing' or a 'dacent drink' as recompense for taking him on. If the apprentice did not purchase the drinks, fellow workers were 'shy to answer'; they would refuse to answer his questions when the master was absent. For this reason, Dunlop said, 'even widowed mothers will stretch every nerve to provide for the apprentice footing'.

After a house was completed, builders hoisted a flag to indicate it was time for the owner to bring the workers to the pub for a 'treat' or a 'mug', and it would not be taken down until they got it. If they left the job untreated, they would ensure 'some parts of the building would be left spoiled or defective'. When a child was born to an operative, he had to buy his workmates a drink; this was called 'socket money'. When it was time to use candles in the workshop in winter, the master gave the men money to go to the pub for a drink – a 'way goose'. Cabinetmakers operated similarly. The last man who had paid his footings was called 'the constable' until replaced by someone newer. It was the constable's job to organise the night out with the footings of the new man. Like the carpenters, they had a system of 'drink fines'. It was administered by the oldest worker in the shop, who was immune from sanction. They all went for a night out when the fines had sufficiently accumulated. Fines were incurred for the most inane offences: leaving windows open, putting tools in the wrong place or wearing a dirty shirt to work on Monday. Ropemakers were fined for coming to work unshaven. If a worker refused to pay his fines, he was treated miserably: his tools were covered in candle grease, water was thrown at him or trapdoors were made to ensnare him. If he persisted in refusing payment, his tools were taken to the pawn shop; this was referred to as 'sending the articles to my uncle' or 'putting them up the spout'.

Dunlop had an informant among the shoemakers who told of unpleasant scenes he had witnessed when wives came looking for their husbands in the pubs: 'They are bate out of the public houses, they are bate home, and they are bate at home for coming after their husbands to the public houses.' Dock workers were particularly vicious in exacting retribution from workmates, according to Dunlop. In Dublin port, a coal porter had to treat all his friends when he got married: 'Should he refuse to comply, he is forcibly mounted on a long pole, sometimes square, and sometimes round, and then is carried up and down the quays and neighbourhood for two or three hours.' If he paid up, he was set at liberty. Among the farmers, Dunlop reported 'a barbarous and pernicious system of drinking'. They celebrated harvests and transacted business over drink. He found 'the supposed necessity of a wet bargain' universal and many farmers only bought or sold animals in the pub. Scriveners' clerks, he wrote, were 'habitual drunkards' because of the nature of their job. Although literate and educated, their work was irregular. When they had not any work, 'the poorer classes of them' were permitted to wait in a public house. If they got paid work, they were expected to return to the pub and buy drink or pay for any that had been advanced. Pay nights were problematic across the trades: 'There is much drinking on the pay night. Some masters or foremen keep a public house where they excite men to take drinks upon credit and stop it off the week's wages. This is said to be "bringing sucken to their own mill".'

Dunlop recounted the 'ludicrous tradition' prevalent among butchers in Dublin called 'whipping the herring'. On the last Saturday in Lent, one of their number dressed in sheepskin, to which was attached 'the animal's legs, dangling about so as to represent drapery'. The guts of a pig were put on top of the sheepskin. The pig guts were 'blown, and tied at every six inches' distance, to appear like chain-work'. He also wore a 'hideous-looking mask' and a cocked hat, and was put sitting on an ass with a wand in his hand. He was addressed as 'His Majesty' by his associates, one of whom held a pole, on top of which were 'two hoops crossing each other perpendicularly'. A sheep's head was placed on top of these, with a number of herring suspended underneath. In the other hand, he held a small birch broom, with which he occasionally struck the herrings. Each time he did so, he repeated a verse: 'We come from Merrin, to whip the herring, and wish you a happy Easter.' They went from shop to shop, 'followed by a crowd of the lowest rabble' and on each stop 'the laureate of the party' asked for a financial contribution, usually given to get rid of the nuisance. At the end of the night, they adjourned to the pub and drank the money.

In an enquiry into rioting at the 1857 elections in Drogheda, publican Joseph Harris was questioned about the running of his premises by the chairman, Mr Power:

Power: Is there any dancing at your house?

Harris: We have in Ireland what we call a holiday when we have music, St Patrick's or St Mary's Day, or any day we please.

Power: That is a long way from an answer to my question; I asked you whether you have dancing on in your house, and you told me in answer to that, that on St Patrick's day and some others in Ireland, you have music; have you dancing at your house?

Harris: Yes.

Power: You keep a dancing place there, do you not?

Harris: I do.

Power: You keep a public house, and you have dancing there?

Harris: Certainly and so do scores like me. That is the custom in Ireland; it is the custom to have music.

Isaac Welds, author of the 1832 book *A Statistical Survey of the County of Roscommon*, spoke to a Dr Stern about the tradition of holding 'cake dances' beside the local public houses. They were so named because a large cake was awarded to the best pair of dancers. Dr Stern was unsettled because he had seen the cake awarded to a man at a recent dance. The winner gave it to his partner and carried her and the cake 'into the public house contiguous to which all the dances were held'. He divided the cake among the crowd and continued drinking 'carousing to intoxification and in uncontrolled dissipation'. Stern objected to drinking because men spent more money than they could afford, leading to 'burglaries, robberies and other outrages on society'. These gatherings were far from an innocent peasant pastime; they were, he wrote, 'the baleful sources of such vices as flow from them, ramified into numerous branches of moral turpitude and political evil'.

Cake dances were particularly popular in the east of Ireland. The cake was usually positioned on a 10-foot-high pole surrounded by ribbons. Generally, the publican's wife baked the cake, and the participants paid for both it and the musicians by placing money in a hole beside the pole. Dancers moved around the pole in a circle, and usually the couple who lasted the longest 'took the cake' – the possible origin of the phrase 'to take the biscuit'. Sir Henry Piers, MP and First Baronet of Tristernagh Abbey in County Westmeath, described a typical cake dance in 1682 in *Chronological Description of the County of Westmeath*:

> The most ordinary sort of people meet in the afternoon near the alehouse . . . here to be sure the piper fails not of diligent attendance; the cake to be danced for is provided at the charge of the alewife

and it is advanced to a board on the top of a pike about ten feet high; this board is round and from it riseth a type of garland, beset and tied around with meadow flowers, if it be early in the summer; if later, the garland has the addition of apples set round on pegs fastened unto it; the whole number of dancers begin at once in a large ring, a man and a woman, and dance about the bush, so is this garland called, and the piper, as long as they are able to hold out, they that hold out longest at the exercise, win the cake and apples and then the alewife's trade goes on.

Even this scant information gives lie to the commonly held belief that pubs were drab, lifeless, all-male preserves. In the nineteenth century, there is also evidence of higher female ownership of pubs than became the norm in the twentieth century. Slater's *National Commercial Directory of Ireland* of 1846 lists thirty-eight female publicans in Cork city, out of a total of 236. In the same year, a Mrs Cassidy from Mullingar was advised to leave her work as a publican by her doctor, and her premises was advertised in the national newspapers. The business was 'extensive and remunerative', and the building included five bedrooms, an elegant drawing room, a parlour, a kitchen, a stable and a walled garden, as well as a taproom, spirit stores and a grocery shop. In 1889, Beamish & Crawford listed those publicans who had ended their association with the brewery over the previous five years; twelve were women.

There is evidence, too, in the writing of William Carleton of female publicans. *Traits and Stories of the Irish Peasantry* of 1843 – while fictional – was closely based on his upbringing in Clogher, County Tyrone. He wrote that McKeown's public house was beside the church in Kilruddery, County Wicklow, and a popular gathering place after Mass: 'The public house was filled to the door posts, with those who wanted to get a sample of Nancy's *Iska-behagh* [whiskey]; and many a time has little Father Ned himself, of a frosty day, after having performed Mass . . . come in to Nancy, nearly frostbitten, to get his breakfast, and a toothful of mountain dew to drive the cold out of his stomach.'

Despite regularly partaking of drink in Nancy's pub, Father Ned was slow to pay and was eventually refused credit. He retaliated by threatening to move the congregation to the other side of the town. There, he said, he would set his nephew up as a publican, to the detriment of Nancy's flourishing establishment, 'and don't you know if I remove my flock to Ballymagowan you'll sing to another tune'. Carleton – who referred to himself as 'a historian of their [the peasants'] habits and manners, their feelings, their prejudices, their superstitions and their crimes' – was not universally loved for his tales by the Irish, many of whom found his depictions simplistic and demeaning.

The Famine changed the demographics of public-house attendance. The widespread belief among many British politicians and some Irish clerics held that the promiscuous and lazy Irish brought the disaster on themselves. This school of thought was particularly strong in the Catholic Church, where the self-blaming doctrines of the Bishop of Ypres, Cornelius Jansen, had garnered support. Jansenists emphasised original sin and the fallen nature of humankind. According to this movement, promiscuous sexual desire was the cause of overpopulation and famine; only strict adherence to clerical guidelines could save the Irish from themselves. This included the denial of enjoyment, and the exit of women from the public sphere, including the public house. The Jansenists were expelled from France after the revolution, but many were recruited by the national seminary in Maynooth, County Kildare, and their beliefs came to dominate ecclesiastical thought in Ireland. The solution was to promote celibacy, strictly prohibit sex outside marriage, and delay marriage and childbirth for as long as possible. The long-term effects of this sexual repression were devastating: high rates of mental illness, alcoholism, loneliness, social isolation and emigration. It created a huge bachelor class, a fundamental characteristic of Irish drinking culture.

Madame Marie Anne de Bovet, a French traveller who recorded her thoughts in *Three Months in Ireland* (1891), is one of the few writers who described the inside of a pub, and even that was through the window. Madame de Bovet was travelling by carriage through the streets of night-time Dublin in 1890 when she saw 'a great flare of gas, accompanied with the sound of voices', but was taken aback by the unpleasant sight of a drinking establishment. It reminded her of some of the public houses she had seen in England, 'places which are little more than gin shops of the lowest order'. The people looked poor and miserable, 'huddled together like a flock of sheep'. They were all standing about, leaning on the counter or up against the wall, in an 'atmosphere poisoned by alcoholic vapours, thick with tobacco smoke, and reeking with the exhalations of foul humanity', an indication of the lack of seating and comfort in public houses at the time. At first they talked quietly enough, then the noise increased, songs were sung in hoarse voices intermixed with wild yells, and it soon became an 'eternal Sabbath'. The landlord removed the inebriates with the help of the few sober customers. These wretches staggered away 'to their hovels, to sleep off the fumes of the whiskey, provided that before this they had not already tumbled down in some corner, there to snore till morning'. There were a few women in the pub, and while she found a drunken man repulsive, it was nothing compared to the sickening sight of an inebriated woman. Her sensibilities were further affronted when a drunken woman was thrown out into the street beside her carriage: 'It is a hideous spectacle – this miserable, emaciated creature; her gaunt limbs, which tremble convulsively, are hardly covered by her dirty rags; her eye is fixed, and she has the mad look of a wild beast, having been brutally jostled by the sneering crowd. She has just thrown herself down in a heap on the dirty pavement; and had not the special Providence that watches over drunkards saved her, she most certainly would have broken her head.'

The obsession of many nineteenth-century travellers and diarists with temperance was absolute. In *Memorandums Made in Ireland in the Autumn of 1852*, Dr John Forbes, physician to Queen Victoria and translator of the famous French medical text *De L'Auscultation Mediate* by René Laënnec (the inventor of the stethoscope), noted three temperance halls in Kilkenny, and was impressed by the library of 400 volumes in one. If there was wider diffusion of this practice, he wrote, all men could 'improve their personal health and save money for the good of the family'. He described teetotallers as 'better men in all the relations of social life, better members of society, and better citizens, than they were before they became teetotallers . . . they are superior in all respects to any other body of men of the same numerical extent and in the same class of society'.

When people acquired temperance, he said, they were not only improved, but they were on the sure path to much greater improvements in the future. He was disappointed in Limerick, where the number of Temperance Society members at one branch had dropped from 1,100 to 300. A spirit shop owner and member of the society brought him on a tour of the local Temperance Hall. It made sense to Forbes that a publican should be a member of the movement. The publican saw the evils of intemperance every day, and 'found it requisite to have some extraneous aid, such as the pledge', to keep him on the right path. Publicans were aware of the disgusting vices to which the working population were addicted, and the 'still more pestiferous atmosphere of the gin shops'. Forbes called on his wealthy friends to establish 'Temperance Hotels' for the poor, 'places much more attractive than the ordinary public house, which by their superior conveniences, comforts and cheapness would rob the former of many of their habitual visitors'.

Samuel Carter Hall and his wife travelled around Ireland in 1840 and their collaborative account, *Ireland: Its Scenery, Character, Etc.* – a book described in *Dublin University Magazine* as 'neither a guide-book, a tale, a history, or a book of travels . . . containing instruction for the tourist, amusement for the novel reader, information for the student, and novelties for the curious' – is replete with accounts of temperance. Originally published in three volumes, it is regarded by some as the best account of travel in nineteenth-century Ireland. The Halls were aware of the stereotype of the drunken Irishman in popular culture: 'For centuries past, drunkenness was the shame and the bane of the Irish; an Irishman has become proverbial for intoxification, and that without reference to his rank in society'. To truly picture an Irishman, 'by words, on canvas or on the stage', it was considered indispensable that he should be drunk.

The Halls had travelled through Ireland ten years previously, and documented the changes that had occurred since. Mrs Hall – Anna Maria Fielding from County Wexford, 'a lady in whose commendation we believe men of all parties can cordially unite', according to the *Dublin University Magazine* – was a noted author of two previous works of non-fiction on Ireland: *Mrs Hall's Sketches of Irish Character*, published in 1829, and *Light and Shadows of Irish Life*, published in 1838. She also wrote nine novels.

The Halls were happy to see increased temperance in Irish society. Previously, 'the extent of the evil was almost beyond belief . . . in the towns and villages, every other house was licensed to sell spirits or sold them without a licence'. According to the Halls, all wakes, funerals and fairs ended in fights, all murders were caused by excessive whiskey drinking, and all 'mischievous tendencies of the lower Irish' could be traced to their habitual intoxification. Alcohol originated and propagated their poverty and wretchedness, 'withering and destroying all it could reach'. All of the songs sung were in praise of alcohol, and drunkenness was seen as 'a merit, almost as a duty'. The rich had songs about alcohol, too, but at least these were in 'delicately turned rhymes' such as 'to wreathe the bowl with flowers of soul'. The poor were lured to drunkenness by the 'rude lays of their village poets', with lines like 'a glass of whiskey to make us frisky'. They claimed to have met a man staggering home from Limerick 'whirling his shillelagh' and every now and then sending a 'shout-a whoop hurra' over the mountains, as he finished his song of a single verse, describing the class to which he belonged:

> There's never a day I have for drink,
> But Saturday, Sunday, Monday,
> Tuesday, Wednesday, Thursday, Friday –
> Och! The dickens a day I have for drink,
> But Saturday, Sunday, Monday,
> Whoop, hurrah –
> Tuesday, Wednesday, Thursday, Friday!

On their first trip, they had seen pathetic inebriates everywhere: a man who swore he would not drink for a month, then soaked his bread in spirits and ate it; another who swore he would never drink on Earth again, then got drunk in a tree; and a man who vowed never 'to drink indoors or out' again, then put one foot outside the door and the other inside, and proceeded to get drunk, pointing out that he was not breaking his promise. There was another who swore he would not 'touch liquor in the parish again', then went to get a sod of turf from the next. Mr and Mrs Hall were shocked and delighted by the new-found sobriety on their second visit: 'even the boatmen at Killarney, proverbial for drunkenness, insubordination and recklessness of life', declined the whiskey they had brought along. In fact, drunkenness was now a reproach where formerly it was a glory, and there was no longer any tolerance or sympathy for an intoxicated person; he was now looked upon with 'absolute disgust', and was pointed out to children 'as the Spartans did their helots, as a lesson not to be forgotten, against vice'.

Things were much better now than on their previous visit, when they had arranged to go fishing on the River Shannon. The boat owner had given their guide, Terrence, money to buy some new clothes to appear decent to 'the strangers'. Terrence turned up in rags and proceeded to give an excuse about his wife taking the money. The owner insisted on going to Terrence's cottage to see the situation, and brought along the Halls. When they entered his cabin, 'his wife was stretched still insensible on the wet floor; his children were crying on a mass of damp straw in the corner; nothing like food was to be seen; the man was half stupefied from the effects of the night's debauch; a more deplorable illustration of the effects of drunkenness we could not have obtained in Ireland'. The Halls asked for a different guide, but Terrence was the best the boat owner had: the rest were habitual drunkards. They came back a few days later to find Terrence had been jailed for beating his wife. She was also drunk, and had bitten his hand badly. In their kindness, the Halls paid to have him released, made him take an oath to forgo alcohol, and arranged to go fishing the following day. The next morning, Terrence turned up so drunk that they decided it would be too dangerous to take him out on the river. They never saw him again. Three months later, they heard the great news that he had taken the pledge under Father Mathew, the founder of the Temperance movement, and was 'altogether reformed, and his wife with him'; their children were 'well clad, amply fed and their cottage clean, comfortable and amply furnished'. He now visited the savings bank, never went to the pawn office and 'a finer or healthier looking fellow never steered a boat among the perilous breakers of the rapid Shannon'.

Still, the Halls wanted more concrete evidence of temperance. They went to the banks in the towns they visited to see if this new-found sobriety was reflected in personal saving accounts. In Cork, there were 5,215 small deposits in 1838. This had increased to 6,457 by the end of the following year. They could not obtain the records for the following year, but delivered a portentous warning; they did not expect the returns to be good because the autumn of that year was 'a season of frightful want, one of those periodical visitations of poverty to which Ireland has unhappily been subject'. Potatoes in the south were so bad in quality that often a third of them were unfit for use. If there had been less temperance, the Halls wrote, the results would have been so much worse: 'If this want of food had been added to the evils of intemperance, the consequences would have been frightful. Yet during the three months the famine prevailed . . . there was scarcely an instance of breach of the peace.' They saw no clouds on the horizon. They never knew Ireland to be 'so contented, so tranquil, or so likely to become prosperous' as they found it during the summer of 1840, five years before the complete failure of the potato crop.

They met Father Mathew, and were introduced to a man transformed by temperance. He was a faction leader from Kerry, 'whose head was scarred in at least a dozen places' from fighting. He told them of the savage fights between the Colleens and Lawlors, 'whose names had figured in every criminal calendar a century back'. Things had been hopeless. If any of the families wanted to fight 'they'd leave the hay half cut, or the oats to be shelled by the four winds of heaven; and taking the hay fork, the reaping hook, and the scythe in their hands, they'd rush out to massacre each other'. What caused this brutality? 'Tubs of "potheen" drunk hot from the mountain stills' resulted in some of them falling down and drowning in the sea with drunkenness. However, the fair at Tralee had just passed and there was not a stick lifted. There was peace between the factions: the Colleens and the Lawlors met and for the first time ever there was not a 'dead boy to be carried home to the widow's cabin'. The Halls summed up the effects of temperance on the country:

> We saw bigotry losing its hold; the undue or baneful influence of one mind over another mind ceasing; habits of thrift and forethought becoming constitutional; industry receiving its full recompense; cultivation passing over the bogs and mountains; the law recognised as a guardian and protector; the rights of property fully understood and acknowledged; the rich trusting the poor, and the poor confiding with the rich; absenteeism no longer a weight of evil; and capital circulating freely and securely, so as to render the great natural resources of Ireland available to the commercial, the agricultural and manufacturing interests of the United Kingdom.

At the peak of the temperance movement, some Establishment figures saw it as part of a plot to unseat the ruling Tory Party by depriving it of tax revenues. Teetotalism became identified with the Irish nationalist cause in their minds. Writing in *The Nation* in 1843, the Young Irelander Thomas Davis described drunkenness as 'the luxury of despair and the saturnalia of slaves': temperance, on the other hand, was the 'first fruit of deep-sown hope, the offering of incipient freedom'.

Temperance festivals were hugely popular in the nineteenth century. Great numbers watched the processions on St Patrick's Day. Men came out of the pubs, drinks in hand, to have a look. Not everyone appreciated the changes; loud music played by teetotallers outside Sunday services annoyed some. Tory newspapers portrayed the Irish working class as a drunken rabble, but nothing worried them more than the sight of less well-off Dubliners marching through the city streets in temperance parades. To the *Dublin Evening Mail*, the parades were 'demonstrations of a treasonable conspiracy'.

In 1840, the Zoological Garden in Dublin's Phoenix Park opened after morning Church services in an attempt to divert people from attending public houses. In 1854, Mr James Haughton, a 'merchant of the highest standing in Dublin' was questioned about the success of this venture in the House of Commons:

> **Chairman:** You have had occasion to know the effect of opening places of amusement on Sunday, I believe, in Dublin?
>
> **Haughton:** To a moderate extent . . . I have some information on the subject.
>
> [. . .]
>
> **Chairman:** Was it [the Zoological Garden] opened at the suggestion of persons who observed that the people were in the habit of resorting to public houses, and with a view to attract them to that place?

Haughton: Yes.

[. . .]

Chairman: Would a large class of persons be found in the public houses if they were not amusing themselves in this way?

Haughton: Certainly; they consist chiefly of tradesmen, accompanied by their wives and daughters.

Chairman: Do you infer from that, if people had other attractions, and had not the temptation of public houses and beer houses open to them, they would resort to those places?

Haughton: To a very large extent. I have no doubt that the temptation of a public house is so great that I cannot imagine anything short of closing them entirely would do away with the evil.

James Haughton, a prominent social reformer and temperance campaigner, was a singular character. He was so averse to alcohol that he signed his letters 'Son of a Water Drinker', and was called an 'anyeverythingarian' by a Dublin newspaper for his contrarian views. He was also the first President of the Vegetarian Society of Great Britain, and was instrumental in the abolition of Donnybrook Fair, long a notorious occasion of drinking in Dublin. Haughton frequently contributed papers to the *Journal of the Statistical and Social Inquiry Society of Ireland*. His submissions included concerns about alcohol-related crime, the social costs of alcohol abuse, the role of education in altering behaviour, punishments for alcohol misuse, the treatment of alcoholics, vested interests in the alcohol trade, links between alcohol and poverty, the hereditary nature of alcoholism, alcohol abuse as a national characteristic and alcohol legislation. E. D. Daly was also a frequent contributor. He submitted a paper to the journal identifying three groups with vested but conflicting interests in the use of alcohol. These were, he wrote, the Revenue Commissioners, which favoured more licences for more excise duties, the Temperance Party, which was strongly against more outlets, and the liquor trade, which wanted free trade but restrictions on new licences: 'The traders were not unwilling to enjoy the increased value of existing licences by prohibiting new ones,' but were happy to 'fight fiercely against further restrictions on their present establishments'. Haughton discussed the hereditary nature of alcohol abuse in his 1858 paper 'Progressively Deteriorating Influence of Alcoholic Stimulants'. He believed generation after generation drank more than their predecessors. Another contributor, John Osborne, agreed, but felt the congenital tendency to alcoholism often skipped a generation, so it could be inherited from grandparents. Osborne thought state intervention was necessary to reform marriage laws, and quoted Dr Newman Smith: 'The facts of heredity justify the state forbidding marriages which threaten to become sources of disease and crime. Marriage licences should not be given to inebriates, those who have had delirium tremens or addiction problems.'

The Statistical and Social Inquiry Society of Ireland has a unique place in the study of the Irish economy and Irish society. Since its foundation in the autumn of 1847, the society has analysed changes in population, employment, legal and administrative systems, and social services in Ireland. No other single source provides such a comprehensive picture of social change over such a long period. In his 1897 paper 'The Struggle between the Drunkard and Society', Daly discussed the effects of alcohol-related legislation. In the past, whoever became a habitual drunkard, or 'brawler', or 'rogue alehouse keeper', was prosecuted and punished. This principle had now changed, he believed, with the law tending to focus on the trader rather than the drunkard. Daly called for more punishment for the drunkard, including making drunkenness by employees a breach of personal service. Daly argued that fines imposed by magistrates were too lenient and often unequal to the crime. At the end of the 1890s, 'selling drink to be drunk on the premises to a child involves a penalty of only twenty shillings, while neglecting to have a name over the door is ten pounds'. There was no fine for a publican serving more drink to an inebriated person, but they could be fined £50 for diluting their beer.

Other papers presented to the society included studies of the high rates of alcoholism among Irish exiles, the effects of environmental factors such as damp climate and inclement weather, and the lack of alternatives to drink. Excessive availability of alcohol was frequently discussed. So, too, were racial disposition to alcoholism and the role of alcohol in social interaction. Haughton returned to the topic of alcoholism in August 1857, with his paper 'On the Necessity for Prompt Measures for the Suppression of Intemperance and Drunkenness'. He provided statistics from twenty-four English counties. These counties, where the ratio of public houses to population was highest, also had a level of crime above the national average. Haughton believed legislation should be aimed at the destruction, and not the regulation, of alcohol.

In 1844, James Johnson MD, an expert on tropical diseases and doctor to the late King William IV, travelled around Ireland and wrote *A Tour in Ireland: With Meditations and Reflections*. He, too, recounted Father Mathew's actions and the wonders wrought by his temperance organisation. Father Matthew was a popular priest for wedding ceremonies, he wrote, but, more importantly, 'PAT is daily and hourly petitioning his Reverence for a divorce from POTEEN!!' Johnson wrote of alcohol as a legal defendant: '[Pat] accuses her of all sorts of crimes and misdemeanours. She has repeatedly prompted him to break his neighbour's head, and, of course, get his own head broken in return – to neglect his family and his affairs – to spend his time and money in the shebeen – to break the law of his country – to disobey the exhortations of his priest – to take unlawful oaths – and even to commit murder itself!' The defendant appealed in vain: 'Am I not the offspring of my accuser's brain – the very work of his own hands?' Father Mathew was unmoved and decreed a divorce. The result was miraculous: 'Pat, now, instead of scalding his stomach and firing his brain with ardent spirits, has turned his attention to cultivation of the ear, and attuned his auditory nerves to the concord of sweet sounds.' Now, wherever Dr Johnson went, he heard 'the notes of heavenly music floating on the evening breeze while crowds of peasantry gather round the band to hear the delicious airs'. Only Father Mathew could have achieved this. He was 'the very beau ideal of the Evangelist'. There was something 'so noble in his countenance, so eloquent in his speech, so zealous in his manner, and so persuasive in his exhortations' that people could only wonder at his unparalleled success.

Like other writers of his time, Dr Johnson worried that this new-found sobriety would result in political organisation, and uprising against the British King, but, confident in the knowledge that no uprising would be successful against the superior royal forces, he hoped the Irish would not, in sorrow, fall back into intemperate ways. The pub was a place where civil and political unrest could be fomented, while temperance could allow the natives to organise themselves politically. Some years later, in 1891, Madame de Bovet praised Fr Mathew, but was not convinced of the long-term likelihood of temperance surviving: 'As to Paddy and his wife, if they still too frequently brutalise themselves with drink, at least they now know they are doing wrong, which is the first step towards reformation; and in their simple though fatalistic piety, they pray that the Lord may save them from evil.'

On Friday 8 February 1902, William Lawson gave a talk to the Irish Temperance Society on licensing and public-house reform in Ireland. He quoted from a pastoral letter by Dr Thomas MacRedmond, the Bishop of Killaloe, which he had read to his flock on the subject of alcohol and the proliferation of public-house licences. In 1845, according to the Bishop's figures, there were 15,000 licences and a population of just over 8 million. Now, in 1902, he told his congregation, there were almost 19,000 licences for a population of 4 million. It was not just the numbers that concerned him. The quality of drink was also problematic. There were so many outlets that it frequently induced 'the poor and most unscrupulous class of publicans to adulterate the inferior drink they sell, or to substitute for it a concoction, which drives the unsuspecting consumer mad, and creates scandalous scenes of drunken riot'. He appealed to the authorities to stop issuing licences and close down those breaking the law. Lawson broke down the figure of 19,000 licences given by the Bishop: 17,300 publicans or spirit retailers, 57 beer retailers, 116 wine and beer retailers, 29 wine and sweet retailers, and 1,349 off-licences. He also quoted Dr Edward O'Dwyer, the Bishop of Limerick, who had informed his congregation that out of a total of 3,000 arrests in Limerick city in the previous year, 907 men were convicted for drunkenness. This was a 'shocking and abominable vice', wreaking havoc all over the town, according to the Bishop, and 'until the torrent of liquor flowing over Limerick was stopped the city would remain as it was – beggarly, filthy, wretched and impoverished'.

Lawson abhorred the number of licences allowed, and quoted a 'witness' from Tralee in County Kerry, who had told him, 'If a man was blindfolded and put standing in the centre of the street, and spun around a couple of times and started off in no particular direction, he could not go twenty yards without striking a public house.' If one pub was able to cater for the needs of a hundred families, Lawson argued, Limerick should have 499 licence holders instead of 1,551; Belfast, 416 instead of 1,110; Waterford, 44 instead of 232; Clonmel, 18 instead of 113. However, the problem was not the numbers alone. The 'state and character' of the buildings shocked him. The rateable value of the premises indicated their poor state. In Cork, 307 premises were valued at £15 or less, and thirteen of those at less than £5. In Thurles, County Tipperary, thirty-eight of seventy-seven premises were valued at less than £10. By analysing the legal records, he informed his audience, he could tell that the lower the value of properties in Londonderry, the greater the number of crimes committed in them. He bemoaned the lack of food in these establishments – 'not even bread or butter' – which made the effect of alcohol worse. He finished by quoting the 'eloquent words' of a Mr Whitaker:

> The nearer men are to public houses, and the greater the opportunities and facilities are for obtaining liquor, other things being equal, the higher is the death rate. Abounding facilities are an ever-present temptation. In the very nature of things the weak, the helpless, the unsuccessful, the incompetent, the lazy and the criminal, are those who drift into the casual, irregular and more or less doubtful and unsatisfactory employments. [. . .] They are the classes who are most deficient in moral force and power. It is precisely where they live and work, and close to their doors, that our licensing system has planted public houses most thickly, as though it had been the intention of the Legislature and of the licensing authorities to take advantage of their weakness and to provide facilities for luring them to deeper degradation by tempting them to indulgence which only renders them more helpless and hopeless, and makes them fall easy victims to disease and death.

In *A Short Essay on the Grievous Crime of Drunkenness* (1823), Father Henry Young described alcohol as 'a witch to the senses, a thief to the purse, a wife's woe, the husband's misery, the parent's disgrace, the children's sorrow, and the beggar's companion'. Publicans, he warned, 'have a most dreadful account to render in the divine tribunal of our Sovereign Judge after death'. Father Young set up stalls selling coffee and buttermilk in Dublin in an effort to combat the evil of drinking establishments, but was largely unsuccessful.

Father Theobald Mathew, the first leading light of the Irish temperance movement, began his work in Cork in 1838 where he joined the Teetotal Abstinence Society. In less than a year, he signed up 130,000 members in Cork alone. By 1843, an estimated half of Ireland's adult population had signed the pledge to stop drinking alcohol. The mantra was simple: 'I promise to abstain from all intoxicating drinks, except used medically and by the order of a medical man, and to discountenance the cause and practice of in-temper-ance.' He later removed the medical clause. Members were rewarded with a numbered pledge card and a medal. A happy family sitting by a fireside is etched on one side of the medal. The husband holds a banner proclaiming 'Prosperity', while his wife holds one that reads 'Domestic Comfort'. Doves fly overhead. On the reverse side, a drunken man, frothing at the mouth, is about to strike his wife on the head with a hammer. A supporting cast of serpents and vultures cheer on his efforts. 'Demon Whiskey' is written on a scroll over their heads.

The temperance movement seems to have brought about marked effects on levels of criminality: murders fell from 247 in 1838 to 105 in 184, while 'assaults on police' fell from ninety-one in 1837 to fifty-eight in 1841. Similarly, the incidents of 'incendiary fires' and robberies fell dramatic-ally. The effect of sobriety on 'faction fights' was significant; they fell from twenty in 1839 to eight in 1841. However,

Mathew did not ignite the imagination of the middle and upper classes, and was not given unqualified support by the Church. The formidable and influential Archbishop of Tuam John McHale was a particularly trenchant critic. Ostensibly, he objected to the movement's association with Protestantism, but he had an antipathy towards Mathew, possibly because he could not bear anyone else being a powerful voice among Ireland's overwhelmingly Catholic population. In the early years of his campaign, Mathew held mass rallies and spectacular parades throughout the country. The population of Dublin was not as intoxicated by his charms, and, coupled with financial mismanagement, this led to the movement petering out. In 1884, Mathew was arrested for his mounting debts. Somewhat ironically, there is a pub in Cork today called Sober Lane, recalling Father Mathew; it is named after the lane on which it stands, which in turn was named to honour the temperance campaign that began nearby.

The Great Famine of 1845 to 1851 changed everything. Temperance was sidelined. The sole concern for many was to stay alive. Those who survived the Famine and did not emigrate were often left with insurmountable poverty, a desolated countryside and the possibility they and their family would be evicted from their land at short notice. Many Irish people turned to alcohol as an assuaging force in their disrupted lives. Cathy Caruth, in *Trauma: Explorations in Memory*, writes that an event such as a famine can lead to 'wide-scale depression and an entirely changed society'. Trauma, according to Caruth, is 'an overwhelming experience of sudden or catastrophic events, in which the response to the event occurs in the often delayed and uncontrolled repetitive occurrence of hallucinations and other intrusive phenomena'. Alcohol abuse is commonly one such intrusive phenomenon. Caruth goes on to say that 'the traumatised carry an impossible history within them, or they become themselves the symptom of a history they cannot entirely possess'.

It is unsurprising that a new temperance movement arose from the ashes of the old. Father James Cullen founded the Pioneer Total Abstinence Association (PTAA) in 1898. He was motivated by seeing the enormous social damage done to families by alcohol in his parish in Dublin. Poverty was widespread, but addiction to alcohol frequently brought destitution. At first, the Jesuit priest accepted only women into his organisation. He believed they were inherently more spiritual and had witnessed the destruction alcohol wrought on the men, but he later relented, allowing men to join the ranks. Cullen was not a mass-rally crusader like Father Mathew. The members of the PTAA wore a pin with an image of the Sacred Heart, and took a pledge to abstain from alcohol for life. Along with this 'heroic sacrifice', as Cullen called it, members were required to say a special prayer twice a day. In 1905, there were 43,000 members. In 1906, there were 70,000, and by 1910, 100,000 had signed up. In 1917, even though a considerable number had been expelled for failure to live up to the pledge, membership stood at 250,000. Cullen also founded the *Irish Messenger of the Sacred Heart*, a religious magazine with enormous circulation in Catholic Ireland, which he used to further his message of temperance. He linked temperance to patriotism, blaming the loss of the Battle of Vinegar Hill in his native County Wexford on the 'treachery of drink'. In the 1950s, as many as one in three Irish adults were members, and even though membership has declined considerably since then, there are still more than 100,000 Pioneers in Ireland.

As a legacy of the glory days of Ireland's temperance movements, the country still has a higher percentage of teetotallers than many other developed nations; it also has a high percentage of heavy drinkers. In a postcolonial country where subterfuge and getting one over on authority have always been national sports, prohibition would probably have failed abysmally. The Irish pub industry has never lacked in inventiveness, as the next chapter will show.

Special Exemptions:

Spirit Grocers, Early Houses and Bona Fides

Spirit Grocers

In his 1902 paper presented to the Irish Temperance Society on 'Licensing and Public-House Reform in Ireland', William Lawson identified the problem of groceries mixed with draper's shops, with licences to sell alcohol, as a particular social evil. In Dublin, 90 per cent of the trade was mixed in this way, which he felt allowed women to put drink on grocery accounts and put families into debt. This type of pub – a spirit grocer – has played a significant role in the history of licensed premises in Ireland, and continues to be a design motif in new Irish pubs. Spirit grocers were originally a response to the emergent temperance movement of the mid nineteenth century and the consequent drop in sales of spirits. Publicans sought to diversify, and were allowed to trade in another area, or areas, of their own choosing: meat, hardware, drapery and groceries all became common complementary businesses.

In his 1835 report to the House of Commons on the public-house licensing situation in Ireland, John Edgar was critical of the moral standards of some of those given licences. His friend, Sir Robert Bateson MP, had attempted to prevent the renewal of a licence of a man who had, in one of his fits of drunkenness, taken a spade and 'sallied forth, smashing windows and terrifying the whole neighbourhood'. This 'member of the lower orders' obtained a licence even though he was subsequently condemned for murdering his father. In fact, Edgar had never seen anyone refused a spirit grocer's licence. Nine out of ten owners developed difficulties with alcohol; many of them were run by 'melancholy specimens caused by distilled spirit'. Edgar claimed to know three spirit grocers run by widows whose husbands had committed suicide. The first man had drunk himself to death, the second was transported for stealing while drunk and threw himself overboard, 'and of the family of the third, two sons and four daughters became drunkards'. There was a sign on a Belfast pub that read 'The last shift', and he had no doubt that opening a spirit grocer was the very last shift. Edgar was asked to assess the extent of female drinking in the spirit grocers. These shops had caused 'much mischief', he said, as women who never considered going into an ordinary public house had no compunction in entering the spirit grocer. He was particularly concerned about servants and 'mechanics' wives', and described the situation in Dublin: 'It is quite common, in Dublin particularly, to have at one end of the counter a large pile of tea chests for females to go behind, to be hid from sight; but the dangerous secrecy arises chiefly from the want of suspicion in persons going into grocers' shops; other things may be wanted there, whereas going into a spirit shop, nothing is supposed to be wanted except intoxicating drink.'

The quality of the liquor served in the spirit grocers was poor and often adulterated, said Edgar. He gave an example of a whiskey known as 'kill the beggar' in Belfast because 'it first makes the beggar and then kills the beggar'. There was an even worse concoction called 'corduroy', so named because it gave a rough feeling on the tongue and palate. Adulteration and stretching of the spirits were common. Some spirit sellers could make a gallon of whiskey go three or four times further than others. He had heard it stated that there were persons travelling around to the different spirit sellers, offering their services at a certain rate for 'adulterating spirituous liquors'.

R. J. White, retired High Sheriff and Army Contractor of Dublin, was called to provide evidence on the frequenters of public houses in the city. He knew of one pub near St Stephen's Green that over 300 female servants attended every Sunday. Instead of going to a place of worship, 'they are met by men of different kinds and they support these fellows from their earnings as female servants'. J. C. Graves of the Dublin Metropolitan Police was questioned about crime statistics for drunkenness and brawling. He painted a grim picture. The previous year, 20,000 people had been arrested, and he believed that the continued proliferation of spirit grocers would worsen the situation. He was reliably informed that many of the labouring classes spent over a quarter of their wages on alcohol. George Whitmore Carr was asked for his thoughts on spirit consumption in Ireland. He, too, singled out the threat to women, particularly servants: 'Many servants, formerly respectable, especially female and confidential servants, have been thus brought to ruin; a screen of tea chests in the grocer's shop allows the cordial, which is given as a mark of regard and gratitude for good custom, to be taken by the female unseen and unsuspected. The grocer who gives the drams will be sure of ill-gotten trade; and an unprincipled servant, made so by the love of spirits, will not fail to invent an excuse for giving him the preference.'

At the end of proceedings, John Edgar was asked to sum up his thoughts. There should, he said, be 'a refusal to give permission to grocers in Ireland to sell spirituous liquors by retail' because it was a violation of the actual law of the country. Edgar thought much of the legislation framed in England for Ireland aimed to extract the maximum taxes without taking the people into consideration. In England, spirits with alcohol content above 17 per cent could not be sold, but the limit was 25 per cent in Ireland, on which three times as much duty had to be paid. Above all else, the proliferation of spirit grocers had to stop:

> The multitude of spirit shops I have already mentioned, but I cannot mention it too often as a pestilent source of mischief and ruin. Each new spirit shop is a new pest-house, no matter what be its own respectability or the respectability of the owner. Each new spirit shop is a source of temptation; temptation to its keeper and all his connection; temptation to the whole neighbourhood. Many of our spirit shops are of the basest character; night houses, houses of assignation, the nurseries of

prostitution and crime; for in Ireland the same truth holds good which was so strongly expressed by an aged and influential distiller in England, who gave as a toast at a public dinner for the trade in the metropolis, 'The distiller's best friends – the poor whores of London.'

In 1854, when James Haughton was giving evidence to a House of Commons enquiry on public houses, he was asked about licensing laws for spirit grocers:

Chairman: Are all public houses licensed in Dublin?

Haughton: Yes . . . Grocers get licences on easier terms than publicans, but they are prohibited from selling by retail, or from allowing spirits to be drunk on the premises. I understand grocers get licences more freely, and there is not the same strict examination.

Chairman: Can a grocer sell any spirits?

Haughton: Yes, but not by retail. He may sell it to persons coming in and carrying it away; I do not know what the quantity is.

Chairman: He may not have it drunk on the premises?

Haughton: No.

Chairman: May he sell any quantity to be taken away?

Haughton: Yes, to be taken away by the purchaser.

Chairman: Is there any mischief in this practice?

Haughton: A great deal of mischief attends that practice. The giving of licences to grocers is a thing which requires particular attention; in fact, it was intended with so much evil that at one time the grocers in Ireland were prohibited altogether from selling spirits; but they managed to sell them by taking a house next door or by dividing their premises and having a party selling who was not the ostensible owner of the grocer's establishment.

The Chairman expressed surprise:

Chairman: It is a distinct evasion of the law?

Haughton: A distinct evasion of the law, for which several have been published.

Chairman: Do you say that they frequently give their customers drink?

Haughton: It is imagined that they give drink to their customers for nothing, and the servants coming in this way, are very often made accustomed to drink, and the appetite for it is created, and the women servants are very much injured in consequence of the practice.

Chairman: Do you think that that results from allowing grocers to sell spirits, or from the inveterate habits of drinking which those persons have who go to the grocers' shops?

Haughton: I think the habit is created by going to the grocers' shops and getting the spirits. When once the habit is created, we know how difficult it is to eradicate. I do not think that any restriction by Parliament could prevent that evil: I do not know of any mode of preventing the evil except by entire prohibition of the manufacture of strong drinks.

Chairman: Does this practice you have described prevail much in Dublin?

Haughton: Yes.

In 1868, Robert Lindsay, a Belfast publican, reckoned only 5 per cent of the city's 102 spirit grocers were genuine grocers selling tea, coffee and sugar in substantial amounts; the rest relied almost solely on the trade of spirits. Legally, spirit grocers were only allowed to sell alcohol for consumption off the premises and were limited to two quarts of alcohol per person, but both edicts were widely ignored. Grocers commonly served drinks on the premises, and sent the patrons out the back door when alerted by lookouts with whistles that police were in the vicinity. While spirit grocers generally sold tea and coffee, this was 'more a blind than anything else'. Any person, Lindsay said, could pay £10 and obtain a licence without any reference to their character or the nature of the premises.

The Chief Commissioner of the Dublin Metropolitan Police, J. L. O'Ferrell, admitted spirit grocers stayed open all hours, served drink on the premises and refused no one. They even stayed open on Christmas Day, Good Friday and every Sunday. The standard public houses were much more orderly, he said, but the spirit grocers were a law unto themselves. The police were powerless to prevent this drinking. They had to prove a financial transaction was involved, which they found impossible to do.

According to the Dublin Metropolitan Police report of 1881, there were 232 spirit grocers in the jurisdiction, of which, they estimated, seventy were breaching the regulations. Summonses were issued against sixty-six establishments, and forty-seven were convicted. In addition to these convictions, seventy-three houses were convicted of selling alcohol without a licence. Interestingly, there were ninety-three coffee houses, up from twenty-seven the previous year – an increase of over 300 per cent. This was part of the effort by Henry Young and his associates in the Dublin temperance movement to widen the social outlets available to the working class, but it did not achieve long-term success. Called 'coffee taverns', they usually had a reading room and a lecture hall where the message of abstinence could be reinforced. Lucas' coffee house on Cork Hill and The Globe on Essex Street were frequented by the upper classes, but The Coffee Palace on Townsend Street was the most ostentatious of these establishments, with a 13-foot, marble-topped bar, gold fish tank, copper urns and a comprehensive library.

In 1887, 310 of the 641 spirit grocers in Ireland were in Dublin. There was political reluctance to grant regular licences because the tax take was significantly higher from spirit grocers. The House of Commons discussed a Sale of Intoxicating Liquor to Children Bill in 1901. It was proposed that children would no longer be allowed to enter public houses, but J. J. Clancy MP argued that this would present particular difficulties in Ireland. Children went into spirit grocers because they sold products other than alcohol, and to prevent them doing so would 'be to inflict disabilities on the people of Ireland such as were not imposed on the people of England'. He warned the parliamentarians not to incur the political wrath of the spirit grocers. He estimated 'three-fourths of the publicans in Ireland' were nationalists, and if there was any 'stress or struggle between the Government and the people', this could prove costly.

The excise records for spirit grocers from July 1838 to July 1844 indicate that most of them were small business concerns – or else paid little tax. *The Statistical Journal and Record of Useful Knowledge* by William Pixley provides a wealth of financial data on Irish publicans of the nineteenth century. Over this five-year period, Malick Fleming of 81 Lower Mount Street, Dublin, paid just over £27 to the Exchequer, while Simon Martin of 4 Lower Dorset Street contributed £18. Mary A. Eaton had a spirit grocer at 4 Lower Mount Street, and paid £2, 7 shillings. There were five spirit grocers listed for Grafton Street: Joe Byrne, William Robert Kennedy, Richard Frances, Francis Faulkner and Richard Jones. Richard Beer of Aungier Street made the top payment of £84, while James McCormack of Portland Place made the lowest, contributing £2 to the state coffers.

Spirit grocers were central to the Irish rural economy in the twentieth century. In 1935, the *Licensed Vintner and Grocer* magazine claimed 'the trade sells 95 per cent of all foodstuffs and consumable household requisites in this country'. Many took particular pride in their tea-blending skills, particularly during the rationing period of the Second World War. Typically, the premises had rows of drawers behind the counter containing spices, flavourings, tea and tobacco, but different spirit grocers had different layouts. Many sold fruit and vegetables. Others had hardware products for sale. Some licence holders bought agricultural goods like eggs and butter from local farmers and sold them on the wholesale market in the cities. Agricultural feed was a common commodity and one of the biggest sellers in many establishments. A common characteristic was the small space left for drinkers and the general lack of comfort in the seating. The vast majority of rural spirit grocers were also the owners' homes. The pub was an extension of the private dwelling, usually one ground-floor room of the owner's house. Today's kitsch-laden replicas promoted by pub manufacturing companies are not generally an accurate representation of the reality. In the majority of cases, it was a much sparser space with few adornments. They tended to have low ceilings and open fires – a necessity in a time before central heating. Novelist William Carleton was a fan of pub fires. He thought they gave the heart 'a finer and more touching notion of enjoyment than the glitter of the theatre or the blaze of the saloon'. The old folk song 'A Jug O' Punch' describes the attraction of the combination of a fire and alcohol:

> What more diversion can a man desire
> Than to sit him down by an alehouse fire
> Upon his knee a pretty wench
> And upon the table a jug o' punch

From the 1960s on, spirit grocers faced competition from supermarkets, as well as from farming cooperative societies, which began to sell farm supplies and animal feedstuffs. After the partition of Ireland, spirit grocers in the newly created Northern Ireland had to choose between operating as standard shops or as full public houses, selling alcohol only. This accounts for the relative rarity of the interior architecture of spirit grocers there. Some of the most iconic pubs in Ireland were spirit grocers – some still are – and frequently make it onto lists of 'must see' places for tourists: Dick Mack's in Dingle, County Kerry, is also a cobbler's shop; Morrissey's in Abbeyleix, County Laois, has a grocery section.

One of the most sought-after styles from the Irish Pub Company – the biggest player in the 'Irish Pub' overseas boom – is the 'country shop' model. All over the world, there are pubs with shelves and drawers designed to hold groceries and haberdashery, which will never sell a loaf of bread or a button. There are few spirit grocers left in Ireland selling groceries or anything else. In *Sea Legs: Hitchhiking the Coast of Ireland Alone*, Rosita Boland spoke to Mary Ann Saint George in Ballyvaughan, County Clare: 'People would come in and do their shopping and then have a drink before they went on their way. But then the supermarket came and I wasn't able to compete with it . . . I decided to close it down. And it was a pity. Because people liked coming here, and I liked being here, and hearing all the bits of chat . . . you're five years too late for a drink, dear.'

New spirit grocer's licences were no longer issued after 1910, but there is nothing stopping premises with previous licences from selling produce other than alcohol.

Early Houses

From 1927, 'early house' pubs were allowed to open at 7 a.m. in Ireland. Originally granted to serve dock workers, market traders, milkmen, bakers and others who were up to work early in the morning, there are roughly fifteen remaining early-house licences in Dublin, with none granted since 1962. In 2008, plans were mooted to abolish them, but the legislation remains the same. The Minister for Justice at the time, Dermot Ahern, while not well disposed to such pubs, was prevailed upon to keep the status quo. The advisory committee – with the encouragement of the Vintners Federation – took cognisance of changing demographics and increasing patterns of night-shift work. There are approximately fifty early-house licences left in the country, but anecdotal evidence suggests many of them are only used occasionally, and some not at all.

The now-defunct satirical magazine *The Slate* ran an article on Dublin early houses in 2003. The first rule of early houses, they said, is 'never talk to anyone with a plastic bag on the table in the front of them. This could contain a gun, some heroin, a dead baby or their soiled underpants – none of which you want to engage with at that stage of a night out.' Neither should you try to put on a Dublin accent, because 'you will have your head kicked in if you pretend to be a local while talking about the oneness of life and gurning your head off'. Written at the height of the ecstasy-fuelled rave culture, the piece also warned the reader not to be the first person to start dancing as 'there will almost always be some clueless West Brit who can take that role on instead' and 'dancing around in sunglasses may seem appropriate to your exhausted brain, everybody else will be saying "that dickhead thinks he's George Michael".'

The magazine reviewed a number of the Dublin early houses. The Chancery Inn on Inns Quay – supposedly the first stop for prisoners released from Mountjoy Prison – they said, was the sort of place where you would probably have to be 'Mike Tyson or Johnny Adair to get turned away'. Adair was a notorious loyalist thug. The magazine could not recommend The Chancery Inn to night workers looking for a quiet pint at the end of a shift, because 'dancing clubbers are surrounded by everyone from Ballyfermot lesbians on smack to locals sinking ten quick ones before the day gets going'. In 2010, a reviewer on the website Yelp recommended it as the best early house in Dublin. She warned it was also the 'scaldiest' place she had ever been: 'It's a crapshoot whether you'll get in – often they have a "regulars only" policy, which means they exclude anyone with a full set of teeth and who doesn't look like life has completely ruined them. If you prefer to keep rape as a fantasy, you might not want to risk the Chancery, but if you're looking for material for your Basketball Diaries, it's a great place for a drink at 7 a.m.'

The Slate also reviewed the Windjammer of Townsend Street: 'With a name like the Windjammer you might think this is Dublin's only gay early house. And for one day a year, after the Trinity Ball, you wouldn't be far wrong as this is a traditional post-ball favourite for posh dicks in tuxedos.'

Slattery's on Capel Street offers a more rarefied experience. Full breakfast is served from opening. The Galway Hooker in Heuston train station is a popular haunt for early starters, and is a good place to find non-travelling ticket holders on Good Friday (when it is illegal for the majority of establishments to sell alcohol). The *Come Here to Me!* blog lists thirteen active early houses in Dublin city as of 2015. As well as Slattery's and The Galway Hooker, it mentions The Pádraig Pearse, The Windjammer, The Chancery Inn, Ned

Scanlon's, The Dark Horse, Molloy's, The Metro, The Capel, The Boar's Head, M. Hughes and Delaney's. The Fisherman's Bar in Howth is, it says, the only active early house in the Dublin suburbs.

Bona Fides

Bona fide houses utilised a legal loophole – a hangover from the days of coach travel – that allowed a genuine traveller 3 miles from his place of residence to partake of alcohol outside normal hours. If you lived in Dublin city, the limit extended to 5 miles from your habitual residence. According to the law, the customer had to have 'travelled in good faith', not for the purposes of taking refreshment; travellers could go into an inn for 'refreshment in the course of a journey, whether of business or pleasure'. It was a legally fraught area. In order to prove a public house was taking advantage of it, the court had to prove the publican did not believe his customer was a bona fide traveller when serving outside normal hours.

Famous Dublin bona fides included Lamb Doyle's in the foothills of the Dublin Mountains, Walsh's Sandyford House – then known as the Widow Flavin's – and the Dropping Well in Dartry. Brendan O'Hehir and John Dillon provided an account of Dublin bona fides in *A Classical Lexicon for Finnegans Wake* (1977): 'The law took account of the unhappy wanderer far from home at the dread hour . . . in the sizeable city of Dublin, well furnished with public and private transportation, it became no trick at all for respectable citizens to drink at night in suburban pubs five miles on more from the beds in which they had spent the previous night and would also spend the ensuing night, when the charms of bona fide drinking palled.'

Drinkers in the city centre drove out to the suburbs and vice versa. Flann O'Brien, the great writer and satirist, observed that he drove himself to drink. Neighbouring villagers met each other on the road to swap pubs for the night. In Dublin, you could continue on to one of the 'kips' in the city centre where drink was served illegally and, in most cases, prostitutes were available. 'The Irish Bona Fide Nuisance', an article published in Boston's *The Sacred Heart Review* in September 1902, railed against the system. The anonymous author asserted that, while 'travelers, tramps and tourists' are found everywhere, the 'so-called Bona Fide traveler is peculiar to Ireland'. The author described Blackrock and 'Dunleary' [Dún Laoghaire] as 'blots' on Ireland on a typical Sunday night, when three quarters of the people were there 'for the purpose of indulging in the luxury of treating one another to drink'. Recognising the situation was much worse in English towns, the author declared that was 'no excuse for an Irishman to make himself a bonham [a piglet] because an Englishman makes himself a hog'.

Bona fides were a topic of debate in the Houses of Parliament whenever intoxicating liquor legislation came up for discussion. In discussing the Alcohol Act of Ireland 1902, the House of Commons voted on a motion to regulate them: 'We do not think it necessary to maintain the right of the bona fide traveller to be served during prohibited hours, but the needs of genuine excursionists cannot be entirely left out of sight. We consider that a limited number of licensed premises, where travellers may be served at specified hours, should be selected by the licensing authority, and that a special licence duty should be exacted in respect of this privilege. The statutory distance might be extended to six miles.' The motion was defeated.

In 1906, the issue was again debated. Robert Dillon, MP for Galway and holder of the hereditary peerage Lord Clonbrock, appealed for the ending of bona fides in Ireland or, if the House could not see its way to do this, they should institute a minimum distance of 6 miles, which should be strictly enforced. His views were echoed by Mr Joseph Patrick Nannetti representing the constituency of College Green in Dublin. Nannetti was a committed Home Rule nationalist and a member of the Irish Parliamentary Party. He later became Lord Mayor of Dublin, and appeared as a character in James Joyce's *Ulysses*. Nannetti described the suburbs on Christmas Day as 'reeking with drunkenness' because of 'those slumdwellers' from the city centre coming to avail of the bona fides. However, he had sympathy with these people because their houses were not decently habitable, and the pub served as a 'poor man's club'. Mr T. W. Russell thought the legislation had to be changed because of Ireland's particular nature. Emigration was constantly depleting the population 'and lunacy was increasing at a pace that was causing thoughtful men to tremble'. The bona fide traveller had become such 'a stupendous nuisance that people everywhere were prepared to abolish him right away without any consideration whatever'. Russell believed 'property in Blackrock, Dundrum, and all the suburbs had been depreciated, and the effect of that pandemonium had been to make a great impression'. He dismissed Mr Nanetti's argument, stating that if a man was to provide a properly built and furnished house for his family, surely he would stay at home and save his money rather than go drinking in a public house. Mr Nanetti had said it was good for a workman to go and get some fresh air and refreshment on Saturday night, but Russell wondered why he could not just take a walk 'without tumbling in the door of a public house', where the air was bound to be 'fetid'.

Godfrey Fetherstonhaugh, MP for Fermanagh, considered the bona fide business absurd now that so many people had access to bicycles and motor cars. It caused particular distress to the little towns near the five cities. He recommended no traveller claiming to be bona fide should be served alcohol without also purchasing a meal of at least the same value as the drink. Horatio Bottomley, MP for Hackney, thought the proposed bona fide legislation 'preposterous'; a 14-mile round walk for a glass a beer amounted to 'criminalisation of the working man'. To add insult to injury, MPs were now proposing the man had to order some 'hybrid burlesque of a meal' even if he was not hungry. To his mind, the bill was a 'burlesque of social legislation'. William Redmond accused Bottomley of being 'a burlesque', resulting in some rancour in the House – a not uncommon occurrence if the records are an accurate reflection of proceedings. Mr Patrick Gormley, MP for Londonderry, thought the whole thing a 'sham' and that the bona fide system should be abolished. It was well known, he said, that the most valuable pubs in Ireland were those slightly over 3 miles from the centre of one of the exempted five cities. That the Irishman was different from others was repeated by Mr James Bryce, the Chief Secretary for Ireland. The Irishman was particularly given to hospitality and the proffering of an invitation to have a drink with his friends was 'more tempting than to the Englishman and much more than to the Scotchman'. Poverty exacerbated the problem: 'the poorer a man was, the more wretched he was, and the more apt he was to seek some consolation in drink'.

In 1908, Joseph Devlin, Nationalist MP from west Belfast and renowned orator, told the House he was familiar with the bona fide situation in Greencastle, a fishing village in County Down. There, he said, the police constabulary regularly checked the drinking establishments in an effort to find out if the customers were genuine bona fide travellers, but this had proven problematic. They took people to the adjacent police station to have their names and addresses verified, but found 'very few of the persons so taken gave correct names and addresses in the first instance'.

Sean O'Ciarain recalled coming home to Belmullet from Scotland and making use of the bona fide clause with his friends in his memoir, *Farewell to Mayo* (1992):

> On Saturday I was in the town and I met Pat Conroy and Pat Carey and another man, Lavelle, and we had a few drinks together in McDonnell's. People shook hands and asked us what part of England we had been in . . . We left McDonnell's about midnight and headed down to Forty's and we were not long there when two Guards came in and chased away the locals. We were OK they told us; we were bona fide, and so we could drink on, meaning that we lived more than three miles away, we were travellers and therefore entitled to a drink after hours. And what do you think the Guards did once they got the others away? They came into the

bar for a drink with us, and not only one drink, we had several drinks before we left, and the two men in uniform were as canned as any of us. It was a good old night.

Rosses Point, 5 miles from Sligo town, was a testing ground for bona fide legislation in the 1930s. Redmond John Bruen ran a pub in the village adjacent to the Elsinore dance hall. Mr Bruen believed those who travelled to the dances from Sligo town were bona fide and eligible for passes into the pub. The local police did not agree and he was called to the District Court for serving alcohol after midnight. The district judge demurred, recognising the dancers as genuine bona fide travellers, and threw the case out of court. However, the Attorney General appealed the case to the High Court. This time, the judge held that there had been two journeys, one to Rosses Point and one back, and hence the travellers were allowed the privilege in respect of each journey but not for the time between the two, spent at the dance. The judgement of the district judge was reversed. Mr Bruen did not give up, and appealed the case to the Supreme Court, which found in his favour, adjudging: 'The visitors in the present case were travellers from Sligo and had done nothing to divest themselves of that character by the time the drink was supplied to them.' This placed the onus on the Attorney General to prove that the real purpose for their travels was to get alcohol, and this could not be done. From then on, everybody was there 'for the dance' while the locals could only look on in envy. While he nobly proved the legislation fallible, it is said the cost of the actions brought penury upon Mr Bruen.

The law was finally changed in 1943. Bona fide travellers could no longer be served between midnight and 6 a.m., and the pubs were eventually abolished in 1963. The widespread use of cars brought the curtains down on a unique phase of the Irish pub and social history.

Trad Sessions, Bombs and Gay Bars:
The Irish Pub in the 20th Century

Leopold Bloom, the central character in James Joyce's modernist masterpiece *Ulysses*, famously said it would be a good puzzle to walk across Dublin without passing a pub. The problem was only solved in 2011 by software developer Rory McCann, using a computer algorithm. There are fewer pubs now than on Bloomsday, 16 June 1904. On his first attempt, McCann could not find a route that did not pass a hotel. He did, however, rule out restaurants with licences to serve alcohol. McCann's route runs from Blackhorse Avenue to Baggot Street. It goes through Stoneybatter, past St James's Gate – the home of Guinness – down Bride Street, across York Street, past St Stephen's Green, detouring through the Iveagh Gardens, and down Adelaide Road. He modified this route in 2014 to avoid passing any hotels. Fittingly, it now crosses the James Joyce Bridge.

The late nineteenth century had seen the continued tightening up of legislation for public houses, against a background of urban decay and poverty. Over 100,000 people lived in shockingly substandard tenements in Dublin, and the pub was one of the few escapes available, as described by an unnamed witness at the Select Committee on Intemperance in 1876: 'Public houses are chiefly established, I think, for the use of those who have no private houses, and two thirds of the population of Dublin have literally no dwellings, no private houses; they have simply a place to sleep in and if you consider a man with a wife and children and perhaps the children a little cross occasionally . . . what are they to do? They cannot go and sit on the flags in the open street . . . the accommodation that they have in a well conducted public house in proportion to their circumstances is as good as gentlemen have in a club.'

A 'witness from the professional classes' used a sporting analogy: 'Thousands upon thousands of the multitudes in this city live and die in places whence a humane sportsman would be ashamed to whistle forth his spaniels. Surely it is vain that I, or such as I, should bid them, steeped in squalor and besieged by diseases, joyless, hopeless, Godless, not seek the light and warmth of the Gin Palace, and the oblivion, however temporary and baneful, they can purchase therein.'

Sir Charles Cameron, Chief Medical Officer for Dublin Corporation, was in agreement: 'The workman is blamed for visiting the public house, but it is to him what the club is to the rich man. If he spends a reasonable proportion of his earnings in the public house he is more likely to be condemned than the prosperous shopkeeper or professional man who drinks expensive wines at the club or restaurant.'

A full history of the legislation pertaining to public houses and alcohol enacted in the twentieth century would be unwieldy, but some of the major changes mirror wider societal changes. Rev. H. J. Johnson of Longford addressed the Irish Temperance Society in 1901, and told those assembled that fifteen licences had been sought and granted at recent licensing sessions in Boyle, County Roscommon, and Ballinamore, County Leitrim, despite a number of objections. This, he fulminated, was beyond the boundaries of common sense. There were now seventy-two public houses in Ballaghaderreen, County Roscommon, a town with a population of 1,360. Nearby Rooskey had nine pubs and a population of 174, but two more were granted on the plea of 'the advent of tourists'. This created a ratio of a pub for every sixteen residents, and the local constable reported that he had only seen two tourists in the entire year. He quoted the editor of a local newspaper, who called the granting of eleven licences to the village of Ballinlough in County Roscommon 'one of the most glaring travesties of justice'. This brought the total number of pubs in the village up to seventeen, and there was a population of only 200. The editor fumed: 'Is there no regard for the welfare of the country in the minds of magistrates who lend themselves to the indiscriminate distribution of licences?' There were 17,695 licensed premises in the country in 1901, up almost 400 from two years previously. The laws were being ignored almost everywhere.

The year 1902 was a watershed in the history of alcohol-related legislation in Ireland. From then on, the emphasis was on controlling the number of licences, and they were never to reach the same heights again. The significant and immediate impact of the 1902 Alcohol Act of Ireland in reducing the number of premises can be seen in the 1925 Report of the Intoxicating Liquor Commission, which stated that the number of people per pub in Dublin had risen to 700. According to the 1926 census, the population of Dublin – county and borough – was 505,654. With 700 people per pub, this roughly translates to 722 pubs in Dublin in 1925. This was a considerable drop of 35 per cent since the intro-duction of the 1902 Act.

In 1906, legislation curtailed drinking hours, with earlier Saturday closing and a two-hour reduction in Sunday hours in the cities. Mr T. W. Russell, Vice President of the Department of Agriculture and MP for Tyrone, spoke to the House of Commons on the effects of earlier closing times on Saturday night since the legislation had changed. He went to each of the five cities to check the situation: 'The effect in Dublin of ten o'clock closing on Saturday night instead of eleven o'clock had been that almost every shop closed at half past ten o'clock. In the old days, poor women in thousands were wont to watch their men leave the public houses at eleven o'clock, and then had to go to market afterwards. Now, however, the streets of Dublin were as quiet as Westminster Hall after ten o'clock.' Arrests for drunk and disorderly conduct were down in all of the cities: 'What was true of Dublin was true also of Belfast, Cork, Limerick and Waterford.' Russell also spoke of the changes wrought by the reduced Sunday hours:

First of all, it was eleven on Sunday night; that was reduced to nine, then to seven, and in 1906 it was reduced to five. Now what was the effect? When it was seven o'clock closing, the crowds were just coming out of the public houses as the people were going to places of worship, and nothing could be more intolerable than that. Now the public houses were closed in these large towns at five o'clock on Sunday evening, and they had only three hours' sale during the whole of Sunday, and the streets were as orderly and peaceful as they could be.

Mr Patrick White, MP for Meath, did not see things through the same rose-coloured lens. He claimed Ireland had changed for a different reason, and he asked his Tyrone colleague if he was aware that the population had decreased by 10 per cent; 'that in a decade, half a million people had vanished'; that it was a period of acute distress; that the reduction of alcoholic drink was due to 'the moral suasion of the clergy'.

Publicans successfully blocked restrictions on opening hours during the First World War. Lloyd George felt drink was a 'deadly enemy', hampering munitions production and damaging potential recruits. He tried to impose higher taxes on beer and wine, and double taxes on spirits as well as diluting their alcohol content by 35 per cent. This was regarded as an attack on the economic life of the country, and united clergy, politicians and the drink trade in an unusual common cause. Dr Fogarty, Bishop of Killaloe, delivered his protest during a confirmation Mass, during which children were taking the pledge to abstain from alcohol.

Eddie Bohan, a Dublin publican, has written about the role of Dublin pubs in the 1916 Rising, the insurgency that sparked a chain of events ultimately resulting in the establishment of the Irish Free State in 1922. The rebels of 1916 began their action by seizing the General Post Office (GPO) in the city centre. Immediately, the commanders sent a detachment to secure other buildings in the immediate area. The owner of nearby Mooney's public house would not allow them access and, despite firing a shot at the door lock, they failed to gain entry. They proceeded to the nearby Ship Tavern, where they found a friendlier reception. It was a public house long associated with nationalist sympathisers.

William Daly, a commandant of the insurgents, recorded the approach rebels took towards alcohol on their mission: 'In passing, I wish to record with pride that a few of the men I was in company with, although hardened drinkers, were stationed in the Ship Tavern and had the taking of anything that was there, did not touch anything and refused the offerings of the barmen.' The pub was later destroyed by British bombing. J. T. Davy's pub in Portobello, on the route between Portobello Barracks and the city centre, was also commandeered by the rebels. They planned to disrupt the movement of troops towards the fighting zone by using the premises as a sniping location. In this, they were successful.

Delahunt's pub on Camden Street was seized on Monday night by the rebels, aided by the republican-minded barman George Heuston. A little further down the street, opposite Jacob's Biscuit Factory, The Swan pub was seized. Michael Molloy was called to testify at an enquiry after the Rising, and spoke of proceedings in the pub: 'Orders were also given that we were to burrow through from Jacob's to a public house at the corner facing Aungier Street. We had two masons in our party and the burrowing was made easy. Strict instructions were given that no Volunteer was to take any drink from the public house. And although I am not a drinking man myself, I must say that this order was strictly obeyed.'

On Monday night, rebel forces retreating from the now abandoned J. T. Davy's pub seized Philip Little's pub. Nearby, Bowe's pub on William Street was also commandeered, but quickly evacuated. In their haste, some of the rebels left behind their weapons, which were bravely retrieved by members of Cumann na mBan, as described by Annie O'Brien, a member of the women's organisation:

> Word came in from a sniping post, a public house called Bowe's at the corner of William St and Coppinger Row, and that the two snipers at that post had evacuated it, leaving their arms behind them, and they sent word to Dawson St to have their arms collected and put into safekeeping. The two of us went to the post and found the house locked up. We went to the house next door where we found a friendly man who showed us up to the skylight, which we got through and onto the roof of the public house. Its skylight was a bit small and only my sister, who was small, was able to get through. She went down and opened the door of the public house for the rest of us. We had to search the whole of the house for the arms and at last we found the two loaded rifles in an office.

Not all pub-related activity during that fateful week was commendable. Looting was common. Two rebels sent out by Pádraig Pearse to deter looters heard roaring and shouting as they passed Meagher's pub on North Earl Street. On investigation, they found a group of old women –

colloquially known as 'shawlies' because of the shawls they wore around their shoulders – deliriously drunk in the cellar. The soldiers pleaded with them to take account of events: 'In the name of the Irish Republic you need to leave this pub and go home to your families.' The rebels were subjected to a barrage of bottles and verbal abuse, and returned to the GPO. When they informed Pearse of the episode, he asked them why they had not followed his orders, to which they replied, 'We would rather fight the British guns than tackle those three auld ones.'

On the north side of the city, O'Reilly's pub on North King Street (now The Tap pub) was seized by the rebels to slow the progress of the British troops from the Royal Barracks (now Collins Barracks). Lambe's on Richmond Road (now Meagher's of Ballybough) was commandeered by another group of rebels attempting to halt the advance of British troops from a training camp on Bull Island towards the city centre. They held the pub until they were ordered to fall back to the GPO. The British Army seized Egan's public house in Smithfield and used it as a firing position on Church Street and North King Street.

By the end of the week's uprising, the collateral damage suffered by the city's hostelries was substantial. Some of the pubs completely destroyed or severely damaged as a result of fire from both sides included Mooney's, McGreevy's and Moore's on Eden Quay, J. Humphrey's and Fee's on Moore Street, Farrell's of Marlboro Street, Kavanagh's on Lower Bridgefoot Street and the famous Brazen Head. The Oval on Abbey Street was destroyed by the end of the week. The pub had been purchased in 1902 by John Egan and, after a major refurbishment, reopened in 1903. It was very popular with both the local journalists and with rebels in the lead-up to the Rising. After the rebellion, the pub remained closed for six years.

Combined with their use by Michael Collins and his Irish Republican Army associates to hold secret meetings and plan attacks during the War of Independence, the pubs of Dublin can justifiably claim an important role in the battle for Irish freedom. The Confession Box – once called the Maid of Erin – is a small pub in the shadow of St Mary's Pro-Cathedral, which had a rarely mentioned role in the War of Independence. The Catholic Church took exception to its members' involvement in the conflict, and some were excommunicated, largely at the behest of Bishop Daniel Cohalan of Cork. Michael Collins was numbered among them. In this pub, sympathetic priests provided the black sheep with communion and confession – hence its present name.

In 1924, the Irish Free State's Intoxicating Liquor Act once again tried to tackle the problem of the illicit distillation, sale and consumption of alcohol in establishments without licences. The police were given significantly enhanced powers to close down shebeens. The Minister for Justice, Kevin O'Higgins, introduced two-hour midday closing time – the 'holy hour' – to keep urban workers from lunch-time drinking. To reduce the number of liquor outlets, it was first established that no additional licences would be allowed. The Competition Authority was asked to close pubs with only marginal trading. As a result, 299 licences were eliminated by 1927, at a cost of just over £50,000. This was not cost-effective, as publicans were compensated for the loss of livelihood, and many of the pubs closed under this legislation had been barely operational. This practice was not officially repealed until some thirty years later, with the Intoxicating Liquor Act of 1960. In 1925, the Government commissioned a report on various matters relating to the pub. The writer George Russell (A. E.), writing in *The Irish Statesman*, was dubious:

> It is merely absurd that a country trying to find its feet should attempt to maintain, in proportion to its population, twice as many licensed houses as England and three times as many as Scotland. The statistics for individual towns are still more startling. In Charlestown and Ballaghadereen, every third house is licensed to sell liquor. Ballyhaunis, with a total population of a thousand, has a drink shop for every twenty of its inhabitants, and Strokestown and Mohill run it close with one for every twenty-six. We wish Mr Kevin O'Higgins had informed the commission how many of these towns can boast a bookshop, a gymnasium, a public swimming bath or a village hall. Throughout the greater parts of rural Ireland, such things are looked upon as ridiculous luxuries, and the mark of social progress is demonstrated by the opening of two public houses where one would normally suffice.

The commission did recognise that there were 119 towns and villages in the country with an excessive number of public houses, but did little about it. There was plenty of debate, but little change. John Troy, the District Judge for Tipperary, argued that there were too many pubs in his area of operation, with the result that many of them stayed open at all hours to generate trade. The chairman, J. J. Horgan, agreed, and added that it was almost impossible for the police to regulate the situation. There ensued the typical tortured debate about Sunday opening. Judge Troy said he looked upon habitual drunkenness more as a disease than anything else – a view ahead of its time.

The main focus of legislators from the foundation of the Irish Free State was on licensing, or what Minister for Home Affairs Kevin O'Higgins referred to in 1923 as the need for 'a genuine licensing code, not a bewildering maze of statutes and decisions, which, while creating offences, also provided ingenious means of escape for unscrupulous people and for people otherwise honest but who were driven to lie and worse in the struggle for existence'. O'Higgins was careful in the language he used, insisting he was not hostile to the licensed trade or prepared to indulge prohibitionists. He pushed through different legislation, but was vague in addressing the question of whether Ireland was a nation of drunks. Speaking in the Dáil in 1927, he said excessive drinking was a 'question of angles'. He did not take it 'that excessive drinking means that you fall over a man every five yards on your way home', but 'if we are drinking beyond our resources there is excessive drinking'. He pointed out that £17.5 million was spent on drink in the financial year of 1925–6, and wondered if this was excessive drinking: 'Some people would say no. Some people would say very differently. At any rate, I object to the criterion that drunkenness and drunkenness alone is to be the test of whether or not there is excessive drinking.'

In 1927, an end was put to the sale of drink on Christmas Day, Good Friday and Saint Patrick's Day. Publicans and alcohol were reviled by many in authority in the new state, and this is reflected in some of the laws enacted. A female teacher could not marry 'the owner, part owner or occupier of a public house, or an assistant therein or other persons having an interest therein'. Teachers were not permitted to work in any business or occupation that could 'impair their usefulness'. They were especially forbidden to keep 'public houses for the sale of spirituous liquors or to live in any such house'.

In 1956, the Minister for Justice appointed a commission of enquiry consisting of twenty-two people, including representatives of the licensed trade, the Pioneer Total Abstinence Association (PTAA) and the Dáil, to review the licensing laws. Garda authorities recommended the liberalisation of the existing Sunday opening hours. They were difficult to enforce, and drunkenness was no longer a major problem in the country, they argued. The Garda Commissioner provided figures to back up the assertion: in 1955, 3,782 people were prosecuted for drunkenness, compared with 7,165 in 1925 and 45,670 in 1912. The general tone of the report was progressive; it suggested a mature democracy should not have to behave paternalistically towards its citizens in alcohol-related legislation. The Catholic Church demurred: 'Increased facilities for obtaining intoxicating liquor by the extension of the general opening hours will inevitably lead to a greater extension of alcoholism, which, in modern conditions, has most serious moral and social effects in the increase of delinquency and in widespread dangerous behaviour.' The issuance of a new public-house licence in both urban and rural areas would be dependent on the extinction of two existing licences. Hotels could have a public bar forthwith on the extinction of a public-house licence. Seán Lemass, the Taoiseach at the time, diverted criticism when he said 'drunkenness is a sin for which men are responsible to a higher court than ours'.

In the Intoxicating Liquor Act of 1960, further restrictions were placed on the geographical mobility of licences. A licence issued to a rural pub was required to remain in a rural setting. Urban licences could only be purchased for use in other urban areas. In 1962, less restrictive opening hours were introduced, as was the concept of ten minutes' 'drinking-up time'. From 1979, a 'substantial meal worth £2 or more' had to be served to obtain a late extension. This was an attempt to address the problem of abuses of special exemptions. The 1988 Intoxicating Liquors Act extended opening hours and drinking-up time. It also granted restaurants special licences to serve alcohol.

Tim Pat Coogan, historian and journalist, noted the changes taking place in Irish pubs during the 1960s. In 1966, he wrote, 'ladies are now frequently seen in pubs unescorted by men, though not yet true in country areas. The entrance of the fair sex into so traditional a male preserve as the pub is certainly a sign that male attitudes are beginning to change.' Change in Irish society was a slow process. In an interview in 1995, publican Mary O'Connor from Edenderry, County Offaly, told a story that illustrates the prevailing mores of the 1960s. In 1994, a couple came to her pub for a drink and said they were celebrating their twenty-fifth wedding anniversary by cruising the Grand Canal, a repeat of the journey they had made on their honeymoon in 1969. On the original trip, they had also called to the Harbour Bar and were refused service by Mary's father, but 'this time she drank Guinness until she fell out the door'. Mary recalled that women were never seen in the bar when she was growing up unless there was a very specific reason. They were immediately brought into the taproom, a small space annexed to the bar where the beer kegs were stored, and had to ring a bell for attention. Tony O'Donoghue, a local historian from Crossmolina, County Mayo, recalled an episode from 1958. Three Englishwomen holidaying in the vicinity went into a public house in Enniscrone, County Sligo, and ordered pints of Guinness. The incident was a talking point for miles around, and one of the local clergy was so incensed he saw fit to denounce the women from the altar of the church.

In his 1968 book *James Larkin: Irish Labour Leader, 1876–1947*, Emmet J. Larkin provided an analysis of the life and influence of the labour advocate, but at one stage he became sidetracked into the issue of women and children in pubs. He and his team observed twenty-two pubs over a fortnight in 1967 and categorised the people entering them. Over the fortnight, 44,574 women and 27,999 children went into the pubs. Of the children, 5,087 were babies in arms, which he found 'lamentable'.

The Limerick Rural Survey was a landmark sociological project carried out in the early 1960s under the auspices of Muintir na Tíre and directed by Maynooth College philosophy graduate Patrick McNabb. Founded in 1937 by a Tipperary priest, Canon John Hayes, Muintir na Tíre proclaimed itself to be 'a movement for the promotion of the true welfare, spiritual, cultural and material, of Ireland and, in particular, of its rural people, through the application of Christian social principles'. Despite the national scope of its aspirations, the movement's main work took place in Cork, Limerick and Tipperary between 1937 and 1958. The national headquarters of the movement was – and still is –

in Tipperary town, close to the Bansha parish of Canon Hayes. The survey was comprised of seven reports produced between 1960 and 1964: 'Migration' in 1960 by McNabb, 'Physical Geography and Geology' in 1961 by P. J. Meghen and others, 'Social Structure' by McNabb in 1962, 'Social Provision and Rural Centrality' by Jeremiah Newman in 1963, and 'Social History' by P. J. Meghen in 1964. Also in 1964, a volume collecting all the reports was edited by Jeremiah Newman – a future Bishop of the Limerick Diocese. McNabb briefly addressed the role of the pub in the report on social structure: 'A respectable woman would never set foot inside one of those places unless there is a grocery store attached. She certainly never drinks in the local bar.' McNabb did not like the nature of some of the male communication patterns in pubs, and particularly deplored 'the habit of taking a rise out of someone'. He thought the inside of the rural Limerick pubs 'gloomy and functional'. Alcohol was a rite of passage in the male fraternity. When a young man took his first drink, it was a coming of age: 'This was a sign that he had grown up and was acceptable to the male community.'

American anthropologist John Cowan Messenger spent nineteen months between 1958 and 1966 intermittently living on Inisheer, one of the Aran Islands off the west coast of Galway, and documented his findings in *Inis Beag: Isle of Ireland* and later in *Inis Beag Revisited*. He studied the social life, customs and family structures of the islanders. He attended storytelling nights in the islanders' houses and spent time in the pub. The all-male pub patrons played cards, sang and drank. The two most influential people on the island, according to Messenger, were the head schoolteacher and the head barman of the island's only pub who was known as 'the King'. This man, he wrote, was politically active and had 'great business acumen'; he was 'a friend of priests, politicians and civil servants'. The traditional pastime of visiting each other's houses was dying out and only remained common among the elderly men. The main findings of Messenger's report described the sexual repression evident on the island: a taboo on breastfeeding and nudity, sex viewed as a purely mechanical process of reproduction, no swimming, and sexual intercourse confined to the missionary position with anything else viewed as 'deviant and sinful'. Messenger concluded this repression resulted in 'high levels of masturbation, drinking and alcohol-fuelled fights'. The islanders viewed his work as a betrayal of trust and regretted the access they had granted him – a not uncommon after-effect of ethnography.

Rosemary Harris' *Prejudice and Tolerance in Ulster* studied social behaviours and attitudes among rural communities in south County Tyrone from 1952 to 1965. It compared the lives of Protestants and Catholics, prosperous lowland dwellers and poor hill farmers. Women did not socialise outside the home except at Church services; the four pubs in Ballybeg were the sole preserve of men. Harris did not mention socialising patterns, but commented extensively on religious fault lines, which were reflected in different affiliations and viewpoints. It was an area characterised by subtle sectarian divisions, but not yet sundered by the violence that would come with the Troubles in the 1970s. The Catholics regarded the Protestants as 'materialists and philistines': the Catholics, in turn, were considered 'self-indulgent and indolent' by their Protestant neighbours.

In 1948, and again in 1950, Martin Corry, a Fianna Fáil TD, attempted to bring in legislation to liberalise Sunday pub opening hours. The bills were defeated – not because of worries about public health, but on moral grounds. The Catholic Church denounced them, and that was enough for the majority of parliamentarians. Oliver J. Flanagan, a Fine Gael TD from Mountmellick in County Laois and a voice of conservative Catholic rural Ireland, commented: 'Does he desire to see a state of affairs prevail in this country whereby on the dark wintry Sundays in rural districts, the young boys and the young men, immediately they leave mass, plunge their way into various public houses and remain there? . . . Does he know that intemperance exists to a very great extent in this country at the moment? . . . Does he know that champagne is cheaper today than it has been for a considerable time in the past, thanks to Fianna Fáil?'

When the Intoxicating Liquor Act of 1960 finally allowed all pubs to open on Sunday, it was viewed, in some quarters, as the first piece of legislation in the Irish State to ignore the advice of the Catholic Church. Despite a memorandum from the Irish bishops penned by the powerful Archbishop of Dublin, John Charles McQuaid, arguing that increased access to alcohol would result in a steep rise in alcohol-related illness, the Government pressed ahead. Times were changing. Tomas Ó Maoláin, a Labour Senator, greeted the bill thus: 'This is the sixth decade of the twentieth century and this is a civilised community. We are no better and we are no worse than others, but certainly we are as well conducted as any. We are building up a modern progressive democracy. There is no reason why we should fear to get in line with other modern progressive States, which trust their people to be rational in using wisely the liberal facilities they provide for drinking.'

Until 1988, pubs in Dublin and Cork had to observe a weekday 'holy hour' between 2.30 p.m. and 3.30 p.m. All other pubs had been allowed to open at this time since 1962. The holy hour had endured since it was introduced by Minister Kevin O'Higgins in 1924. He was assassinated in 1927 in an episode that was a hangover from the Civil War and not, as some wags said, for introducing the detested legislation. Today, pubs without a late licence can open between 10.30 a.m. and 11.30 p.m. on Monday, Tuesday and Wednesday, between 10.30 a.m. and 12.30 a.m. on Thursday, Friday and Saturday, and between 12.30 p.m. and 11.30 p.m. on Sunday. These opening hours were legislated for in 2000, with one small exception: from 2003, pubs without a late licence had to close at 11.30 p.m. on Thursdays. On the eve of public holidays, opening hours can be extended by an hour. Up until 2000, there were distinctions between 'summer' and 'not summer' opening hours, whereby pubs had to close a half hour earlier during the latter period.

Before the 1950s, it had become uncommon to hear music in bars in Ireland. Despite the encouragement of the Gaelic Revivalists, traditional Irish music in public settings had long been in the descendant. Anything that might have provided enjoyment for people was discouraged in the virtually theocratic state. Traditional music and dancing returned to the cottages and houses of Ireland. This had not always been the case. In 1825 Thomas Armory wrote about a tavern called The Conniving House in his novel *The Life of John Buncle*. He described it as 'a delightful place of a summer's evening' and mentioned the music. Buncle liked to listen to the 'famous Larry Gogan who played on the bagpipes extremely well' and his friend 'dear Jack Latten, matchless on the fiddle'. The Conniving House was in an area of Dublin then known as Brickfields – modern-day Sandymount. Buncle was a fictional student at Trinity College, and the novel recounted his observations and reflections on his travels through Ireland and the north of England. While much of the story is fanciful – he is an expert at pole-vaulting down mountains and has seven wives – the urban geography of Dublin is factual.

The *fleadh cheoil* movement was integral to the revival of traditional Irish music. Competitions organised by Comhaltas Ceoltóirí Éireann (Society of the Musicians of Ireland) were first held in Mullingar, County Westmeath, in 1951 and proved so popular that informal pub and street music sessions became an integral part of the festival within five years. Above anyone else, Seán Ó Riada had the most profound effect on traditional Irish music. Ó Riada had a wide knowledge of Western art music, and while working as a music lecturer at University College Cork, he became interested in Irish traditional music. As his interest grew, he began to explore it in greater depth. He set up a band of traditional musicians in the early 1960s called Ceoltóirí Chualann, with the aim of creating a new music built on the tradition. He made use of classical music forms within the workings of the band, which was made up of fiddle, flute, uillean pipes, accordion and bodhrán, and came up with a formula of playing solos within the group. The poet Thomas Kinsella was effusive in his praise of his friend: 'He reached out and swiftly captured a national audience, lifted the level of music practice and appreciation, restored to his people an entire cultural dimension and added no little to the gaiety of the nation.' Ó Riada's music was played to be listened to and not danced to, thus bringing it across a social divide; it was no longer associated solely with rural areas and poverty – he gave it cultural validity.

Irish traditional music sessions in pubs were popular overseas before they took off in Ireland. The website Session claims the very first Irish music session to take place in a pub was in the Devonshire Arms in Kentish Town, London, in 1948. The practice was equally strong in the big cities of the eastern United States. Folk music became hugely popular in Ireland from the mid 1960s. The Clancy Brothers, the Chieftains, the Dubliners, the Dublin City Ramblers, the Wolfe Tones and later Sweeney's Men and Planxty were some of the more successful bands. Planxty was a key band in Irish musical development because it welded traditional form to contemporary folk music, a style carried on by Moving Hearts among others.

The old dance halls were not suitable venues for traditional music, and Irish pubs began to reconfigure their space to accommodate music sessions. During the showband era, which began in the 1950s, large bands had played the hits of the day in alcohol-free dance halls. It was predicated entirely on dancing, and drunkenness was not tolerated. The buildings were largely breeze block, cold and strictly functional. In the mid 1960s, there were around 700 full- and part-time showbands earning their living from the business. It peaked in the early 1970s. Tastes changed, and people wanted a more sophisticated environment, with comfort and alcohol. Historical buildings housing ancient bars were frequently destroyed and replaced by flat-roofed bunkers, but there were comfortable chairs and carpets. The surroundings were becoming more like a comfortable home. The 'lounge bar' had arrived in Ireland.

It was not just folk music that was growing in popularity; country and western had a great appeal for rural audiences. Publicans had to decide which way to go. Mary O'Connor from Edenderry, County Offaly, remembers sitting down with her family in the early 1970s to consider the future of the pub: 'In the end we decided not to modernise as we were a small family concern but after that the trade dropped badly.' Another publican, Mary Rose Egan, was raised in Egan's pub in Mount Temple, County Westmeath. She recalled the early 1970s as 'the age of beauty board'. The family pub was not doing very well, and they decided to modernise: 'We were losing business to the new lounge bars in nearby Moate and we decided to change. Women were starting to go into new lounges but they wouldn't come into our bar. The grocery and petrol pumps were replaced by a new lounge.' Lounge bars, singing bars and cabarets came to dominate the social scene.

The 1970s in Ireland was a time of increasing prosperity. The national debt had been eradicated for the first time in the history of the state, there was an increase in returning emigrants, and many people now had disposable income. Ireland joined the European Economic Community in 1973, and the national mood was generally positive; future prosperity was envisioned. Women were also going to work in greater numbers and had more money to spend. Families were getting smaller, and people had more time for a social life. The per capita consumption of alcohol doubled between 1960 and 1975, despite a 25 per cent increase in the cost. Television was also becoming more widely available. Images of feminism and liberalism flooded the living rooms of Ireland. Many women were no longer prepared to accept the patriarchal structure of Irish society. The advent of mass tourism resulted in more visitors wanting to hear traditional music. There had been a huge folk revival in America and antennae were sensitised to ethnic sounds. Music became commodified and slickly presented, and was now a viable livelihood for musicians. The relationship between publican and musician had become a professional one in many cases. Musicians left traditional *céilí* bands and formed duets, trios or quartets to play in the pubs. Typically, a quartet included a singer, guitarist, drummer and accordionist. There were still informal sessions, but pubs began to advertise music nights to entertain locals and tourists alike. Repertoires changed and became more eclectic. Lounge bar musicians had to satisfy the tastes of the public, and needed to be able to play jives and jigs, waltzes and quicksteps, as well as to sing ballads. In rural areas, it was particularly important to know a selection of country-and-western songs. Television was key in sparking the ballad boom. The Clancy Brothers from Tipperary along with Tommy Makem from County Armagh achieved phenomenal success in America. They played the bars of Greenwich Village in New York City side by side with such folk luminaries as Bob Dylan, Joan Baez and Pete Seeger.

The net result of these factors was a change in the way people lived their social lives in Ireland. As Eugene Lennon wrote in *The Irish Times*, it seemed 'the popular definition of what constituted a pub had expanded from a narrow parochial viewpoint to a valid and valuable leisure activity. The pub scene had become the pub culture.'

In *Alcohol, Drugs and Health Promotion in Modern*

Ireland, a report by Shane Butler for the Institute of Public Administration in 2002, psychiatrist Patricia Casey argues drinking can be a political act:

> Given the colonial relationship between Ireland and Britain and continued tensions over Northern Ireland, it is possible that for young Irish people, drinking is a political act of defiance . . . In the past, the pub provided a safe haven but with a more confident community today, drinking could be a defiant gesture rather than a retreat. Communal drinking may be a form of everyday resistance, which affords a sense of power or equality. It may facilitate a separate and Irish identity through sharing and resistance against an authoritative and controlling "nanny" state.

The pub bomb was perhaps the most callous and brutal of all the tactics used in the Northern Ireland Troubles, and was responsible for some of the single greatest losses of lives. The Ulster Volunteer Force (UVF), a loyalist paramilitary organisation, attacked McGurk's bar (also called the Tramore Bar) in North Queen Street, Belfast, on Saturday night, 4 December 1971, killing fifteen people. It was not their original target, as the nearby Gem bar had strong connections with the Irish Republican Army (IRA). When the bombers could not get past the security guards there, they went to the nearest bar frequented by Catholics. It was the single deadliest attack in Belfast during the Troubles.

On the night of Saturday 5 October 1974, the IRA set off two bombs at pubs in Guilford in Surrey, claiming the lives of five young people and injuring more than sixty-five others. The first blast was at 8.50 p.m. at the Horse and

Groom in North Street; the second was at the Seven Stars in Swan Lane thirty-five minutes later. No warning was given of either explosion. The army presence in nearby Stoughton and Aldershot meant the town centre was a popular destination for soldiers. The Horse and Groom was popular because it was reputed to have the cheapest beer in town, while the Seven Stars had a disco. Servicemen and women would start their evening at the Horse and Groom and then move on to the Seven Stars. Of the five people killed, four were teenagers. It was the first major act of terrorism in Surrey and the police panicked, rushing to find those guilty. They had little knowledge of the situation in Northern Ireland or of the IRA. Four people – Paul Hill, Gerry Conlon, Paddy Armstrong and Carole Richardson – were wrongly jailed for life for the bombings. Their convictions were quashed in 1989.

The King's Arms pub in Woolwich is a landmark on the London Marathon route. On 7 November 1974, a gelignite bomb containing shrapnel was thrown through a window into the bar, where it killed two men. An active service unit of the IRA claimed responsibility. On 21 November of the same year, a duffel bag containing a bomb was hidden at the Mulberry Bush, a popular pub in downtown Birmingham. A second bomb was left at the nearby Tavern in the Town. It was a Saturday night and both bars were crowded. Shortly after 8 p.m., a vague warning was phoned to the *Birmingham Post* and *Mail* offices, but within minutes the two bombs exploded. Ten people were killed in the Mulberry Bush blast, eleven were killed in the Tavern in the Town and almost 200 were injured between the two explosions. Following the bombings, anti-Irish sentiment ran high in

Britain, especially in Birmingham, which had a substantial Irish immigrant community. By late November, six Irish immigrants had been arrested and charged with the bombings. Hugh Callaghan, Patrick Hill, Gerry Hunter, Richard McIlkenny, Billy Power and Johnny Walker became known as the 'Birmingham Six'. They were convicted in August 1975 and sentenced to life imprisonment. In 1991, after a long campaign conducted on their behalf, an appeals court overturned all six convictions, citing police mishandling of the evidence and indications that the confessions had been coerced.

On 6 December 1982, six civilians, four of them women, and eleven soldiers were killed when a bomb was detonated by the Irish National Liberation Army (INLA), a republican terrorist group, at the Droppin' Well bar in Ballykelly, County Derry. Thirty others were injured. The pub was targeted because it had a disco attended by members of the British Army from the nearby Shackleton Barracks. In June 1986, two men and two women were convicted for their involvement. In the aftermath of the bombing, the INLA released a statement: 'We believe that it is only attacks of such a nature that bring it home to people in Britain and the British establishment. The shooting of an individual soldier, for the people of Britain, has very little effect in terms of the media or in terms of the British administration.' Many people were particularly aggrieved when they described the women as 'consorts'. Shortly afterwards, the Irish Government banned the INLA. Membership was to be punished by seven years in prison. INLA leader Dominic McGlinchey, known as 'Mad Dog', said the owner and the patrons 'knew full well that the warnings had been given and that the place was going to be bombed at some stage'.

Seven people died when three gunmen from the Ulster Defence Association (UDA), a loyalist terrorist group, opened fire on 30 October 1993 in the Rising Sun pub in Greysteel, County Derry, as the patrons waited for a country-and-western band to come on stage. The two men were dressed in boiler suits and balaclavas when they entered the pub. One of the gunmen, Stephen Irwin, shouted 'Trick or treat' and opened fire with an AK-47 rifle. By the time it was over, forty-five shots had been fired, seven people lay dead and a further nineteen were injured. The UDA claimed responsibility, stating it was a revenge attack for a bombing carried out a week previously by the IRA in the Shankhill Road, Belfast, which killed ten people at a fishmonger's. Within two weeks, four men were arrested and appeared at Limavady Magistrates Court charged with the murders. The pub is still open and owned by the family of James Moore, one of those killed in the massacre. There is a memorial to the victims outside the building, which reads: 'May their sacrifice be our path to peace.'

The bombing at Greysteel is regarded as a pivotal incident in the Northern Ireland Troubles. There was widespread concern that the country was facing all-out civil war, and it was the catalyst for another effort to achieve a political solution. Within a year, both the IRA and loyalist para-militaries announced a ceasefire. In 2013, a journalist from *The Belfast Telegraph* approached the Moore family for an interview, but was politely refused: 'We as a family vowed twenty years ago we wouldn't speak out about what happened and that hasn't changed. You are more than welcome here, but you are wasting your time. We all just want to get on with our lives.'

The Northern Ireland Troubles occasionally reached into the Republic. On 21 May 1994, members of the UVF brought a bomb in a holdall to Widow Scallan's pub on Pearse Street, Dublin. At the time, there was a fundraising event for republican prisoners and their families taking place upstairs in the pub. The doorman, Martin Doherty, challenged the bombers and was shot dead. If the bomb had gone off, it would have caused 'carnage', a Garda spokesman said.

On 18 June 1994, a number of terrorists from the UVF, dressed in boiler suits and balaclavas, burst into The Heights pub in Loughinisland, County Down, and opened fire. Six civilians were killed and five more seriously injured. The pub was targeted because it was frequented by Catholics. On the night of the attack, the Republic of Ireland soccer team was playing Italy in the FIFA World Cup. There have been persistent allegations of collusion, and widespread disillusionment with the police and political enquiries. The Police Ombudsman criticised the police investigation. The Ombudsman's report was termed 'a whitewash' by supporters of the victims. One of the victims – Barney Greene, aged eighty-seven – was the oldest person killed in the Troubles. The attack garnered international media attention, and messages of sympathy were sent by the Pope and the British Queen, among other world leaders. Six days later, the UDA tried to repeat the attack at the Hawthorn Inn in the nearby village of Annaclone. This time, the doors were locked, and seven people were injured when the gunmen shot through the windows instead.

The use of pubs as political targets is a reflection of the

centrality of public drinking culture in Irish and British society. As the Troubles in Northern Ireland ratcheted up, pubs and clubs became increasingly divided along sectarian lines. Many of the social clubs created by both sides were methods of generating income for terrorist activities. Some were even used as torture chambers. Despite pubs' visibility and vulnerability as targets for terrorists, they continued to trade through the worst of the Troubles. Thankfully, those violent days are now fading into the past.

Homosexuality was finally legalised in Ireland in 1993. For many years, The George pub and nightclub on South Great George's Street in Dublin was by far the best-known gay bar in the country. Since it first opened in 1985, the country has developed much greater tolerance (gay marriage was legalised in 2015) and a more diverse gay scene, but The George remains at the centre of gay life in Dublin. Not everyone is tolerant, however. In June 2008, on the evening of the Dublin Gay Pride Festival, a bomb scare at The George turned out to be a hoax.

The only previous dedicated gay bar in Dublin, The Viking on Dame Street, operated from 1979 to 1987. Other bars, such as Bartley Dunne's and Rice's, attracted gay clientele in the 1960s, but did not openly trade as gay bars. Both were close to St Stephen's Green and the Gaiety theatre, the best-known gay cruising areas in the city at the time. The Bailey on Duke Street was also a meeting place for gay men on a Saturday morning. The 1958 *Fielders Travel Guide to Europe* described it as 'full of hippies and Gayboys'. David Norris, Senator, gay rights activist and former presidential candidate, described his first encounter with Bartley Dunne's in his memoir *A Kick Against the Pricks*:

Towards the end of my schooldays, I started to explore a little. I had a kindred spirit in school, and we occasionally visited a city centre bar called Bartley Dunne's, which was a notorious haunt of the homosexual *demi-monde*. It was an Aladdin's cave to me, its wicker-clad Chianti bottles stiff with dribbled candle-wax, tea chests covered in red and white chequered cloths, heavy scarlet velvet drapes and an immense collection of multi-coloured liqueurs glinting away in their bottles. The place was peopled by theatrical old queens, with the barmen clad in bum-freezer uniforms. While not being gay themselves, as far as I know, the Dunne brothers were quite theatrical in their own way. Barry would hand out little cards bearing the legend 'Bartley Dunne's, reminiscent of a left bank Paris bistro, haunt of aristocrats, poets and artists'. Whatever about that, Saturday night certainly resembled an amateur opera in full swing. There only ever seemed to be two records played over the sound system: 'Non, Je Ne Regrette Rien' by Edith Piaf, and Ray Charles' 'Take These Chains from My Heart'.

Bartley Dunne's offered sake, tequila and ouzo before any other venue in the city. Mary Frances Kennedy, writing in *The Irish Times* on 15 July 1960, was amazed at the range of wines available: 'Bull's Blood of Eger; Balatoni Riesling; Tokak Aszu and Samos Muscatel'. Dunne referred to his patrons as 'avant garde' and 'bohemian'. The playwright Aodhan Madden described the pub in his memoir *Fear and Loathing in Dublin* (2009) as 'a known haunt of gays, theatrical types, criminals and what passed for the Dublin Bohemian set' and wrote 'it exuded a seedy air . . . drag queens, policemen, judges and doctors all lived out their fantasies here knowing that just beyond the front door was a hostile world'. It was sold in 1990, and mutated into a superpub called Break for the Border.

Rice's stood on the corner of St Stephen's Green, where the entrance to the eponymous shopping centre is now. Anthony Redmond wrote to *The Irish Times* in January 1986, remembering it as 'a place of great warmth, character and charm . . . nothing garish, brash or kitsch about its decor'. It accommodated both gay and straight patrons. Those congregated in the front bar were often blessed by the presence of Ireland's most famous and accepted gay couple, Hilton Edwards and Micheál Mac Liammóir, joint founders of the Gate Theatre.

In 1982, the Charles Self murder case focused unwelcome attention on Bartley Dunne's. Self, a set designer with Raidió Teilifís Éireann (RTÉ), was found murdered in his flat on Brighton Avenue in Monkstown in affluent south Dublin. He had been stabbed fourteen times; six of the wounds were so vicious they went through his back. He was last seen coming out of Dunne's talking to another man before they got in a taxi. There were allegations by the Gardaí that the mainly underground gay community closed ranks and would not cooperate with enquiries, while members of the gay community accused some members of the Gardaí of being homophobic – a fact admitted by an anonymous detective in Stephen Rae's book *Killers: Murders in Ireland*. Nobody has ever been charged with the murder. Contemporary observers and members of the gay community remember it as a tense time when the latent homophobia in Irish society became more palpable and violent 'gay bashings' more common.

'Overt sexual behaviour and European House music isn't accepted everywhere,' according to Jeff Dudgeon in his article 'Mapping 100 Years of Belfast Gay Life' for *The Vacuum* newspaper. He described Maurice Leitch's portrayal of the Royal Avenue Bar in the 1965 novel *The Liberty Lad* as the earliest description of a gay bar in Irish literature. It was the first in the city, operating from the early 1950s, and was often shared with deaf and dumb customers, who occupied the front of the bar. In the novel, Frank, the schoolteacher narrator, is taken to the bar by his gay friend Terry, and is at first nonplussed by the clientele: 'Teds and labourers in clean blue serge donkey jackets with leatherette shoulder patches beside quietly dressed middle aged men and a lot of thinnish younger men who looked like clerks or shop assistants.' After a while, he realises he is in a different environment and is seeing a new version of his friend: 'Here he was with his own kind. Before that night I'd always thought of him as being different, as the misfit in the society in which we moved back home but now it was me who was out of place. It was a strange feeling to have.'

The Chariot Rooms in Lower North Street was the first gay-run bar in Belfast. It was in the central gated area (a 'ring of steel' surrounding the central business district. All those who entered this area were searched), where no other nightlife had existed for several years. Dudgeon describes a night out: 'We had to be processed by the civilian searchers to enter the central area, leading to many camp and ribald remarks. The reasons for the Chariot Rooms closing are obscure although it was well frequented and much loved even by soldiers who duck patrolled through the dance floor, lingering in the warmth and safety.' In the remainder of his article, Dudgeon lists and describes the city's subsequent gay bars: the Whip and Saddle in the Europa, the Crow's Nest in Skipper Street (locally referred to as the Raven's Rectum), the Orpheus Bar in York Street, the Dunbar Arms in Dunbar Links and its replacement the Parliament Bar (now being run as Mynt), the Kremlin in Upper Donegall Street and Dubarry's in Gresham Street.

Scott De Buitléir, founder of the online magazine *EILE*, wrote an article in 2013 on the role of the pub in the Irish gay scene:

> Whether we like it or loathe it, the pub is an intrinsic part of any Irish community . . . the pub still reigns supreme . . . Despite any stereotypical image of a gaggle of gays sitting around their favourite gay bar with a Cosmo, the pub culture applies just as well to the Irish gay community too. The local gay rugby or football team will cheer on Ireland in their sponsor bar, just like a gang of lads (or girls!) will cheer on their local GAA, soccer or rugby team in any other pub in the country. There's genuinely no difference . . . I even know of the odd 'straight' venue that does bingo nights with drag queens . . . when the Sun goes down and you're in the mood for a laugh, the gay bar takes over the role of our community centre, just like any other pub in Ireland.

In December 2014, then Taoiseach Enda Kenny visited members of LGBT Fine Gael in Pantibar – the most 'notorious gay bar' in north Dublin city, according to *Lonely Planet* – where the organisation was having a Christmas party. When Rory O'Neill, the owner and famous drag queen Panti Bliss, was asked why he put photographs of the visit on his Facebook page, he replied: 'Because the Taoiseach in a gay bar is a first. It's significant because only a few years ago a Taoiseach wouldn't have dared, so it shows how times have changed.'

Sean Mullen, the owner of Dignity, a gay bar in Waterford city, told *The Sunday Times* in 2013 that it was getting more difficult to run his business. He opened up two further franchise operations in Galway and Kilkenny, but both subsequently closed. He attributed this to societal changes and social media: 'There isn't the stigma towards showing affection in public as there once was,' he said. He pointed out that it is much easier for people to meet now through social networking and location-based dating apps like Grindr. In the same article, Brian Finnegan of *Gay Community News* suggested there may be an oversupply of venues, and punters have remained loyal to industry stalwarts like The George.

It is unlikely that a bar in Washington will ever become a byword for a school of economics to guide the American government but, arguably, such a thing happened in Ireland during the 1980s. Doheny & Nesbitt on Lower Baggot Street in Dublin is a pub of the old school: a stone floor, a couple of snugs, wooden partitions and dim lights. In 1976, Ronan Foster described it in *In Dublin* magazine: 'There are a lot of people in this town who seem to be unable to enjoy a drink in anything other than uncomfortable surroundings; many of them can be found here. That said, it must also be said that this is a very pleasant pub indeed, even if it often proves difficult to raise your elbow above your waist.' He recommended the snugs: 'These small enclosed rooms, each with access to the bar, are ideal for a quiet drink away from the bustling crowd outside. The trick is getting into one before someone else, and that is no mean feat.' Originally owned by two Tipperary men, Ned Doheny and Tom Nesbitt, how it came to be the gathering point of political and economic opinion-shapers is a story told by John Waters in *Jiving at the Crossroads*, his memoir of the social, political and cultural landscape of Ireland in the 1980s. Niall Fleming worked in Madigan's pub in Donnybrook, near RTÉ. He was friendly with many influential employees of the state broadcaster, such as journalists and producers, and obliged people by cashing cheques in the bar during a postal strike in the 1970s. When he left to work in a bar in Upper Baggot Street, some of his friends followed him. They did not take to his new workplace, but soon discovered the nearby Doheny & Nesbitt. It became the home of some influential people.

Waters lists the principle habitués: Paul Tansey, the economics correspondent with *The Irish Times*; Sean Barrett, a lecturer in economics at Trinity College Dublin; and Colm McCarthy, who had worked for the Central Bank and the Economic Social and Research Institute (ESRI). Journalists, high-ranking civil servants, members of the legal profession and certain politicians also frequented the establishment. Vincent Browne, then editor of *Magill* magazine, provided a link to the media for the voices emerging from this social think tank. Paul Tansey was also able to publish his thoughts in *The Irish Times*. McCarthy later became a paid adviser to Fianna Fáil, sitting on a committee established to rein in public spending, which acquired the name An Bord Snip ('the snipping board'). The group of people who dominated the gatherings at Doheny & Nesbitt viewed Ireland as an economic basket case. According to Waters, Vincent Browne wearied of them and stopped socialising there. He told Waters:

> On the whole, and in many cases individually they are a terrible pain in the ass. They think they have the answer to everything. They also think they are very funny . . . They are tickled to death by meeting people they otherwise deride – for instance they get so chuffed if Charlie [the then leader of the Government, Charles Haughey] speaks to them. They rush around to Doheny's to tell the others all about it, and what brilliant witticisms they said back etc. Pathetic really . . . They also love to go on television and they will tell you again and again how clever and witty they were and how foolish they made others look and all that . . . none of these fellows gives a bugger about anyone who is poor.

The Irish pub came of age in the twentieth century. It evolved from a male-dominated space to a more democratic institution where gender and sexual orientation were no barrier to participation. Its sickening use as a political target in the long winter of the Northern Ireland Troubles points to its central role in Irish society. It is an institution that is ever evolving, and has reflected the development of the nation, warts and all.

'Neurotic and Mercurial':
Alcohol and the Irish

There has been remarkably little research on the role of pubs in Irish society. While this book is not concerned with the health and social effects of alcohol or quantifying alcoholism in Ireland – that is best left to the health professionals – it is important to recognise different cultural attitudes towards alcohol because these have a direct bearing on the pub culture. All societies equip citizens with attitudes and rules in relation to patterns of behaviour. Deliberately flouting the rules is viewed negatively. Drinking alcohol is a learned social act. Different cultures and ethnic groups drink differently. David Pittman, a cultural anthropologist and expert on alcohol policy, has studied drinking cultures all over the world, and noted, 'The Irish have a long and picturesque history with alcohol – a history in which the use of alcohol has penetrated deeply into nearly every aspect of their social life.' He famously divided cultures into four types based on their treatment of alcohol: abstinent, ambivalent, permissive and over-permissive.

In an abstinent culture or subculture, the dominant attitude is negative and prohibitive towards any ingestion of alcohol, and its use arouses strong feeling. Islamic, Hindu and ascetic Protestant traditions have varying degrees of abstinence. The level of prohibition and the sanctions imposed for breaking the rules vary from culture to culture. In India, a predominantly Hindu society, the principle of abstinence and prohibition is reflected in the constitution, and both custom and law have combined to create a culture that frowns upon alcohol use. In the ascetic Protestant Churches of northern Europe, the United States and Canada, among others, there has been a deep-rooted history of temperance and intolerance of alcohol abuse. Many smaller religious groupings, such as the Seventh-Day Adventists, Mormons, Christian Scientists and some Baptist sects, strongly prohibit alcohol. Drinking alcohol is illegal in Iran, Libya and Saudi Arabia, and can result in severe sanctions.

An ambivalent cultural attitude towards alcohol usage is one of 'conflict between co-existing value structures'. This is where Ireland fits in, according to Pittman – and many other researchers. On the one hand, there has been a strong temperance movement, yet many Irish people drink heavily. This ambivalence can be conducive to alcoholism, Pittman argues. Binge drinking is a common characteristic of ambivalent cultures.

In a permissive culture, the attitude towards alcohol is favourable, but the attitude towards drunkenness and other drinking pathologies is negative. These countries are also termed 'positive' or 'integrated' drinking cultures. Pittman mentions Spain, Portugal, Italy, Japan, and Jewish and Chinese New Yorkers. Italians, he points out, think it strange to go to a pub and drink alcohol without eating. Wine consumption in Italy has dropped over the last two decades. Many people no longer take a drink at lunchtime, but the alcohol consumed still tends to be with food.

In an over-permissive culture, the attitude is permissive towards drinking, behaviours that occur when intoxicated and drinking pathologies. Japan is mentioned again by Pittman, along with Bolivia and France.

Recent research suggests there is a shift towards more ambivalent drinking attitudes in some cultures that were traditionally permissive. The rise of binge drinking among Spanish teenagers is one such phenomenon. Many would argue that the treatment of alcohol in Irish society has moved from ambivalent to over-permissive.

Pittman suggests there are near-universal similarities in all drinking cultures: proscription of solitary drinking, prescription of sociability, social control of consumption and behaviour, and restrictions on female and underage drinking. While values and sanctions vary, these self-imposed societal norms have more influence on drinking patterns than any legislation. There are no longer any significant social sanctions on female drinking in Ireland, but recent research and indicators point to increased female drinking, with negative health outcomes. Criticism of underage drinking is universal.

In a 1944 study, *Attitudes Towards Drinking in Irish Culture,* Robert Bales examined the array of occasions in Ireland at which alcohol was consumed. He contended that drinking in Ireland started in childhood and continued throughout life at dances, festivals, markets, fair days and family celebrations. Bales' work was based on literary sources from the early sixteenth century to the late nineteenth century, and on a famous study of north Clare during the 1930s by two American anthropologists, Conrad Maynadier Arensberg and Solon Toothaker Kimball, called *Family and Community in Ireland*. Bales has been criticised for making an implicit assumption that his results were particular to the Irish situation, and for viewing Ireland as an unchanging primitive society. Subsequent research has shown little difference between drinking practices in Ireland and England. This limitation was not unique to Bales' work. Many foreign scholars viewed Ireland as an unchanging country of universal consensus, social harmony and social isolation. Some came with preconceived notions of what they would find in rural Irish communities and ignored any contrary findings.

Bales distinguished between the symbolic use of alcohol accompanying spiritual activities and the celebratory use of alcohol in social rituals in Irish culture. He gave the example of a baptism. The drinking 'was convivial, not part of the ritual . . . though it had a social meaning. He who offered liberally was regarded as "a good fellow" and his offering implied that he regarded the other as a "good fellow".' The exchange was symbolic of social solidarity and acceptability on both sides, without explicit religious meaning. Drinking in the Jewish-American culture, Bales argued, was spiritually and physically symbolic, but in Ireland 'the individual does not express anything about his relation to the sacred in drinking. His drinking or not drinking has no determinate relationship to religious ideas and sentiments which are part of his own or others' orientation.'

Bales also argued that the Irish sometimes substituted alcohol for food. This, he thought, was a legacy of the Famine. This observation had previously been made by G. C. Lewis (among others), in his 1836 *Observations on the Habits of the Labouring Classes in Ireland*: 'They get drunk on Saturday evening and Sunday; having eaten very little during the week, a small quantity of spirits has much effect on them. They fight with one another in the public houses and streets.'

Bales accepted the widespread view that the Irish were particularly prone to alcohol problems without any analysis. However, when he looked at the statistics, he found them 'puzzling'. He expected to see high death rates from alcoholism, but the low figures reported by doctors seemed an anomaly. He believed the answer lay with the medical community. Because of the ambivalent attitude to alcohol, he argued, deaths from alcoholism in Ireland were not reported correctly and could not be compared accurately with statistics from other countries. Doctors felt uncomfortable declaring alcohol abuse as the cause of death. For many, it was a shame and should be hidden away and not mentioned – a common feature of an ambivalent alcohol culture. To back up his argument, he consulted police records and demonstrated that far more people were arrested for drunk and disorderly behaviour in Ireland than in England. This could be construed as a suspect argument. The records he quoted were prior to Ireland achieving independence. The Irish were still being policed by a colonial power and the policing of a colony is inherently different from that of fellow citizens.

Teetotallers were, Bales said, potential sexual deviants because they did not sublimate their sexual tensions into drinking like the other members of the bachelor group. However, Richard Stivers, in his book about Irish-American drinking habits, *Hair of the Dog,* noted abstainers viewed drinkers as potential dangers; the lack of inhibition brought on by alcohol could lead to the same end. Stivers also argued that heavy drinking among males in Irish-American society was the result of 'cultural remission': family structures had started to decline after the Famine and continued apace. Dimitra Gefou of the Panteion University of Social and Political Science in Athens also compared drinking in Jewish and Irish cultures. She argued that while Jewish communities have a permissive attitude to alcohol, it is regulated through family structures, and is largely limited to set social and religious situations: 'Learning to drink in the context of family and religious rituals acted as a protecting factor, making Jews moderate drinkers while lack of family rituals and the tendency for bar drinking combined with economic frustration made alcoholism and heavy drinking acceptable among the Irish.' Irish drinking, she continued, became attached to a place outside the home and embedded in the social networks of the community. The focus was on group cohesion and community solidarity, which may, she reasonably argued, inevitably lead to excessive drinking in some cases.

The consensus from the research community seems to be that the Irish attitude to alcohol consumption is ambivalent, the focus is on conviviality and it is overwhelmingly public. Offaly publican Mary O'Connor recalled a time in the early 1970s when her father decided to surprise some of his most valued customers by having alcohol delivered to their homes. He was shocked when some of them brought it back to the bar, telling him they did not drink at home, and then proceeding to buy drink in the pub. According to a 1999 study, 80 per cent of alcohol consumption in Ireland took place in public. That was the reverse of the United States, where just over 20 per cent of drinking took place in public situations. The study also found that 74 per cent of alcohol purchased in Denmark was consumed at home. The French consumed 65 per cent at home, the Dutch 62 per cent and the Spanish 25 per cent. At that time, the British consumed 20 per cent at home. In 2013, consumption patterns had changed dramatically in Ireland, according to a study by the Central Statistics Office. Now 43 per cent of alcohol purchased in Ireland was consumed at home. Of the remainder, 10 per cent was consumed in hotels and restaurants, and 42 per cent in pubs and nightclubs (the remaining 5 per cent is unaccounted for in the study). In a comprehensive study by Ipsos MRBI, sponsored by the Irish Department of Health and carried out in 2013, 75 per cent of all the alcohol consumed in Ireland was in a binge-drinking session – a key characteristic of an ambivalent drinking culture. A binge is defined as drinking more than six standard drinks in a row.

Robert Bales made a distinction between 'convivial' and 'utilitarian' strands in Irish drinking culture. He defined the latter as the 'use of intoxication, whether of the self or other, in order to gain some personal advantage over the other or to bring relief or satisfaction of self-oriented or self-contained needs'. He made an eclectic list: drinking for warmth, lessening of hangovers, rewarding children, releasing sexual and emotional tensions, resolving emotional problems, sealing bargains and as a sleep inducer. He summed up the net effect of both convivial and utilitarian drinking in Irish culture by comparing it with the American Jewish community: 'This complex of utilitarian ideas and sentiments, deeply internalised through overt actions in which the ideas and sentiments are objectively represented, "sets the stage" as it were for certain further articulation and reinforcement on the individual level, and that is thus primarily responsible for the notably higher rate of alcohol addiction among the Irish as compared to the Orthodox Jews.'

In more recent times, Professor Robin Room divided cultures into 'wet' and 'dry'. In this model, 'wet cultures' are characterised by a weak temperance history, a low proportion of total abstainers, a pattern of drinking that can sometimes be heavy but is never usually binge-orientated, a relatively low level of death from alcohol poisoning, a low level of violence associated with drinking and an almost total absence of illegal alcohol production. 'Dry' cultures are the opposite. Room considered Nordic countries as the most extreme examples of dry cultures and Mediterranean countries as the epitome of wet cultures. Ireland is a dry culture. Both models have limitations. There can be regional variations in a country, and attitudes and norms can change over time. New political regimes can impose sanctions against the use of alcohol. This happened in Afghanistan when the Taliban took power, for example, and banned alcohol. Countries can be divided along ethnic lines, with people of different ethnicities treating alcohol differently. This is also the case with religion. Both Iran and Saudi Arabia inherited a substantial body of cultural artefacts celebrating the joys of alcohol and drunkenness, but now ostensibly have a total ban on alcohol. Many countries had periods of prohibition, including the United States and Great Britain. Sweden introduced alcohol rationing between 1917 and 1955, but found it impossible to police.

The ritualistic consumption of alcohol is a cross-cultural phenomenon. Births, birthdays, graduations, job promotions, engagements, weddings and funerals are celebrated with alcohol almost throughout the world. The interdependency between alcohol and festivity is nearly universal, but is particularly strong in ambivalent cultures. Occasions like weddings, birthdays and anniversaries tend to involve a lot of alcohol. Bales concluded his study on Irish drinking by comparing it to more integrated cultures, where 'festivity isn't a justification for every drinking occasion: a celebration usually requires alcohol, but every drink does not require a celebration'.

Dr T. J. O'Meara addressed the Irish Temperance Society in 1904 on alcohol and the Irish. Intemperance, he said, was a national trait because of the Irishman's 'excitable, high-strung, nervous temperament'. The Irishman was 'essentially neurotic and mercurial . . . easily overjoyed and as easily depressed and accustomed to treat both conditions by whiskey'. Dr Garrett O'Connor, an academic psychiatrist and an authority on addiction, writing in *Irish America* magazine, linked a number of factors that he believes form a predilection for alcohol among the Irish community:

> The net effect of religious persecution, land rape, extreme poverty and intermittent abuse of military power by English colonists in Ireland during 700 years of continuous occupation was to produce a national inferiority complex in Irish Catholics which I identify as cultural malignant shame, characterised by chronic fear, suppressed rage, self-loathing, procrastination, low self-esteem, false pride and a

vulnerability to use alcohol as remission for suffering
– past and present.

Nineteenth-century Irish emigrants to American and British industrial cities were generally landless labourers, who were illiterate, Catholic and, in some cases, spoke only Irish. They arrived in an English-speaking, urban, industrial and puritanical society, which often regarded them as barbaric and backwards. Dislocation, poverty, alienation and a sense of failure are common feelings among migrant groups, and may have proven fertile ground for the escapism offered by alcohol. As the image of the drunken Irishman developed, he reacted to and fed the myth until reality and image became indistinguishable. The alienated Irish emigrant in a foreign country found a psychological home in the pub and in alcohol; here was a cultural role offering something other than hard labour.

Garrett O'Connor's article, 'Breaking the Code of Silence: The Irish and Drink', addresses the abuse of alcohol in Irish-American communities. He writes eloquently of the tendency of the Irish-American family to hide alcoholism because of the stigma. This stigma, he argues, is greater for the Irish American than other ethnic groups because of the historical stereotype of the drunken, feckless Irishman. He estimates one million American children live in families of Irish descent, and describes the profound effects alcoholism had on his own life before he became sober and raised questions about the role of alcohol in the lives of the Irish in America.

When President Bill Clinton was describing progress in the Northern Ireland peace process in 1999, he used a drinking analogy: 'Every time they make an agreement to do it, they're like a couple of drunks walking out of a bar for the last time – when they get to the swinging door they turn around and go back in and say, "I just can't quite get there."' The simile might be interpreted as evidence of how deeply the stereotype of the Irish drinker is rooted in American culture. According to Tom Hayden in his book *Irish on the Inside: In Search of the Soul of Irish America*, 'You drink because you're Irish . . . which soon became you're Irish because you drink.' Hayden was brought up to believe the Irish drank in the same way the Mexicans were said to eat tacos. Drinking was a way of coming to terms with a new culture: 'Hey, I'm Irish so of course I drink. What's wrong with that? Paddy can hold his drink, right?'

Maurice Parmalee studied Irish-American drinking habits in 1909. He analysed the number of arrests for public drunkenness among the different ethnic groups in New York City. The number was substantially higher for the Irish than any other group. A study of admissions to all hospitals in New York between 1929 and 1931 concluded that alcohol-related admissions of Irish people were substantially higher than those for all other ethnic groups. A 1950 study of arrests for drunkenness in Connecticut found Irish Americans had the highest percentage of arrests among the ten ethnic groups studied. When Richard Stivers studied alcohol consumption rates during 1960, those with an Irish background were the heaviest drinkers. In a 1985 study, G. L. Muhen found 51 per cent of the Irish-born males admitted to New York psychiatric hospitals had alcohol-related diagnoses, whereas only 4 per cent of Italian-born men had similar diagnoses. A recent study by the National Opinion Research Centre found 40 per cent of Irish Americans indicated a drinking problem existed in their homes during their childhood. In a comparative study between Irish and Canadian drinking habits, John Teehan found the Irish drank for relief from painful feelings or for mood alteration, whereas the Canadians drank for social facilitation and sexual enhancement. The 'painful feelings' listed included guilt, low self-esteem and anxiety. Professor Robin Room studied Irish-American drinking patterns in the 1960s using the United States census data of 1890. He found more Irish married females than married males died from alcohol abuse. The opposite was the case for German immigrants. Single Irishmen died more often from alcohol-related illness than single females. Room suggested a high percentage of the single women were in service and had restricted access to alcohol.

The stereotype of the Irish drunkard and alcoholic is ancient and persistent. In Shakespeare's *Henry V*, Macmorris, an army captain of Irish origin, asks in a slurred voice, 'What ish my nation? Ish a villain, and a bastard, and a knave and a rascal?' In a cartoon titled 'St Patrick's Day 1867' published in an early edition of American magasine *Harper's Weekly*, Thomas Nast depicted Irish immigrants as ape-like barbarians prone to lawlessness, laziness and drunken rioting with police. The etymology of some Irish loanwords used in American English is bound up in stereotype. Fighting and drunkenness are 'shenanigans', and if things go too far, people are taken away in a 'paddy wagon'. The stereotype must be acknowledged, and in all stereotypes, it is said, there is a kernel of truth. Irish drinking is much more visible than in other cultures, and it is easier to stereotype the visible.

A 'Third Place':

The Social Significance of the Pub

'Officially and politically Dublin and Belfast are
Ireland's capitals but the true centre of Irish life
for centuries has been her pubs . . . the pub has
served many functions: grocery store, funeral
parlour, concert hall, restaurant, bar, political forum,
congenial meeting place, courting corner and most
of all a place for talk.' – Sybil Taylor in *The Life
and Lore of Ireland Through Its Finest Pubs.*

In his 1989 book *The Great Good Place*, Ray Oldenburgh,
an American urban sociologist, argues 'a third place' is
central to keeping a community alive. The first place is home;
the second is work, but it is in the third, or neutral, space
that social capital is accrued. It is here that civil society,
democracy, civic engagement and a sense of place are

enhanced. Oldenburgh contends the pub is a perfect third place: a neutral ground, a leveller, defined by conversation and accessibility, with a group of regular customers. Often it is plain and unpretentious, keeps a low profile and permits a level of playfulness – 'a home away from home'. The unique potential of the public drinking establishment to become this third place of informal public life, he says, derives from a 'fundamental synergism' that comes into play whenever 'alcoholic beverages and good company come together'. Oldenburgh has a chapter on the English pub that is equally applicable to Ireland. A good pub, he says, can be the epicentre of community interaction and conviviality, where you can meet other locals and friends, access the news, and discuss national and international issues of the day. Oldenburgh observed the decline of bars in America as the loss of a significant third place:

> Few trends in American life are as pronounced as the rejection of the public drinking establishment. Despite the greater comfort offered, despite the flocked wallpaper, giant televisions . . . two for the price of one drinks, a lower drinking age, appeals to women who appeal to men, rock musicians . . . and a host of other lures, American drinking establishments are losing ground to the private consumption of alcoholic beverages . . . The tavern is a failing institution, perhaps even an endangered species . . . While avoiding few, if any, of the problems surrounding alcoholic beverages the nation is losing the socially solidifying rituals of public drinking within inclusive and democratic settings.

Despite 2,000 closings in the last fifteen years, there are still roughly 7,500 pubs in Ireland. In a report from the University of York funded by the Vintners Federation of Ireland on the role of pubs in creating economic development and social well-being in rural Ireland, the authors, Dr Ignazio Cabras and Dr Michael Mount, asked publicans to consider their role in the locality. The first man interviewed ranged widely: 'Well, we have the bridge club, the poker night . . . always with eight lads . . . we have tip retirement night and in two weeks' time we start Spanish classes, conversation . . . the drama group use our room for their practices . . . there is another man that does a lot of charity work and he uses our spaces, and that's very exciting because you get involved in these things.'

A second was equally forthcoming: 'You have an idea yourself and you bring it . . . propose it and see whether we can support it . . . we have a quiz night for a children's charity, we do fundraising for getting extra food every week . . . and it is nice when you can get part of the community and do something actively for others.'

In a similar vein, a third landlord alluded to his sponsorship of all the local sports teams over his time in the business, but, he said, 'these evenings are so seldom now, it's a treasure when it happens'. If he did not support the teams, he could not think of anyone else who would. The researchers also conducted interviews with rural dwellers, asking them about the importance of the pub in their lives. The replies were various; the first respondent went to the pub to find company because he lived on his own and he needed to get out of the house. A man from Dingle, County Kerry, went to 'find the spark' and 'the same homey atmosphere'. He emphasised – as many others did – that it was not necessarily about alcohol. A woman from the town of Killaloe/Ballina on the border between Clare and Tipperary described her local pub as 'a free place where you can say whatever'. She compared the social role of the pub and the church: 'I cannot meet people socially at the church, I mean talk with them . . . you know, you would not have any bad language, any gossip there . . . you would not really know what is going on by standing at the church, but you go across the road [to the pub] and then maybe . . . It is also important for people that live on their own; the pub is a place with no judgement, no questions asked.'

A man from Ballyporeen in County Tipperary said the church was only a place to listen, but 'inside the pub you can have an argument and talk freely and express your feelings'. A resident of Castletownbere, County Cork, called his local pub the community's 'crafted version of Facebook'. It is the locus of information sharing and gossip, according to another: 'See you go to the pub here . . . they like to know what's happening in the area and find out what's going on in the village . . . if you are in town you may just go out for a drink and don't care about what's happening around the streets . . . but here in rural areas the pub provides us with information about everything and anything.'

The traditions of *bothántaíocht* and *béaloideas* are significant components of Irish cultural inheritance. *Bothántaíocht* is an Irish word meaning 'visiting other people in their houses'. A *bothán* was a small house, and *bothántaíocht* translates as going from house to house to visit and talk. In an era before television and electricity, there was very little else to do. *Béaloideas* translates as 'education by mouth'. The culture of Ireland, a bardic culture, was passed down orally: stories, poems, myths and legends were transmitted from person to person through storytelling. In its purest form, this oral tradition was regulated by *seanchaithe* or 'storytellers'. Pubs may be viewed as a natural progression of this oral culture. As an ethnic group, the Irish have frequently gathered together in one place to trade stories.

The story of Irish pub culture in the late nineteenth century and much of the twentieth century is overwhelmingly a study of Irish manhood. This is not unique to Ireland, but the creation of a huge bachelor cohort at this time gave rural Ireland a remarkably skewed demographic profile. Primogeniture – the inheritance of land by one child, usually the eldest male – created a substantial bachelor class, men who did not get married until later in life, if at all. They had to wait to inherit the land, and oftentimes their circumstances were not conducive to marriage by then. They may have just lost interest, found it difficult to find someone or dissipated their lives through alcohol abuse and personal neglect. The loneliness could be sublimated in alcohol and the companionship and solidarity of the pub with other men in the same situation. It was a rite of passage to show you could 'hold your drink' as well as the next man. Once initiated into the hard-drinking bachelor fraternity, you had reached manhood. The company was male and the norm was heavy drinking. Richard Stivers put it well:

> Young men were socialised into all-male groups whose older members established avuncular-type relationships with younger members . . . social and

emotional needs of young men, especially those of friendship, guidance and recreation, were met in that male group. It provided a context for the intimate mutual relationship between males of different generations. Thus the generations were linked in a relationship of authority and subordination, father-son, and in a relationship of friendship, maternal uncle-nephew.

In 1933, a parliamentarian raised considerable amusement in the national newspapers when he used the country idiom of 'boy' to describe country bachelors. Speaking on a bill on land division, he asked for 'special treatment for boys of forty-five or over'. 'Boy' had been used as a legal term in the nineteenth century for men in this situation. These 'boys' made up only one section of society, but it was the dominant group in Irish rural pubs. In many rural areas, there was a gender imbalance – young women emigrated in large numbers. The bachelor had no responsibilities to a young family and no wife to manage a domestic budget. Coupled with the prohibition on sexual expression engendered by an overweening Catholic Church, the chances of a balanced life for these men were slim. Sublimation of frustrated sexuality has been a constant theme in Irish literature. The final verse of '*An Crúiscín Lán*' ('the full jug') – a well-known Irish lament – translates as 'the love of my heart is my full jug, here's health to my darling girl'.

In her 1979 book *Saints, Scholars and Schizophrenics*, Nancy Hughes argued the rural pub provides a sense of solidarity and community for the 'dispirited' men of the locality. Among the bachelors isolated in their lonely cottages, drinking was 'endemic'. This led her to conclude it was these men who were responsible for Irish people being hospitalised twelve times more often for drink problems than their English counterparts. Hughes' book was not without its critics. Based on fieldwork carried out on the Dingle Peninsula in County Kerry, it attempted to show how the sociocultural structures of the society were conducive to high degrees of mental illness. She interviewed local people about mental health issues, focusing particularly on the older bachelors. The interviewees were upset when the book was published, and she was accused of exaggerating. Four of the six pubs in the village catered exclusively to single men, who gathered 'in little clubs most evenings of the week but in greatest numbers on weekends, fair days and funeral days'. She believed the majority of the village bachelors were able to make 'an adequate adjustment to the demands of their stoical existence through male bonding patterns as evidenced in round drinking in the pubs' but the overriding atmosphere was one of 'tension, anxiety and disequilibrium'. They were shamed by their 'backwardness'.

> Throughout the long and discouraging winter, Ballybran farmers gathered into clusters at the pub . . . to listen to radio or public television reports decry and deride the 'backwardness' and 'conservatism' of the western coastal farmers, who were characterised as living like parasites off welfare handouts, grants and subsidies, who were opposed to progress, and who hung greedily and tenaciously onto their unproductive and miserable farms. The spectre of forced and early retirement hovered over

the nightly pub sessions in Ballybran and a puritanical gloom settled like a mist into each man's pint of bitter porter. 'Well lads, 'tis we're finished up for sure,' was a commonly heard refrain. The local residents read about their lives and livelihoods discussed in national newspapers as so much debris and deadweight.

In a similar study by Hugh Brody, *Inishkillane: Change and Decline in the West of Ireland,* the picture of the bachelor group painted was even more pitiful:

> When they do drink and the effects of the drinking begin to appear, despondency becomes more extreme and its behavioural indices more overt. Such a group creates a tight circle of privacy around itself, a privacy physically expressed by the arms that lay across each other's shoulders. Then with faces almost touching they appear to join together in evident despair. This despair is not expressed in discussion among the drinkers; rather they exchange silences as if they were words, and words in brief expressions of their loneliness.

Émile Durkheim, the father of modern sociology, described *anomie* as an imperfect relationship between man and the social context in which he lives, caused by rapid social change, leaving a vacuum in which a state of 'normlessness' or lack of rules exists. Nancy Hughes argued *anomie* was the dominant feeling in Ballybran: 'The combined effect of the steady erosion of the community through childlessness and emigration, the disintegration of traditional values and familism, the constriction of village social life and institutions and the national policy to retire even young and able-bodied farmers can be observed in the contagious spread of a spirit of despair and *anomie* in Ballybran.'

This feeling, she ventured, was expressed in drinking patterns and alcoholism, in sexual devitalisation and the high incidence of mental illness – especially schizophrenia – among middle-aged bachelors. Hugh Brody used the term demoralisation: 'In Inishkillane people are demoralised: they feel outside their social system and have no faith in it continuing. They are lonely and withdrawn . . . to be demoralised for such a people is to lose belief in the social advantage or moral worth of their own small society. The demoralisation is aggravated by continuing to live in a milieu which, in the view of the Inishkillane people, offers neither real advantage nor compensatory dignity.'

Brody lived in various parts of rural western Ireland from 1966 to 1971, working in bars, on farms and on fishing boats. The fictitious parish of Inishkillane is a composite of the communities he studied, set in the rough and mountainous land of west Clare. Like most parts of the west of Ireland, this area lost a high percentage of its population through emigration. Of the 231 households in the parish, only forty-six had children living at home and helping on the farm. Thirty-two were occupied bachelors, four by spinsters, thirteen by widowers and thirteen by widows living alone. Brody estimated that only 20 per cent of the farms had any possibility of lasting another generation. The outlook was appalling: chain emigration, old people reliant on remittances from those abroad and a breakdown in the system of collective help previously central to the community. Now 'privacy itself has come to be associated with sophistication. The home which is forever busy with the neighbour's comings and goings is seen as poor and old fashioned.' The bar had become the community centre for those committed to life on the land, married men and ageing bachelors. The shop had a similar function for those on the periphery of the farming society – young girls and boys. In the summer, the tourists who came to Inishkillane visited the pub and, according to Brody, brought some reassurance to the men, providing 'approval from outside for the traditional way of life'.

Cultural anthropology and ethnography can be as much about the writer as the subjects studied. Hugh Brody was supposedly attacked in a pub in Allihies on the Beara Peninsula in County Cork. He had spent time there and some of the locals believed he deliberately set out with an agenda to show a community in terminal decline populated by people with pathological illnesses.

Many Irish rural bars are still largely a male preserve. When Rosita Boland got to Clifden in County Galway on her hitchhiking journey around Ireland's coast, she contemplated the issue: 'In Mannion's that Friday evening the men represented 100 per cent of the customers. I found myself in this situation many, many times. As a single woman I had two choices. I could either sit quietly or read a newspaper or a book while I was having a drink or I could talk to people . . . In pubs, I ended up speaking almost exclusively to men, since they were nearly always the only other customers.'

Hugh Brody recounted an incident in which a young woman returned to Inishkillane, having been away in America for nine years. She was 'removed from the old ways' and asked her mother to take down all the holy pictures from the walls and insisted on going out drinking in the bars in the evening: 'With a son selling cattle at the fair and a daughter out drinking . . . traditional family life is overthrown.'

In 1930, two American anthropologists, Conrad Maynadier Arensberg and Solon Toothaker Kimball, came to live among the people of rural north Clare and the town dwellers of the county's capital, Ennis. Their famous socio-logical study, *Family and Community in Ireland*, analysed family structures and roles, division of labour and employ-ment, inheritance and the comings and goings of everyday life. It is still regarded as a landmark ethnographic study. When Arensberg – the main author – first came to Ireland to assess the research possibilities and establish information sources, he was immediately daunted by the amount of socialising he would have to do: 'It is impossible to have a conversation with anyone without whiskey, and if I've got to fight off the effects of whiskey is addition to all this . . . Christ! I would gladly sink all of the drink in Ireland under the sea.'

Arensberg and Kimball were interested in the pub as a place of social ritual and commerce. They noted match-making and the buying and selling of farm animals in particular. Arensberg also noted the use of alcohol as an emotional suppressant, and was told any emotional difficulty of young men was believed best treated by advising them to drink it off. Drowning one's sorrows was 'the expected means of relief, much as prayer among women and young children or among the older people'.

According to Arensberg, one custom for maintaining a successful pub involved matchmaking arrangements between 'country and town folk'. Traditionally, married pub owners sought country girls to marry their sons. Country girls were preferred to city girls as they were believed to be hard workers who already knew how to cook and clean, and 'had no grand ideas'. After they got married, the newly-weds would typically take over the pub when the parents retired. This transfer, the researchers were told, injected new life into the business and the local community. Regular pub goers would continue to go to the grocery bar, but the wife's family and friends now came exclusively to her pub. A similar arrangement was made if the original pub owners had no male children. Farmers often sent one son to apprentice under an established pub owner. The best partner for the pub owner's daughter was an experienced apprentice. This generally represented a move up the social ladder for the man. Arensberg also noted some publicans operated as bankers and gave loans to local farmers. The researchers met publicans they viewed as community leaders, some of whom were politically active. Arensberg contended the customers believed the publican had their best interests at heart because he interacted with them regularly and they perceived him as their friend. Arensberg believed this close relationship between customer and publican enhanced 'national unity'.

Mildred Warner came to stay in Ennis with the scholars in the summer of 1932, and wrote:

> Our headquarters were in the Queen's Hotel where Lloyd [Mildred's husband and supervisor of the project] had engaged rooms for Connie Arensberg and for us, with an extra room to serve as an office ... Connie studied the market and I did the statistical

work on his reports . . . A good researcher, Connie joined in the customs of the country and had drinks with the men beginning when they arrived at market, carrying on from there. He often treated and learned, almost too late, that it was the custom for the person buying the first drink to buy the last. He had unwittingly been prolonging sessions at the bar.

Arensberg found the drinking habits of the Irish were not conducive to quick research. He recounted his first trip to the capital city: 'I had a very pleasant week in Dublin but I don't know how profitable it was for the job I am supposed to do here. Nevertheless it was filled with a great variety of calls upon people. It seems I already have quite a connection here and the traditional Irish hospitality doesn't fail. I saw two professors, three civil servants, a judge, a doctor, a student, lots of them, some fox-hunting aristocrats, some stout-drinking democrats and the United States chargé d'affaires.'

In a letter to his girlfriend in New York, Arensberg wrote of the local bars as 'sorts of men's clubs here'. In an interesting reflection of the work of Arensberg and Kimball, a research project by Chris Curtin and Colm Ryan on the pubs and clubs of Ennis in the 1980s, *Clubs, Pubs and Private Houses in a Clare Town,* concluded there was 'a distinct pattern of the attending of pubs and lounges . . . more than half the bars in Ennis can be classified as working-class only establishments and local pubs continue to function as semi-exclusive social clubs'. They went further:

The discreet middle-class bar where the clientele speak in low, educated tones of lofty issues only recreates for worker the formal rules of the workplace. He is not barred from these pubs and he can afford to buy his drink like the rest, but he cannot participate fully nor does he want to. Public places such as pubs and lounge bars in this way become class specific according to informal codes which are just as effective in shaping the character of social life in the town as were the formal codes associated with member-only clubs of the 1930s.

They suggested a breakdown: 16 per cent of the pubs were exclusively middle class; 50 per cent were exclusively working class; 12 per cent were classified as country pubs and 22 per cent as having a mixed clientele. Some years earlier, Arnsberg had noted class distinctions in the drinking establishments in Ennis: 'The sociability provided in the nightly gatherings at the men's clubs is restricted to contacts with those of comparable manners and social position.'

In Britain, historically the pub has largely been the province of the working-class man, and has been well researched. In the late 1930s, Tom Harrisson and his colleagues at Mass-Observation, a social research organisation, conducted an extensive study of pub-going in Britain. The organisation was established to record the everyday life of Britons at work, on the street, at public occasions, at sporting and religious events, and in social situations. The work was partly funded by Victor Gollancz, publisher and founder of the Left Book Club, although only one book, *The Pub and the People,* was produced as a result of the research. It followed Gollancz's commissioning of George Orwell to visit Wigan and other northern towns in 1936 to write a 'condition of England' piece, which was published in 1937 as *The Road to Wigan Pier*. Tom Harrisson reflected in 1970: 'We sought to fully penetrate the society we were studying, to live in it as effective members of it and to percolate into every corner of every day and every night.' Observations and interviews were written up by volunteers and observers. Centred on 'Worktown' (Bolton) and Blackpool in the holiday season, the team of social anthropologists did little else for nearly two years but sit in pubs, observe behaviour and interview the patrons. *The Pub and the People* was not published until the Second World War was nearly over, ostensibly because of paper shortages, but more probably because the country had other matters on its mind. Here is a typical transcribed account of a night in the pub, complete with some casual misogyny:

> The Great Birthday Night. Went in about 7.35. Approx 80 people, trade brisk, barmen skipping about like mad, large skinny black dog running about getting under people's feet and being patted. Great barrels being rolled around. Cheerful air, conversation loud. Mostly working-class people, men and women, women all over 40 except for one little tart with colleague of about 35 both standing with frozen smiles in one place not drinking. The birthday port going like mad, toothglasses half full for 5d. I had one; it was thick, sweet, and goose-berryish. It didn't taste any different to the ordinary threepenny a small glass stuff. While I was there

another barrel of it was being heaved and shoved into position, the first one being almost empty, tilted down very far. Chaps coming up and saying give me three glasses of the Christmas stuff, I mean the birthday stuff. Everything very brisk, very animated. Barmen grinning and standing in a straight row behind the bar as if waiting for heavy work.

Harrisson and his colleagues showed the pub as a British institution that towered over its rivals for attention and commitment. Of all the social institutions that moulded men's lives between home and work in an industrial town, the pub, they wrote, 'has more buildings, holds more people, takes more of their money, than church, cinema, dance hall, and political organisations put together'. The most often quoted paragraph from his work is equally applicable to Ireland: 'The only kind of public building used by large numbers of ordinary people where their thoughts and actions are not being in some way arranged for them; in the other kinds of public building they are the audiences, watchers of political, religious, dramatic, cinematic, instructional or athletic spectacles. But within the four walls of the pub, once a man has bought or been bought his glass of beer, he has entered an environment in which he is a participator rather than a spectator.'

One man interviewed spoke of social equality: 'There's something quite democratic about the pub because you might well say, "Are you coming along to that restaurant?" and I might say, "Sorry, no I can't afford it." But you would never say that about a pub would you? "No, I'm not going because I can't afford it" . . . So you're not excluded on account of price really, whereas you might be in a restaurant. I could go to the pub with a fiver in my pocket, whereas I couldn't go to a restaurant with a fiver in my pocket.'

In a review of the book, George Orwell – a great fan of the pub – bemoaned the decline of the pub in British society, and predicted it would 'gradually be replaced by the passive, drug-like pleasures of the cinema and the radio.' Thankfully, this has not yet come to pass.

The 'Start' and the Finished:

The Pub and Irish Emigrants in Britain and the United States

Britain

As far back as 1817, the Select Committee on the Police of the Metropolis debated the issue of the Irish and alcohol in London. An unnamed witness provided his opinion: 'The effects of liquor upon the Irish in every scene of depredation and murder needs only to be adverted to. It is certain that the abuse of this destructive stimulus foments and keeps alive the most atrocious and appalling crimes.' It was widely believed alcohol affected the Irish differently than the natives, and their predilection for whiskey made them more dangerous again. A Manchester magistrate spoke on the issue in 1834 to the House of Commons: 'If there be a company of English men drinking in a beer shop, they are very good friends if they get drunk together, and they can go home with each other and behave with the utmost kindness; but if it be a party of Irish drinking whiskey or spirits, they will quarrel or fight before they get home.' In the same report, a Manchester clergyman referred to this bias, and damned the Irish with faint praise. 'The Irish', he said, 'have more a reputation for drunkenness than they deserve because they are so noisy and brawling . . . they give money to one another when in distress and sickness, and send money to their poor relations in Ireland.' The living conditions of most of these immigrants were poor. In 1849, the Chief Constable of Wolverhampton commented on the issue: 'Many are tempted to spend their time and money in these places from the total want of comfort at their own houses; indeed, many of them have told me, after having been turned out of the public house, that the place in which they lived was in such a miserable state that they would rather remain out in the open air if the weather was not so severe.' According to the report, some migrants brought alcohol with them from Ireland and sold it in lodging houses. The police referred to such places as 'wabble shops' and despaired of counteracting the problem because of warning systems in place.

In 1968, John Healy published *No One Shouted Stop: Death of an Irish Town* about the decline of his native Charlestown in County Mayo. Ireland was in an economic morass and England wanted all types of workers: 'England, hated England, now waved its trident-engraved fresh green money under the noses of all the Charlestowns of the West of Ireland, and from those huge overstocked rich spawning streams . . . the young and the lusty and the eager turned like strong fingerlings and headed downstream and out to sea for the rich feeding grounds of wartime Britain.' He described the pain felt by the families left behind and the wonder of the young emigrants. His memories as a child are of the returning crowds at holiday periods. The buses heading to the north and west of Mayo passed through Charlestown. As soon as the buses pulled up, he remembered, the men would come lurching out and into the bars on 'The Square'. Their wallets were full and they wanted drink, and 'they drank until the buses pulled out again and went on to Swinford where they stopped again and drank again'. They would repeat it again in Foxford and Ballina. They drank their way home, 'those two hundred miles across the face of Ireland'. They were different people from when they had left. Now 'they could buy drinks with the best in the best lounge bars in town. Their money and their earning power was as great, if not greater, than the social hierarchy of the town. They made more than the schoolteachers who could not afford to buy a round of drinks for the house . . . Drink up, mate – there is plenty where this came from . . . Come on, mate! Put them up again, Tom, fill them up: let the last day be the best.' Healy pondered the reasons why so many of these emigrants developed problems with alcohol. He acknowledged they were lonely and living in an alien environment but these were 'stock' answers. Money was an issue, 'the unfamiliarity with money, the handling of money':

Young men who lived in and about our town were lucky to have the handling of a pound note in the week; more likely it was ten shillings, which kept them in the threepenny packet of Woodbines, gave them half a crown for a Sunday night dance, nine pence for the Thursday night picture and left something for the odd bottle of stout . . . The social historian will do well to ponder what happened when, overnight, such a young man found himself in MacAlpine's Fusiliers [in the employ of MacAlpine's building company] with as many pounds in his pocket as he had shillings before.

In *The Men who Built Britain*, Ultan Cowley provides a history of the life of Irish labourers, or 'navvies'. The term 'navvy' came to be used as a catch-all for any labourer, particularly in relation to construction, but its origins were more specific. The commercial canal system laid out in the British Isles in the nineteenth century was known as the Inland Navigation System. The diggers of these canals became known colloquially as 'navigators', which became shortened to 'navvy'. Cowley quotes from a book by David Fitzpatrick, entitled *Irish Emigration 1801–1921*, which described the tensions sometimes created when groups of Irish labourers came to small villages:

They lived for the present; they cared not for any past; they were indifferent to the future. Their pay nights were a Saturnalia of riot and disorder, dreaded by the villagers along the line of works. The irruption of such men into the quiet hamlet of Kilsby . . . produced a very startling effect on the reclusive inhabitants of the place . . . the navvies were little better than heathens . . . For their lodgings, a hut of turf would content them; and in their hours of leisure, the meanest public house would serve for their parlour. Unburdened as they usually were, by domestic ties, softened by family affection, and without much moral or religious training, the navvies came to be distinguished by a sort of savage manners, which contrasted strangely with those of the surrounding population.

The pub was often the first port of call for the emigrant. In England, you could get 'the start' in a pub frequented by other Irish people. 'In every urban centre there were Irish pubs, albeit perhaps called The George, The Crown or The King's Head,' Crowley wrote. Here, emigrants could network, meet old friends, get news from home, establish local contacts, find lodgings or get a job. Loneliness and culture shock drove men to the pub. They desperately sought a sense of community, and it was in the pub they often found it.

Kevin Casey was interviewed by Catherine Dunne in her book *An Unconsidered People* (2003), the story of some Irish emigrants in London. He had an unusual job for an Irishman, working as a valet for a Lord Beatty near Banbury. He recalled his visit to a local pub:

I remember going to a pub one night in King's Sutton and it was full of people. In the crowd was this chap wearing a little shamrock badge. It was what was known as an Aer Lingus badge. I went over to him and asked him if he was Irish. "I am," he said, "from Tipperary." He was a groom from one of the other estates, and we became great pals. It's not that the people weren't sociable – they were and they made us very welcome. But there's something about looking for your own identity, your own

language, your own accent. It's something to home
in on, something familiar.

Drinking numbed the pain of loneliness, acting as an
anaesthetic for many. Another man described the lack of a
home life as the reason he gravitated to the pub: 'When you
come over here, you have no home, you pay for your week's
lodgings, get a bed, your meals maybe . . . you don't fit in,
your culture is different, you go out at night and spend your
money in the pub because there's nowhere else much to go
to, because there's camaraderie there, and there's people, it's
a social kind of life.'

In his research, Cowley received a letter from a man
called 'Callahan', who told him the Irish were not wanted by
the landladies, and were forced into the pub by loneliness,
lack of identity and culture shock. Bill Brennan, who lived
in Arlington House, an iconic homeless hostel in Camden
Town, London, recalled a typical day 'jumpin' out of a van
in the evenin', soakin' wet, into the pub – no such thing as
goin' home to change and the rain soakin' into you . . . that's
why you see all the old men goin' around with sticks and
crutches. When you were young it didn't seem to affect you,
but now it's got into their bones, dried into them.' One
traffic island in Camden Town, close to a popular pub, was
known as Penguin Island. So many Irish men gathered there
waiting for the pub to open on a Sunday morning, dressed
in black suits and white shirts, that they looked like a group
of penguins. Dance halls were the place to go after the pubs.
They were alcohol-free, which often led to binge drinking
in the pubs beforehand. Bill Brennan elaborated on the
theme:

172

I needed the alcohol to be able to ask a woman to dance . . . I had to have a massive amount of alcohol drunk over there in The Good Mixer pub before crossing the road to the Buffalo . . . I was goin' across and no one would dance with me, because I was mad drunk, and I was saying 'What the fuck is wrong with me? I'm young and I've a three piece suit on, and I've got a few bob in my pocket – what the fuck's goin on?' And, of course the answer was I was totally drunk . . . I'd come away totally frustrated. I wasn't socially able to make any of these moves towards a normal life, which a normal human being should have without alcohol.

Phyllis Izzard was the first person interviewed in Catherine Dunne's book. She confirmed Bill's account: 'Some of the dance halls could be rough, and these fellas would be well inebriated. They wouldn't come into the dance hall until late in the night; all of us girls would have been sitting around the wall all evening like wallflowers, and then they'd come in, last knockin's.'

Ultan Cowley sought information from women of their experience of the construction industry in Britain and how it affected relationships with men. In a public appeal, he received only four replies, two of them from the same person. This correspondence is from a lady identified as 'K. Hamilton':

I have a limited recollection of my father's life as a navvy. I remember he would get a draw [an advance] on his wages early in the week – having spent a great portion of his pay cheque the previous weekend in the pubs . . . I'm afraid my father wasn't very articulate on his return home at the end of the day. After his meal he fell asleep. However, had I been able to follow him after work to Ward's House, The Queen's Elm or The Lord Packenham, I'm convinced I would have found out a lot more about his day on the job . . . by today's standard, mine and many other Irish families in England would be classified as dysfunctional – so be it.

He received an embittered letter from a woman who wished to remain unidentified: 'The Irish men, young and old, were drunken thugs who disgraced themselves in every city they worked in. They had no respect for their women at home or on the streets . . . Paddy would not marry, he carried the status of a hard case. He made dirt of his own women in a foreign country . . . The Irish girls coming from Ireland – most didn't drink, smoke or dope. They worked to get a bit to eat and clothes on their back.'

Joe McGarry from Tyrone described the downward spiral that sometimes occurred. The people who had a sense of self became millionaires, while he was 'standin' down a hole, to get money, to buy a drink, so that I could fit in, belong, be normal, and be one of us'. If you did not maintain this togetherness, you were not part of the little group: 'You were one of them, whoever they were.' If you did not drink your money at night, you were seen as mean, 'there was something wrong with you'. After that, McGarry said, men often ended up homeless, working an odd day to get money for alcohol. If there was not any work, they often drank for the entire day. He eloquently described the mindset of these broken men: 'There is a depth of pain that finds its level, among a group of men in a pub, in a park, homeless and drunk, who recognise each other's pain . . . Now I know I'm an island of self, between two places, and I have to identify my own self – what I am, what I can do.'

F. H. Boland, then Ireland's Ambassador to the Court of Saint James, notified Éamon de Valera's government in 1951 of the appalling conditions in which many of the Irish emigrants were living and was critical of the role of the clergy. The Catholic Church wanted the Irish to live together because they believed the atmosphere in English homes might present a moral hazard. Boland cited an example 'where the local Canon approved of having 150 Irishmen living in three smallish houses because the men were kept together in accommodation run by a man of good character'.

In 2013, Longford-born painter Bernard Canavan had this to say about de Valera in an interview with journalist Seamus Enright for the *Anglo Celt* newspaper:

Mr de Valera came over here to Birmingham and said that wages were as high in Ireland as they were in Birmingham. Well, what can you say? What is the answer to that? Why were there boatloads of people coming over? You'd see them weeping, distraught. Why was that happening if the Irish government was providing a world where people could flourish? That's an old question. It's the old, old question. Aristotle asked it, "What is the government for?" It is to allow people to flourish, and we didn't flourish then, did we?

The Crown in Cricklewood is the most iconic and celebrated of the Irish pubs in London. 'The Crown in Cricklewood was our Mecca,' according to one of the interviewees in Catherine Dunne's book. 'If you wanted a job or wanted to know where work was coming up, if you were known as a worker you could always get drink on the slate or a loan of a few quid until you got back on your feet . . . if you were stuck for a place to stay, you had a word with the Guv'ner and there was always a room upstairs for a couple of nights . . . The Crown was like Rick's Cafe in Casablanca – everyone went there sooner or later. People who moved around got their letters from home addressed to The Crown.'

The Crown is now the Clayton Crown Hotel, and bears little relation to the establishment it once was. Established in 1751, it was a coaching tavern, situated on a road notorious for highway robberies. The London General Omnibus Company selected The Crown as a terminus for its horse-drawn double-deckers. From the early nineteenth century, seasonal agricultural labourers came to Cricklewood. The Crown pub was built in 1900 on the site of the original, much smaller, inn, which had been sold in 1898 for £86,000. Magistrates had imposed a strict limit on licensing in the area, even though the population was increasing rapidly. Consequently, The Crown was the only public house in Cricklewood. Between 1940 and 1975, the London areas of Cricklewood, Harlesden and Kilburn became focal points for the rapidly growing Irish community in London, and The Crown became famous for being at the heart of it. Early each morning, groups of Irish tradesmen and labourers gathered in the forecourt looking for 'the start' or 'call on'. Building contractors or subcontractors would turn up with trucks and vans to recruit men out of the crowd for a day's casual labour. If you did not get work, the temptation was to go to the pub. In the early 1960s, Irish songwriter Dominic Behan wrote the ballad 'McAlpine's Fusiliers', which was recorded by The Dubliners:

> Oh, the craic was good in Cricklewood, and they
> wouldn't leave The Crown,
> With glasses flying and Biddy's crying 'cause Paddy
> was going to town
> Oh mother dear, I'm over here and I'm never
> coming back
> What keeps me here is the reek o' beer, the ladies
> and the craic.

In 1998, Tom Moran of the Irish-owned and -operated Moran & Bewley's Hotels purchased and restored the pub. There is still a mural of a group of construction workers inside the building.

Putting drink 'on the slate' may have seemed a kindness, but it was the start of a slippery slope for many. It was common for pubs to cash cheques for workers. Some charged a fee, while others would give a certain amount of cash early in the night and tell the worker to come back for the rest at the end of the night. The subcontractors – or 'subbies' – commonly paid their workers cash in the pubs. Many Irish workers often travelled to urban centres for a weekend or longer after a period spent in work camps in remote areas. They usually had substantial disposable income. One such group, the so-called 'Tunnel Tigers', bored tunnels for roads, railways and hydroelectric schemes, and often earned substantial wages, particularly when overtime was included. Sean O'Ciarain describes their lifestyle: 'The Tunnel Tigers, as they were called, came down at the weekends all rough and scruffy, and badly in need of a bath, but with plenty of money in their pockets . . . The Irishmen were known for flashing the pay slips. A pay envelope showing a high figure of money for a week's work was a thing to keep for showing in pubs in order to impress people.'

The 'Sunday shift' was often a lifeline for the indebted drinker. Sunday was the best day to carry out roadworks, an area of construction in which the Irish were well represented. Workers were often hired in the pub the previous night. In Ultan Cowley's book, Malcolm O'Brien described how it worked:

> I used to work occasionally on Sunday morning for Murphy, pulling cable. On Saturday night a ganger would come into the Half Moon pub on Holloway Road and ask did you want a shift in the morning. If you did, you had to guarantee him a drink the next night. Well, of course everyone did, because it was Sunday only, and it gave you money for your beer, and maybe a good meal of bacon and cabbage. The shift might last from seven o'clock until half past twelve, for about five pounds a shift. No documentation – just a bundle of fivers in the pub . . . Afterwards when you were driven back to London in the wagons, the foreman came in with you and he had possibly ten shillings off each man, and be drunk all day free, and if you didn't go along with that no more Sunday shifts.

Francis Browner compiled the stories of a number of people who left Ireland as young men and women and 'after many years of exile, closed the circle by coming home again'. She published the accounts in *Coming Home,* under the auspices of the Safe-Home Programme established by Dr Jerry Cowley from Mulranny in County Mayo. Cowley became aware of two groups of elderly people who were sidelined in modern society: local people who could no longer take care of themselves, and Irish emigrants who would like to come home to live out their days but did not have the financial means to do so. He built St Brendan's Village in Mulranny, where both of these groups are now catered for. The programme has since expanded to other areas of Ireland. In Browner's book, emigrants spoke of their personal and professional lives, and the difficulties of integrating into the host culture. Interviewees who spoke about the role of the pub in their social life were overwhelmingly males who had emigrated to Britain. David Sinnotte, from Ferns in County Wexford, told a sad tale too often repeated on the streets of British cities, primarily London. He did not feel comfortable when he emigrated, 'but the drink blanked out the memories . . . that's why a person did drink . . . I couldn't live without drink. I had to have a drink even to socialise with people . . . and once you were drinking you just concentrated on working to get money for drink.'

In *An Irish Navvy: The Diary of an Exile*, Dónall Mac Amhlaigh described his life as an unskilled labourer in 1950s Britain. Originally written in Irish as *Dialann Deorai* and published in 1960, it was translated into English by Valentin Iremonger and published in 1964. From the start, Mac

Amhlaigh thought the English pubs inferior to those of his native land, despite the better facilities on offer:

> The pubs were nice and clean and the people pleasant enough but somehow or other I didn't take to them. There were games going on all the time in the pub – darts, skittles and suchlike, with a jukebox screeching away all the time. I couldn't help comparing it with Larry's pub back home – the good, wise chat and the manliness that I shared with those drinking there. The women are as plentiful in the pubs here as there are fleas on a goat and no man can be at ease wherever they are.

Mac Amhlaigh was brought up between Barna and Galway city, moved to Kilkenny when he was fourteen and left for Britain aged twenty-five – a relatively late age to emigrate at that time, particularly so because he had left school at fifteen. It was not long before he found an establishment where he felt more comfortable – among his own people. He had moved from London to Northampton. He was not a native Irish speaker, but had a lifelong affiliation with the people of the Connemara *Gaeltacht*, where Irish was the mother tongue. The Connemara people were notorious for sticking to themselves, according to Mac Amhlaigh. It was not unheard of for a Connemara native to pick up very little English during a lifetime spent in England. Mac Amhlaigh was called to a job in Berkshire one Sunday afternoon, and had arranged to get a lift with his friend Mike Ned, but the inevitable happened: 'Nothing would do Mike Ned but to go across to Camden Town to see if any of the lads from

Rosmuc were knocking around there. In the heel of the hunt, of course, we didn't get out of London at all. We finished up blind drunk in The Black Cap with a crowd from Connemara.' Mike Ned never made it to Berkshire. The author got an early train the next morning, secured his employment and went to work in a labour camp where there was no access to alcohol. Among the workers, conversation inevitably turned to the good times they would have when the work finished. 'Big Bartley' hated the incarceration and told Mac Amhlaigh he could not wait to get to the pubs, and would never come back to the camp: 'I'll be in The Shamrock on Sunday night and I'll be plastered . . . round there by The Elephant we'll have the good time and won't it be wonderful after this deadly camp. I'll never set foot in a camp again as long as I live.'

When Mac Amhlaigh got home to Ireland for a break, he briefly went to see his mother and then went to spend the night in Larry's pub with his father. After he returned to England, he had difficulty getting work and eventually gravitated back to Northampton. He felt lonely and lost until he met up with his former colleagues. He did not have any money, but his friends insisted on bringing him to the pub: 'The three of us moved off down to The Jolly Smokers where we had five or six pints of mild. We met a gang from Connemara there that had been brought down from London by Pat the Tailor to replace the others that were gone . . . and if we hadn't a good time together I don't know what a good time is . . . By the end of the night the spree was great and I hadn't felt so good for many a long day . . . I felt as I went to sleep a great burden had been lifted from my shoulders.'

Mac Amhlaigh gave an account of Saint Patrick's Day in 1957 – it was then still a closed day in the pubs in Ireland. He went to mass, then for something to eat with a few of his friends. There was only one thought on their minds: 'We were dying for the pubs to be open and as soon as they were, we were into The Black Cap like a flash. We laid into the stout and mild with a will and, before long, we all felt nicely enough.' They moved on to The Bedford Arms, a pub well known for traditional Irish music, and later to The Laurel Tree in Camden Town, where the Connemara people gathered: 'Most of them were pretty young and spending money as if they had just picked it off the pavement.' After a debauched three weeks in London, he was offered a job in Daventry. On his first day off he went to The Lion and the Lamb for a bottle of Guinness. This was a different type of pub. It was where the natives drank:

> There were a good crowd in there making so much noise that you'd think they were drinking barrels of beer – which they weren't. They're a close crowd these country people, and even though they go into the pub now and again, they stretch out each drink so long that it's a wonder the landlord gets any profit at all. The pubs in England are kept beautifully clean, the floorboards and every bit of wood well-scrubbed and they have all sort of things to entice customers in: music, darts, skittles and crib and even television in some of the places. The pub here is a meeting place for the people, or for some of them, and parish questions are often hammered out in them.

He concluded there were two things that would never be as good as in Ireland: the great drink and the conversation. His next job was in Rugby. He stayed in Daventry again and recalled going to The Plough and Bell after Sunday mass:

> The back room was full of half frozen old fellows watching each other to see who would be the first to stand a half-pint. They're a queer crowd, the Midlands people, without any 'go' or spunk in them and living rather meanly. Any ordinary workman back home in Ireland on a Saturday night would say: 'To Hell with it! Knock it back! We're alive, aren't we?' God knows if at home they had the money and the comfort people have here, there's not a country that would be better for sheer enjoyment of life.

Reading the accounts of different emigrants, it is clear many of them defined their culture by the life in pubs. If the pub was dominated by Irish patrons, it was better. An Irish pub owner might not be superior to the English in education or wealth, but Irish-owned pubs offered more fun than the staid British alternatives. Emigrants were proud of their ability to have a good time and drink plenty compared to the abstemious Englishman. This copious drinking indicated the presence of 'go', a word normally understood as a work ethic. It was considered a skill to drink heavily, and a proud indicator of ethnicity. The pub was not a place of assimilation or acculturation, but a reinforcer of differences. It was a place to feel a sense of continuity and belonging, but arguably it did little for these Irish people to come to terms with life in a modern, increasingly secular and multicultural country.

Pubs reinforced a false ideal of Ireland, with songs depicting the country as a peasant idyll and not the impoverished, claustrophobic, Catholic-dominated backwater that it was for most. This had repercussions when some of these emigrants returned home to Ireland to find a country completely at variance with the ballads sung drunkenly in pubs across Britain. This had particularly been the case for older Irishmen, many of whom did not engage with the host society beyond earning a wage and spending their spare time in the ethnically divided pubs and cafés.

Sean O'Ciarain described a more abstemious time in Scotland in his memoir *Farewell to Mayo*. He went to the pub only on Saturday nights, and even then only for an hour or two before closing time, but it was important to him: 'Nearly every man I knew in those days who was half a man at all took a drink on either Friday or Saturday night, some on both nights.' Not to take a drink was to be an incomplete Irishman. The licensing laws were different in Scotland, and pubs had to close by half past nine. Protestant temperance ideology always had a stronger foothold in Scotland than England, and was later reflected in the muted drinking culture of Protestant Northern Ireland and the south-western United States, where Ulster Scots emigrated in significant numbers. Restricted opening hours often led to problems: 'Men drank to beat the clock and coming near closing time it was chaos, with all the pushing and shouting, trying to draw the attention of the bartenders and guzzling down drink as if there was no tomorrow.' O'Ciarain pointed out the counterintuitiveness of the legislation. Every time an extension of opening hours was petitioned for, it was vigorously opposed by certain elements of the public, 'very often people who had never been inside a public house in their lives'. These people might not have liked what they saw when men came out at closing time 'stone clobbered', and this O'Ciarain understood, 'but one sure way to make people drunk is to have short drinking hours. Shorter hours serve to increase drunkenness, not to decrease it: that is a proven fact.' He lodged in a house in Glasgow where the landlady did not like the pubs, and claimed she was never inside the door of one in her life, but O'Ciarain was not impressed: 'Well, if that was the way that suited her, good luck to her, it did not suit everybody. There are far worse things a man can do than drink a couple of pints on a Saturday night after having worked hard all week.'

The Irish pubs in London were still vibrant in the late 1980s, largely due to soaring unemployment in Ireland. A contributor to the website An Fear Rua described the scene. The pubs were busy all day long with 'the usual hard cases, lads who had gone overboard the night before, and lads who never seemed to do anything, but always had enough for a few pints and a game of pool'. They got busier in the evening when the vans of the building contractors dropped off workers. It was different on Friday: 'The lads who had worked for the subbies during the week were paid by cheque. Most Irish pubs in Kilburn and Cricklewood cashed them, charging £5 per £100 and, of course, they were expected to buy drink.' Friday evening also saw buses coming up Edgware Road 'stopping at The Crown, with their destinations on the front – Castlebar, Galway, Limerick, heading for Holyhead'. The pub functioned as the bus stop for those on their way home to Ireland. It was the nucleus of the community. In the late 1980s, McGovern's on the Kilburn

High Road cashed 3,000 to 5,000 cheques every week, according to a former manager: 'Over the course of a year that would average out at about £900,000 a week. Some weeks, we were doing £1.5 million in cheques. The queue into the pub used to be five or six hundred yards long, and five or six people deep.'

In 1991, the Irish support and advice centre in Hammersmith, London, published a report on the health and welfare of their clients. They told the story of 'Jim' to illustrate their needs. He had come to England unskilled and spent thirty years working in the construction industry. After injuring his hip, he could no longer work and gradually slipped into a world of alcoholism and ultimately homelessness, before coming under the ambit of the support service.

> If you work on building sites, the pub is the focal
> point of social life: many people then (and now)
> kept to the pubs as a relief from the mistrust and
> dislike they found elsewhere. It was a place to hear
> about the next job in the construction trade and
> where you met the foreman on Friday for your pay.
> The tradition is to treat everyone lavishly when you
> are in the money, and then when you are down on
> your luck they treat you . . . if you won't take part
> in the endless rounds of drinking, you are somehow
> ostracised, you have offended group morale.

In *The Social Contexts of Drinking Among Irishmen in London*, Mary Tilki described the Irishmen she interviewed: 'Their masculinity was constructed around a combination of hard physical labour and heavy drinking, and alcohol became a culturally sanctioned coping strategy for men economically inactive because of injury, degenerative disorders or redundancy, or with underlying mental illness. This could become a downward spiral very quickly. Having spent a lifetime working on the lump and little accrued pension or social insurance rights, their safety net was porous.'

The 1999 *Health Survey for England* included first- and second-generation Irish people for the first time. It found they were more likely to drink alcohol, and drank more frequently, than the general population or other minority ethnic groups. Irish men and women were less likely to be non-drinkers, and both were much more likely to consume alcohol in excess of government recommendations. Tilki interviewed a group of Irishmen in London. 'Seamus' described the experience of living in London in the early 1960s: 'When I came here first . . . the pub was the only place to meet your mates. I was a Pioneer but I was living in an oul' room, coming from work and getting the tea and going out again. Looking at the four walls. The entertainment was basically the pub, there was no other place to go.' The perceived lack of alternatives to the pub is a consistent theme in the accounts of Irish emigrants to England. With substandard accommodation and unfriendly landlords, it is easy to see why this happened. However, it may be argued, the persistence of the pub as the sole social outlet was indicative of people unwilling or unable to acculturate to their new home. British society was replete with opportunities to join clubs and organisations of all types. The arts were well provided for. Cinemas and theatres were common in all urban areas, but the pub held complete sway in the lives of many Irish people. So many had emigrated at such a young

age to such a different environment that they clung to the
only rock they knew. Low education standards and poor
language skills, in some cases, exacerbated the problem.
Racism was an issue, and there were organisations that
would not countenance Irish membership. While many still
held onto their religious beliefs and engaged in activities
through the Church or affiliated social clubs, others drifted
away and the pub became their only meeting ground. It
was a perfect storm that blew apart the lives of so many
unfortunate people.

It would be disingenuous and untrue to look on the pub
culture among emigrant Irish to Britain as entirely negative.
For those who could moderate their drinking, it was a lifeline
to society and a way to meet people. It was largely a democratic space, with what Mary Tilki called a 'flattened social
structure'. It allowed the sub-contractors and foremen to be
teased and 'taken down a peg or two', or at least 'spoken to
without deference and with impunity'. The pub allowed men
to demonstrate skills not otherwise observable, and purchase
some social currency: 'Prowess at conversation, cards or
darts, a good singing voice or the ability to play an instru-
ment afforded men with little status as labourers, a measure
of prestige and self-esteem.' Music became a career for
some, but it too was a trade in close congress with alcohol
and its potential dangers. After reading a number of personal
accounts of Irishmen who had worked in the construction
industry in London, Tilki summed up her findings:

> They describe how men with nicknames like Mule
> Kennedy, Bull Gallagher, Big Mick or Elephant John
> and others 'horsed it out', digging trenches, tunnel-

ling, pulling cable or laying concrete. Masculinity for Irish men was constructed on the basis of physical strength and the ability to consume large volumes of alcohol without staggering, being sick or out of control. It is therefore significant that when men were unable to work because of redundancy or ill-health, their whole image of themselves as men came under pressure.

In 2006, Corinne Silva put together a photo essay called *Róisín Bán: The Irish Diaspora in Leeds*. In it, there is a series of interviews with people from Mayo who emigrated to the greater Leeds area in the 1950s, '60s and '70s. The stories of pub culture are similar to those told by others. Bernard was the first man interviewed, and described the role played by a pub called the Roscoe:

> The Roscoe, when I got there, was the main pub for the Irish because there was always music and you met everyone from home. Everyone knew everyone else going into the Roscoe, a great place for meeting. They called it the Labour Exchange of Leeds because if a lad came over from Ireland, he'd go to the Roscoe and they were able to get him a job. There were people there who were contractors, whatever. So that's where they went to for a job when they went to England . . . They went to the Roscoe.

Inevitably, there was a dark side too. Michael told the 'classic tale' of his uncle Jimmy: 'He just came home from the pub one night, turned on the gas heater and forgot to light it or something because he was drunk and the fumes just killed him. It was quite sad, it was a couple of days before he was found and stuff, because he lived on his own. To me that's just a classic tale of a poor Irish immigrant. It would have been good if he'd been married, just to have somebody.'

Tom felt pity for Irish immigrants: 'I feel sorry for the Irish fellas in Leeds and those places, the cities, that didn't get married . . . Living in flats, it's lonely, you know what I mean. Actually I think it shortens their lives. It's sort of being thrown on the scrapheap and living alone, and that sort of thing . . . I suppose you turn to the drink then for company.' Joe reckoned a lot of the Irish brought problems on themselves: 'The way they carried on, going out and getting drunk and looking for a fight . . . It was a lack of education, that's what it was.'

The United States

Up to 1830, the majority of Irish immigrants to North America were Protestant. By 1840, they accounted for a little over 10 per cent. The 1830s and 1840s were the age of mass emigration of Catholics from Ireland to America. Leaving behind a desolate and famine-ravaged country, the numbers were staggering. From 1840 to 1900, 3.6 million Irish people emigrated to the United States, with over 1.7 million leaving between 1840 and 1860. In each decade between 1820 and 1869, the Irish accounted for over 35 per cent of the immigrants. From 1841 to 1850, the figure was a staggering 46 per cent. After 1860, the figure gradually dropped until it was a little over 2.5 per cent in the decade from 1911 to 1920. Catholic immigrants overwhelmingly settled in urban areas; by 1920, 90 per cent of Irish immigrants to the United States lived in cities and towns. Three quarters lived in seven industrialised urban zones: Massachusetts, New York, New Jersey, Connecticut, Illinois, Pennsylvania and Ohio. The vast majority of these immigrants ended up in low-paid, low-skilled jobs, but for some, saloon keeping was viewed as a road to financial success. The image of a saloon in Ireland and England is generally that of a high Victorian-style establishment with ornate decoration and expensive furnishings, typically located in an urban environment. The Crown Saloon in Belfast is perhaps the most famous and elaborate example. In America, the term was used to describe a wider range of establishments. The Irish, like other ethnic groups, sought to recreate their social environment in a new context. The Italians brought their restaurants; the Irish brought their pubs. Some countries brought a cuisine; the Irish brought their alcohol. Emigration is recognised as a stressful process, and psychologists have long noted the propensity of stressed emigrants to revert to native comfort foods. In a country where most business areas were dominated by Protestants, the ownership of a saloon was a way for an Irish person to gain a foothold in commercial life. The costs of entry were low, and many fine establishments evolved from humble saloons. However, the Irish did not have the pub trade all to themselves. German pubs with beer gardens and elaborate dance floors were popular with the social elites.

At the start of the American Revolution in 1775, there were saloons in Philadelphia called The Faithful Irishman,

The Lamb and Three Jolly Irishmen. By 1820, the Southwark part of the city was heavily populated by Irish immigrants, and of the eighty-three liquor licences in the municipal area, thirty-one of them were held by recognisably Irish names. The situation in nearby Worcester was even more pronounced. By 1880, two thirds of the applicants for licences were Irish, even though they accounted for less than a third of the population. While just one sixth of the city's population was born in Ireland, half of the saloon keepers were Irish and another 10 per cent were Irish American.

As far back as 1868, Michael 'King' McDonald, the so-called 'Gambler King of Clark Street' was a powerful politician, saloon keeper and illegal gambling boss in Chicago. While the German beer gardens tended to the prosperous, the quality of Irish saloons was varied. Richard Lindberg, biographer of Michael McDonald and noted Chicago historian, wrote that they ran the gamut 'from simple, unpretentious basement dives with dirt floors and wooden planks propped up by barrels to elegantly festooned showplaces like the kind Hal Varnell kept on Randolph Street'. 'Prince Hal' was a notorious gambler and political kingmaker who was later appointed warden of the Cook County Insane Asylum. The *Chicago Inter-Ocean* newspaper carried a report on his saloon, writing that it was 'fitted up with the most skilful contrivances and appliances for the perpetration of crimes so dark they cannot be named'.

In her PhD thesis 'Emerald Pub to Silver Saloon: Building an Irish Saloon Community in the American Mining West', Michelle A. Charest studied saloon proprietorship in Virginia City, Nevada, in 1870. She found the Irish were the largest group of ethnic saloon keepers, followed by the Germans. Irishmen controlled eighteen saloons – 26 per cent of the drinking establishments in the city – while Germans owned fourteen, or 19 per cent of the total. However, it was the Germans who were the best represented when total population was taken into account.

In 1899, John Koren studied crime figures in an attempt to see if the widespread vilification of the Irish in America as drunken criminals was statistically valid. The Irish ranked third, behind the Scottish and Canadian ethnic groups, and were on a par with the Polish, English and Americans. He concluded that 'Irish saloons stand for immoderate drinking and drunkenness in greater measure than any other.' A stereotype had been created, and any drunken act by an Irish person was an indication of the nation's propensity for alcohol and criminality, while other ethnic groups with similar statistical profiles were ignored. Koren was an avowed teetotaller, but did not envisage damnation for the drinkers. They were not a riotous company intent upon reducing themselves to drunkenness, but 'a well behaved group of men who play cards together, read, smoke and drink a glass of beer . . . in not a single one of the many such groups observed did drinking seem to be the most important thing'.

The Five Points area of lower Manhattan was once synonymous with the Irish, poverty, violence and alcoholism. In 1835, renowned frontiersman Davy Crockett visited the area. He compared the Irish of his acquaintance in the western states to the Five Pointers: 'In my part of the country, when you meet an Irishman, you find a first-rate gentleman; but these are worse than savages; they are too mean to swab hell's kitchen.' Charles Dickens passed the same way in

1852, and referred to 'hideous tenements which take their names from robbery and murder; all that is loathsome, drooping and decayed is here'. Jocelyn Green described the area in her 2014 novel *Yankee in Atlanta*: 'If Broadway was Manhattan's artery, Five Points was its abscess; swollen with people, infected with pestilence, inflamed with vice and crime. Groggeries, brothels and dance halls put private sin on public display. Although the neighborhood seems fairly self-contained, more fortunate New Yorkers were terrified of Five Points erupting, spreading its contagion to the rest of them.'

The area was originally a pond, filled in by the authorities to build accommodation for the rapidly expanding immigrant population. However, the builders did not take account of the softness of the ground, and the condition of the tenements deteriorated quickly. The Irish population in New York City rose from 961,719 in 1850 to 1,611,304 by 1860, and the vast majority of these newly arrived citizens were housed in these abysmal tenements. The buildings were often little more than outhouses. In the late nineteenth century, a report on tenement life around Five Points counted one bathtub for 1,321 families and one water tap for a floor of apartments. It was an area heavily polluted by industry. Businesses using naphtha, benzene and other flammables made fire a daily hazard. The area was notorious for the number of saloons, brothels and groggeries – the majority of them owned by Irish and Germans.

According to *Wilson's Business Directory of New York City*, the Sixth Ward had a population of 24,000 in 1860. There were 204 groceries and 169 saloons or porterhouses. The groceries – more commonly referred to as groggeries –

were similar to the spirit grocers of the homeland. The *New York Clipper* – the first newspaper in the United States dedicated entirely to the entertainment industry – described a typical establishment as having 'a grease-covered counter' and 'an inevitable bar' at the back. Behind the bar, the set-up was basic: 'a score of tall necked bottles . . . a beer barrel stands in the extreme corner, and in these articles we have the most lucrative portion of the grocer's trade, for no purchaser enters the murky store without indulging in a consolatory drink, be their sex as it may'. Billiard tables and prostitutes were common.

Crowne's Grocery was the best known. It was, according to one of the local Protestant charitable organisations, 'the most redoubtable stronghold of wickedness in Five Points if not in New York', and was memorably described by George Foster in his 1850 book *New York by Gas Light*: 'It is not without difficulty we should effect an entrance through the baskets, barrels and boxes, Irish women and sluttish house keepers, white, black, yellow and brown, thickly crowding the walk right up to the threshold – as if the store were too full of its commodities and customers and some of them had tumbled and rolled outdoors.' He noted piles of cabbages, potatoes, squashes, eggplants, tomatoes, turnips, eggs, dried apples, chestnuts and beans piled around the floor. Hardware was also in evidence: 'boxes containing anthracite and charcoal, nails, plug tobacco, etc, etc, which are dealt out in any quantity from a bushel or a dollar to a cent's worth . . . firewood, seven sticks for six pence, or a cent apiece, and kindling wood three sticks for two cents'. He described the casks of molasses, rum, whiskey, brandy and all sorts of cordials. The latter, he said, were 'carefully manufactured in the back room where a kettle and furnace with all the necessary instruments of spiritual devilment are provided for the purpose'. After describing a myriad of other food stuffs available, he described the bar: 'Across one end of the room runs a long, low, black counter armed at either end with bottles of poisoned firewater, doled out at three cents a glass to the loafers and bloated women who frequent the place.'

Tyler Anbinder provides a description of a typical Irish saloon in *Five Points: The Nineteenth-Century New York Neighbourhood*. It was, he wrote, 'a long, narrow, open space, with a bar running down one wall and an empty floor opposite to accommodate the crowds that might visit at lunch times and in the evening. Sawdust covered the floor to mop up spit tobacco juice and spilt beer and a large stove stood in the centre of the room to provide warmth during the winter.' Many had unsavoury reputations. Armory Hall, owned by Billy McGlory, and The Hurdy Gurdy, owned by Owney Geoghegan, were two of the more maligned. The latter, located in the Bowery, was the headquarters of the notorious Gas House Gang. Other dubious haunts included the Haymarket, Milligan's Hell, Diamond Dan O'Rourke's and the Suicide Hall. The last was patrolled every night by the notorious 'Eat 'Em Up' Jack McManus.

Charles Loring Brace, philanthropist and founder of the American foster care system, compared the standard of tenement accommodation to the attraction of the saloons. In the drinking establishments, the customer could find 'jolly companions, a warmed and lighted room, a newspaper and, above all, a draught which can change poverty into riches and drive care and labor and thoughts of all his burdens and annoyances far away'. The saloon was the 'picture gallery, club, reading room and social salon'. The alcohol was 'the magic transmuter of care to cheerfulness, of penury to plenty, of a low, ignorant, worried life to an existence for the moment buoyant, contented and hopeful'.

Music was common. Saloons employed black fiddlers ready to tune up their 'villainous squeaking for six pence apiece and a treat at the end'. African Americans and Irish Americans mingled in the saloons. Tap-dancing emerged from the cultural stew, a mixture of Irish jigs and the shuffle dance steps typical of early jazz. 'Flash talk' was Irish slang: prostitutes were 'nymphs of the pave' and the police had 'paddy wagons'. Binge-drinking sessions were referred to as 'going on a bender', alcohol as 'lush', talk as 'palaver', clothes as 'duds' and faces were 'physogs'.

Father McSweeney of Saint Brigid's chapel lamented the behaviour of his Irish-American flock:

> Look at the daily newspapers and read the number of stabbings, murders and other crimes that fill the police courts, and from what cause? All, or very nearly all, are from whiskey drinking. In this parish, there are men who never go to bed sober and they abuse themselves by abusing their wives and children. They are not all taken home on a shutter, but stagger in and find faults with their unfortunate wives for not having supper. The cursed habit of rum drinking is bringing destruction on our people.

Some of these establishments were owned by prominent members of the community. Matt Brennan, a well-known

Democrat and later county sheriff, owned Monroe Hall; Yankee Sullivan, a famous prizefighter, owned the Center Street Bar. Saloon keepers with political ambitions were not averse to courting the vote with free alcohol. Different gangs were often associated with particular saloons. Colourful names were a common feature. The Whyos were no exception. In 1880, prominent members included Hoggy Walsh, Fig McGerald, Bill Hurley, Googy Corcoran, Baboon Connolly, Slops Connolly, Dorsey Doyle, Red Rocks Farrell and Piker Ryan. Dandy Johnny Dolan was held in high esteem among fellow gang members and feared by rivals. He invented a copper eye-gouger, which was worn on the thumb, and wore sharpened axe blades embedded in the soles of his shoes as part of his armoury. When Piker Ryan was captured by the police, they found the rate sheet for the gang member's work. A straight-forward punch was worth two dollars. Fifteen dollars was the charge for an ear bitten off, while the 'big job' earned $100. Sporting activities were common in the saloons. Bare-knuckle fighting was an Irish speciality, and gambling on fights was intense. Such was the reputation of the Irish as boxers that men from other ethnic groups assumed Irish names to advance their careers. Future heavyweight champion Jack Sharkey was born Joseph Paul Zukauskas, a son of Lithuanian immigrants. After his fighting career was over, he opened a pub in Boston.

Chicago journalist Finley Peter Dunne became famous for his Mr Dooley articles. The fictional saloon keeper expounded on the political and social issues of the day from his hostelry on the Irish South Side of Chicago. His work was written in the heavily accented voice of an Irish immigrant, and became wildly popular when it was nationally syndicated. The first column appeared in *The Chicago Post* in October 1893, and introduced the setting: 'Business was dull in the liquor shop of Mr Martin Dooley in Archey Road last Wednesday night, and Mr Dooley was sitting back in the rear of the shop holding a newspaper at arm's length and reading the sporting news. In came Mr John McKenna.' McKenna had been on his way to Brighton Park and remembered his friend Colonel McNeerey, who had returned to Ireland. He was lonely, and sought sanctuary in the saloon: 'The lights were shining in the little tavern and the window decorations – green festoons, a single sheet poster of a Parnell meeting in McCormick's Hall and a pyramid of bottles filled with Medford rum and flies – evoked such cheery recollections of earlier years that he hopped off the car and entered briskly.'

Even US President Theodore Roosevelt became a fan of Mr Dooley, despite occasional jokes at his expense. Dunne's columns were read each week at White House cabinet meetings as a barometer of public opinion on current issues. *The New York Times* claimed in 2006 that it was Dooley, rather than Irish-American politician Thomas 'Tip' O'Neill, who coined the phrase 'All politics is local'.

Dunne chronicled the poverty and the role of alcohol among the Irish urban poor. One of his best-known creations was Jack Carey, the 'idle apprentice'. Carey's grandfather had come over from Ireland and lived a solid life. His son Jim was fine at first, until alcohol intervened: 'Jim was as straight as th' r-roads of Kildare but he took to dhrink.' By the time Jack was born, he had become a homeless tramp. As he grew up in Chicago, his life was a

mess: 'It was dhrink an' fight ivry night an' all day Sundah.'
He became immersed in a world of thievery and violence,
ultimately murdering a policeman called Clancy who had
previously sent him to the state penitentiary. Jack, in turn,
was shot and killed by the police force. In his column,
Dooley uses the story – apparently based on fact – to address
the issues of alcohol abuse and lack of proper accommodation and resources in the slums.

Thomas Nast – considered the father of the American
cartoon, and the inventor of the modern image of Santa
Claus – despised the Irish, and frequently represented them
as dirty, riotous, monkey-like and ill educated in the magazine
Harper's Weekly. One cartoon, called 'His First School',
depicted a young Irish boy sitting at a bar surrounded by a
fearsome-looking group of men. Another, called 'His Paddy-
gree' depicted a child in a pigsty brandishing a bottle of
whiskey. Nast converted from Catholicism to Protestantism,
and his anti-Irish sentiment may have been a result of
bullying during his childhood. He also witnessed the
violence between the Irish and the African Americans in the
New York City Draft Riots of 1863, during which the
Colored Orphan Asylum near his home was burned down.

In Maurice Bourgeois's *John Millington Synge and the
Irish Theatre* (1913), he described the typical stage Irishman:

> The stage Irishman habitually bears the general
> name of Pat, Paddy or Teague. He has an atrocious
> Irish brogue, perpetual jokes, blunders and bulls
> in speaking and never fails to utter, by way of
> Hibernian seasoning, some wild screech or oath of
> Gaelic origin at every third word: he has an unsur-

passable gift of blarney and cadges for tips and free drinks. His hair is of a fiery red, he is rosy-cheeked, massive and whiskey loving. His face is one of simian bestiality with an expression of diabolical archness . . . In his right hand he brandishes a stout blackthorn, or a sprig of shillelagh, and threatens to belabour therewith the daring person who will tread on the tails of his coat.

Richard Stivers, among others, argues that the stereotype of the Irish drunkard became more benign as the Irish acculturated and integrated into American society: 'Early in the nineteenth century, a negative identity of drunkard was fostered on the Irish by a cultural stereotype and related institutionalised practices.' As time went by, he suggests, the Irish stereotype converged around a more positive image of the Irish drunk – the 'happy drunk', a stage caricature of an Irishman.

The connection between the Irish, convivial drinking and laughter is found in many songs of the late nineteenth century – particularly those sung in vaudeville. 'Drinking with Daniel Maloney', composed by M. J. Cavanagh in 1884, tells of 'a solid man' whose 'heart and pockets open to assist a fellow man'. In Daniel's company, his drinking partner will 'have the best on the bar, aither drink or cigar'. William Scanlan's 'Irish Potheen' from 1882 makes the same connection: 'Should a friend I chance to meet, I never fail to treat, to that sparkling drink the Irish call potheen.' However, if conviviality is present, violence is often never far away. 'The Irish Spree' describes an Irish gang breaking up a bar:

Smash went the windows and smash went the
　　furniture
Then on the fire we put it for to burn it sure!
Then in the bar we turned the rum and whiskey on,
That's what the boys and the girls got so frisky on.

The police arrived, but were no match for the fighting Irish:

Privates, Detectives, Sergeants and more of them
They were no use because we soon had the best of
　　them;
When they went down we danc'd on every chest of
　　them.

The narrator recounts that sixty of the assembled authorities
were killed by the end of the encounter.

In 'I Haven't Been Home Since Morning', Michael
O'Donovan sings about going on a drinking spree after
getting paid:

Oh I haven't been home since morning or since I got
　　me pay,
I haven't had such an elegant time for many and
　　many a day.
I am just in the humour to treat ye, so come along,
　　boys, with me,
For I've been working overtime and now I'm on a
　　spree.

Founded in New York in 1836, the Ancient Order of
Hibernians (AOH) is a Catholic fraternal organisation for

those of Irish descent or native born. The original purpose of the organisation was to protect Catholic churches from attacks and to help newly arrived immigrants deal with discrimination. It still plays a significant role in the lives of many Irish Americans, albeit largely as a social and charitable society. Another popular vaudevillian song told of the happenings after a parade held by the AOH:

> Then when we were disbanded as quickly as you
>   could wink,
> We all bounced down to Kelley's for to have a drop
>   to drink,
> The whiskey punch flew so wildly for the liquor it
>   was rare,
> In less than fifteen minutes divil a sober man was
>   there.
> And oh such drinking, such drinking, such drinking
>   as was there that night,
> Such drinking, such drinking the boys got awful
>   tight.

All Souls: Growing up in Boston's Irish Ghetto is an account of the poverty, alcoholism, violence and tragedy that marred Michael Patrick McDonald's troubled childhood as a son of Irish parents growing up in the predominantly Irish and Irish-American working-class area of Roxbury in south Boston. His younger brother was a promising boxer, but was killed in a drunken brawl outside a pub. His mother played the accordion in Irish-American bars, begging for small change. He describes one such bar: 'Eddie McGlaughlin's Hole in the Wall on Broadway . . . all boarded up except for the window with a blinking Budweiser sign between some dirty country kitchen curtains. I passed a woman wheeling a baby carriage through the tavern and bumming spare change . . . two older men offering each other out [asking each other outside to fight] . . . I was surrounded by muscled tough boys recounting Frankie's championship matches.'

It is hardly surprising that such bars are declining in popularity. Jason Stein of *New York Daily News* wrote about the passing of 'the Blarney Stone and Blarney Rock and blarney blathering bars'. At their height, he said, 'they were a working man's refuge, with plain food and cold beer and a respite from work and home. Now most of them are struggling desperately to survive.' The Blarney Stone chain had thirty bars in New York – immediately recognisable by their green canopies – but now there are only five. The rents are unsustainable, the product is stale and those left have largely mutated into sports bars. Next door to the Blarney Rock on West 33rd Street is Stout NYC, the largest Irish pub in the city, offering dozens of microbrews, and owned by Martin Whelan. It is where rich young urbanites spend their money. Whelan told *Crain's New York Business* that he deliberately 'dialled down' the Irish element.

Danny McDonald has been credited as the first person to take Irish pubs in a new direction when he opened the Swift Hibernian Lounge in 1995. Candlelit and providing craft beers from all over the world, it was a major departure in style but did not completely do away with museum pieces. There are reclaimed church pews and a pulpit from Jonathan Swift's home parish of Laracor, County Meath. The pub was lauded by *The New York Times* for eschewing television screens. McDonald told journalist Glenn Collins, 'We've never had a television because we wanted to inspire something that is close to the conviviality of pubs in Ireland.' The same situation pertains at The Scratcher, two blocks away, where the only in-house entertainment is a dartboard, a pool table and a jukebox. Joan Mathieu described it in 1997 as a 'trendy Irish bar with a Galway-in-gaslight mood – polished wood floors, crusty wood tables and red-brick walls.' There was, she wrote, 'an earnest heat-defying vitality here as people elbowed back and forth to the bar, becoming ensnared in and disentangled from one conversation to the next.' It had an 'atmosphere of solidarity and security' that made her feel unwelcome as a non-Irish person. She also describes going into one of the traditional 'Blarney bars' in New York on a Friday afternoon. It was populated by 'an assortment of deadbeats, nihilists and the marginally employed, all staring up at a television'. The bartender was a Galway woman, 'a peroxide blonde in a pink sweat suit', who strolled up and down with a cigarette bobbing off the corner of her mouth. Mathieu sat at the end table near the door to read a newspaper. She noticed the man next to her was covered with Vietnam and shamrock tattoos.

On another night, she went with a friend to a bar in Woodside in Queens – an area once synonymous with the Irish – and noticed it was still a first port of call for the newly arrived immigrant:

At one point a young man entered the bar, loaded down with several bags and a mixed expression of confusion, excitement and fear. He nodded uncertainly at the bartender. Everyone at the bar glanced

at him, pegging him for a greenhorn. The barman
gave him an exaggerated up and down glance of
appraisal, then offered his hand. 'How are ye?' The
young man grabbed his hand as if were a lifesaver,
a look of relief washing over his face. He ordered a
pint. 'Just in, are ye?' the barman asked.

New York has its fair share of formulaic new Irish pubs,
but not all are pastiches. In May 2014, Dubliner James
Morrissey opened The Late Late Bar & Spirit Grocer on
Houston Street in the Lower East Side of Manhattan.
Named after the agenda-setting Irish television chat show
originally presented by Gay Byrne, it is furnished in the style
of a 1960s residence, with drinks served in crystal goblets.
Guinness is served over ice with a mint leaf on the top in the
Nigerian style. There is a live feed from a bar in the west of
Ireland 'where time stands still (almost) as tides swell the
harbour as fishermen offload the finest lobster and freshest
fish in Europe' broadcast to the patrons in black and white.
This, the pub's website says, is a true representation of
Ireland today 'in real time'. Morrissey remembers that when
the eponymous chat show was first broadcast in the 1960s,
it tested the boundaries of conservative Roman Catholic
Ireland: 'a disruptive force, which the older audience boy-
cotted and the contemporary young professionals gravitated
towards'. He hopes his bar will have the same appeal today.

The Dead Rabbit Grocery and Grog in Manhattan was
voted the best bar in the world in the 2015 Spirit awards. It
was chosen from over 2,000 entries. It is 'a unique take on
the traditional Irish pub', according to owners Jack McGarry
and Sean Muldoon. The pub takes its name from a street

gang run by the boxer John Morrisscy in the 1850s. It is located in a nineteenth-century red-brick building, and 'seeks to commemorate the history of the area in its name, vintage decor and recreation of historic details'. It is renowned for its cocktails – a long way from the saloons of the Midwest mining towns in the nineteenth century.

McSorley's Old Ale House in Manhattan is a venerable institution. It claims to have been established by Irish immigrant John McSorley in 1854 in the Bowery area of Manhattan, a place synonymous with social strife and criminality in that era. There is, however, conflicting evidence as to the year of its establishment, as John McSorley did not appear in city directories before 1862 and the building it now occupies was not built before 1858. Whatever about the date of establishment, it was definitely called The Old House at Home in its first incarnation. It is the oldest Irish tavern in the United States, and only served women in 1970 after a battle with the National Organisation for Women, which went all the way to the Supreme Court. The toilet was unisex until 1986. There is sawdust on the floor and nothing has been removed from the walls since 1910. They only serve two drinks: light and dark ale. The historic motto was 'Good ale, raw onions, no ladies', but this has been abandoned. Among other things to command attention are Houdini's handcuffs and wishbones left by soldiers going to war. Before they left, they were given a turkey dinner by John McSorley. The bones were to be collected on their return, many of which, sadly, never were.

Quackser and His Cousin:

Cultural Representations of the Irish Pub

Film

In 1970, the American film *Quackser Fortune Has a Cousin in the Bronx* was partially filmed in Kavanagh's pub in Glasnevin, Dublin. The romantic comedy tells the story of an unlikely love affair between a Dublin street seller of manure and an upper-class American student attending Trinity College. Starring Gene Wilder as Quackser and Margot Kidder as Zazel, and directed by Waris Hussein, it was marketed as a screwball comedy. Quackser's parents told him there was no future in selling manure door to door, and he should go and look for a rich woman. This he does, with often hilarious consequences. At one stage, he takes Kidder in his wheelbarrow from Saint Patrick's Cathedral to Glasnevin for a drink at Kavanagh's. When they enter the bar, all the patrons go silent. They are shocked to see a woman in the front bar. Quackser tells Zazel to sit down but the barman immediately intervenes: 'To the ladies' lounge at the back please.' Quacker is surprised but obeys. The barman asks him what he would like to drink and he requests two large bottles of Guinness. The barman presumes these are both for Quackser and asks what the lady would like. When Quackser tells him one is actually for the lady, the barman is taken aback. Not only has a woman entered a strictly male space, she has also ordered a drink judged inappropriate by social mores. A number of the patrons are represented as simplistic and gullible. This lack of intellectual ability is a theme running through representations of the Irish pub in American-made films. Wilder was a co-writer on the script, and took it to Jean Renoir in Paris, who expressed a desire to direct it because he thought Quackser was the 'maddest character' he had seen since Charlie Chaplin. The pub is presented in the film as a place of constant merriment and tall tales that become more fantastical as the night goes on. Wilder's Irish accent is so bad that is frequently found on lists of the worst Irish accents in Hollywood history – a lengthy list indeed.

Whatever about the stereotypical portrayal of the Irish pub in *Quackser*, it pales in comparison to the 1954 *Knock on Wood* starring Danny Kaye. The film – jointly written, directed and produced by Norma Panama and Melvin Frank – tells the story of a vaudevillian ventriloquist unlucky in love. In it, Kaye sings a song called 'Monahan O'Han' – composed by his wife Sylvia Fine – in a pub full of flat-capped Irishmen, some of whom carry shillelaghs. Others are wearing Sons of Hibernia badges. The song tells how he rescued his mother from drowning in a vat of whiskey by drinking it. The scene was described in a review by Bosley Crowther in *The New York Times* on 15 April 1954: 'That bit in the pub, with him staggering among a chorus of lush Hibernians and bawling his long-bowsprited head off to a song called "Monahan O'Han" is a darling exercise in high-class kidding.' It is difficult to see the high-class element in the representation of wide-eyed simpletons listening to a song that grossly stereotypes the Irish. However, it is so over the top that it would be churlish to take umbrage.

Sean Connery's Irish accent in the 1959 Walt Disney film *Darby O'Gill and the Little People* is often cited as the worst in Hollywood history, and the movie as the apogee of stage Irishry. Directed by Robert Stevenson and with a screenplay written by Lawrence Edward Watkin, it was based on a book by Herminie Templeton Kavanagh called *The Ashes of Old Wishes and Other Darby O'Gill Tales*. Albert Sharpe, playing the role of Darby, spends his time telling his friends of his attempts to catch the little people who live on the estate of Lord Fitzpatrick, where he is the caretaker. His tall tales are inevitably recounted in the local pub – the Rathcullen Arms – where the locals stare open-mouthed at him as he recounts his latest efforts to capture King Brian of Knocknasheega and his fellow leprechauns. Once more, the pub is filled with wide-eyed simpletons who gape in wonder.

A leprechaun was also a central character the 1948 film *The Luck of the Irish*. In a somewhat fantastical plot, Stephen Fitzgerald – a newspaper journalist played by Tyrone Power – meets a leprechaun (Cecil Kellaway) and the beautiful Nora (Anne Baxter) on his travels in Ireland. When he returns home, he chances upon them again. The plot revolves around his decision whether to return to his ancestral homeland with the Irish characters or stay in America, where he is guaranteed future wealth through marriage and inheritance. A pivotal scene occurs in a bar at a wedding reception. In the opening shot, an accordion player grins maniacally as dancers whirl around to his music. Stephen sits down to talk to Nora at a table covered in beer mugs. A drunken man sleeps at the table. They are quickly interrupted by the baboon-like Irish fireman Terrence Flaherty, who asks to dance with Nora. Stephen tells Flaherty he smells smoke from the back room and the fireman runs off flailing like a lunatic. After a few minutes, he comes back. Stephen tells him the smoke must be coming from upstairs and he rushes off again. A member of the wedding party comes to the table, puts a drink down in front of Stephen and tells him to break it on his tonsils. Stephen and Nora start a conversation as 'The Rose of Tralee' is sung on the stage. She is going home the next day and he is perturbed. Flaherty returns incensed, asks Stephen if he still smells smoke and proceeds to punch him. A senseless mass brawl breaks out in the bar. The barman climbs out over the counter and breaks a bottle over the head of the nearest man. As the violence intensifies, the music plays on. Stephen is carried out unconscious as the scene fades to black. This barroom scene has almost every element of stage Irishry: a grinning simpleton, a drunken man asleep on a table, an easily confused Irish-American fireman and seemingly pointless violence.

The 1965 *Young Cassidy*, starring Australian actor Rod Taylor, attempted to tell the life story of Irish playwright Sean O'Casey. Cassidy is the name O'Casey gives himself in his third-person writing. John Ford started as director, but his health was failing. Going out drinking in the pubs of Dublin with the sociable Taylor – thirty-five years his junior – did not help. He was replaced by Jack Cardiff. The final credits read: 'A John Ford Film – Directed by Jack Cardiff'. Although Ford only directed four and a half minutes of the finished film, he choreographed the pub brawl scene at the end. To promote the film, MGM released an eight-minute promo. It was an unusual mixture of scenes from the film and information about different aspects of Irish culture, with real-life footage. The narrator described how Taylor met the people to understand Irish society. To a background of raucous scenes in different pubs with Taylor in the middle of the action, the narrator intones: 'To prepare for his role as young Cassidy, Rod Taylor went to meet the people of Dublin. He found them willing to impart their knowledge of customs and traditions and they too found him eager to absorb it all.' Taylor is shown drinking Guinness. There is an external shot of the most iconic – and now defunct – of all Dublin pubs, The Irish House. Even the Gaelic Revivalists, in general not fans of alcohol, loved The Irish House. Built in 1870 at the corner of Winetavern Street and Wood Quay, it was a popular pub and well-known piece of Celtic Revival architecture. Embellished by local stuccodores Burnet and Comerford, the building's façade represented iconic scenes from Irish history and myths. A figure of Éireann wept upon her stringless harp and beside her Daniel O'Connell stood clutching the Catholic Emancipation Act of 1829. Henry Grattan and a seventeen-figure frieze depicting the Act of Union of 1800 were also featured. Round towers surmounted the building, projecting into the sky. It was typical of much

Celtic Revival architecture, in which popular Irish symbolism was used to promote the nationalist cause. It was not universally admired. The *Irish Builder* trade journal of June 1870 commented: 'The genius who designed the unsightly structure now in process of erection at the corner of Winetavern Street has brought into view, by plentiful application of Portland cement, six ludicrous imitations of round towers perched upon its parapet.' The building was also used as a backdrop for Joe Strick's film adaptation of James Joyce's *Ulysses* in 1968. While Joyce's Leopold Bloom had his snack at Davy Byrne's on Duke Street, Strick moved the scene to The Irish House. When Dublin Corporation went to build their Civic Offices at Wood Quay, Lord Moyne, then vice-chairman of the Guinness Brewery, financed a project to save the exterior of The Irish House, the last surviving pub on Winetavern Street. In July 1968, the stuccowork was brought to the Guinness Hopstore. A plan to display it to the public never materialised. In 2003, the exterior of The Irish House was donated by Guinness' new owners Diageo to the Dublin Civic Trust. The remnants of the façade were last seen in pieces in suburban Dublin in 2006.

Pat Cohan's bar in Cong, County Mayo, is a much-loved tourist attraction for fans of the Hollywood film *The Quiet Man*. Directed by Irish-American John Ford and starring John Wayne as retired boxer Sean Thornton and Maureen O'Hara as Mary Kate Danaher, the film tells the story of Thornton's return to his forefathers' native land to purchase the ancestral homestead, White o' Morn cottage in Inisfree. It is by far the Hollywood film most associated with Ireland by older Americans. Shot in 1951 in Mayo and Galway, the film is famous for Winton Hoch's cinematography, which won an Oscar. Ford also won the award for Best Director. The interior of Pat Cohan's bar was built on a Hollywood sound stage, and the outside shots were of John Murphy's grocery shop in Cong. Republic Studios paid him the then princely sum of £5 a day for the right to use his shop for external shots over the four-and-a-half-week shoot. This allowed Ford to mount a sign for Pat Cohan's bar on Murphy's shopfront. After the film crew departed, the Murphy family continued to sell groceries and in later years added a line of *The Quiet Man* memorabilia. In the film, the bar appears in fifteen scenes and takes up almost a quarter of the running time. John Murphy left the shop to his nephew John Connolly, who decided to renovate it as a pub exactly as it appeared in the film. After some difficulties, the doors finally opened on 17 September 2008. It changed hands in 2013 and, under the current stewardship of Ray Kenny and Sharon McGrath, has established an excellent reputation for its food and atmosphere. The lack of memorabilia on the walls inside the pub may come as a surprise to some visitors.

The bar in *The Quiet Man* is a scene of conviviality, community and ribaldry. It is also a location of violence. The protracted saga culminates in a scene in which Thornton takes on his arch-nemesis Will Danaher – Mary Kate's brother, played by Victor McLaglen – in a drunken fight, starting in the pub, to secure the dowry Thornton feels entitled to on his marriage to Mary Kate. It is violence, above all else, which runs through Hollywood depictions of Irish pubs.

The 1970 film *Ryan's Daughter* holds a special place in the hearts of many Irish people. Filmed on the Dingle

Peninsula in County Kerry, it is perhaps best described as an epic romantic drama. Directed by David Lean and starring Christopher Jones as British soldier Major Randolph Doryan and Sarah Miles as Rosy Ryan, it was not rated too highly on its release, but has been reappraised by some influential reviewers in more recent years. Ryan is married to local schoolteacher Charles Shaughnessy, played by Robert Mitchum. The plot revolves around an affair between Doryan the army officer and Rosy Ryan. A pivotal scene occurs in a bar owned by Rosy's father, Tom. Doryan enters and orders a whiskey. Rosy is serving behind the bar. The only other person is a black-toothed, gurning simpleton called Michael who is rhythmically banging his foot off the side of a bench seat. This, we can see, is his constant occupation because he has almost worn a hole in the place where he bangs his foot. The kicking gradually induces nightmare flashbacks in the soldier as he imagines guns shooting and airplanes crashing in scenes of carnage. Doryan falls to the floor, clutching his head in mental anguish. Rosy pushes Michael out the door and soothes Doryan's agony by holding him. They end up kissing, and so begins the central plot of the film.

On the film's release, there was some criticism of the portrayal of the Irish, but the locals hardly cared. At a time when the average wage was £6 a week, they could earn up to £40 a week with overtime on set construction and the wave of prosperity the film brought to the local economy is still talked about. McLean wanted a set built from scratch, and the village was built just north of Dunquin, on the far western part of the peninsula. Unfortunately, it was not made to last, and the only remaining evidence of its existence is some cobbled pathway. Nearby, the wreck of the building used as the old schoolhouse in the film is still extant. One of the many stories told about the production is the arrival of 'pub grub' in Dingle. Members of the crew were drinking in Kate Ashe's pub when the smell of Irish stew came from the kitchen. They enquired if it was possible to buy some, and the rest is local history. Dingle is now known for its beautiful collection of traditional pubs and fine restaurants. Kruger Kavanagh's pub in Dunquin – the most westerly bar in Europe – displays an extensive collection of stills from the film. It was here that many members of the cast and crew drank while on location. It derived its name from the original owner's admiration of the South African Boer leader Paulus Kruger. Neither was averse to using his fists when the need arose. 'Kruger' Kavanagh emigrated to America when he was nineteen and returned to establish his pub in 1920 at the age of twenty-six. The only acting Oscar the film won was for the portrayal of the village idiot, Michael, by John Mills. Once more, the Irish pub had an intellectually subpar patron.

State of Grace, a 1990 film directed by Phil Joanou, explores the world of the notorious 'Westies' criminal gang, a violent group of racketeers and extortionists of Irish origin in Hell's Kitchen, New York. Starring Sean Penn, Ed Harris and Gary Oldman, it was filmed in the Old Town Bar at East 18th Street and Park Avenue, and in the Mulberry Street Bar at Mulberry Street and Broome Street – both in Manhattan. The Old Town bar dates back to 1892. The Mulberry Street Bar – formerly called Mare Chiaro – is a regular on cinema and television screens. *Donnie Brasco, The Sopranos* and *Law and Order* have all used it as a set.

The film's climactic scene takes place during the New York Saint Patrick's Day parade. It is being watched by two men in an Irish pub, who are shot by Sean Penn's character. Once again the volatile mixture of violence and sentimental conviviality is central to the representation of the Irish American and located in the familiar milieu of the bar.

The 1991 film *Backdraft*, directed by Ron Howard, is set in the macho world of Irish-American Chicago firemen. These 'smokies' are not averse to physical confrontation, nor are they shy of drinking. Fully costumed Irish dancers and nuns twirl around to frenetic Irish music at the annual Firemen's Ball. When a fiddler starts to play a mournful dirge, a row breaks out over a family issue. When the drunken protagonist is dragged away, he immediately calls for a drink, while someone in the background opines 'Families are crazy.' Violence, drinking, Irishness, family and conviviality are interlinked and the locus of the action is a pub. The scene was shot at Emmit's Irish Pub on Milwaukee Avenue in Chicago – a real-life haunt of Chicago firemen.

The Boondock Saints, a 1999 crime drama directed by Troy Duffy, was not a critical success on its release, but has achieved cult status over time. The plot revolves around Irish-American fraternal twins Connor and Murphy MacManus – played by Sean Patrick Flanery and Norman Reedus – trying to rid their native Boston of the Russian mafia. In a notable scene, the brothers are celebrating Saint Patrick's Day in McGinty's, their local Irish pub run by Doc, played by the late Irish-Canadian actor Gerard Parkes. Amid raucous scenes, Doc stutteringly tells the men drinking at the bar that he has to close it down, as the Russians are buying the building and not letting him renew his lease. The men offer to help by contacting people, but he refuses, telling them he does not want anyone else to know: 'Well, you know what they say, people in glasshouses sink ships.' One of the boys tells him he needs a proverb book. The banter is interrupted by the sight of a group of Russian heavies, and the inevitable violent fight breaks out. It is far from the final scene of violence in the film.

The theme of violence in Irish-American culture is a consistent motif in American cinema. *The Departed* (2006), starring Jack Nicholson and Leonardo DiCaprio, was a critical and commercial success. Directed by Martin Scorsese, it is based on the life of the Boston Irish-American gangster 'Whitey' Bulger. In one scene, Billy Costigan, the character played by DiCaprio, orders a cranberry juice in a down-at-heel Irish bar. The patron on the next stool – Mr French, played by Ray Winstone – tells the barman it is a natural diuretic and his girlfriend uses it when she has her period. He turns to DiCaprio and asks him if he has his period. DiCaprio contemplates this for a moment, grabs a glass and smashes it over the man's head. An extremely violent fight ensues, but in time-honoured Irish fashion, they turn out to know people in common and end up as friends.

The representation of pubs in Irish films or films directed by an Irish person is usually more nuanced and goes beyond violence, conviviality, sentimentality and simplicity. Irishman Jim Sheridan directed *My Left Foot* (1989), the story of crippled artist, writer and poet Christy Brown. It was one of the great successes of Irish film. Daniel Day-Lewis won an Oscar for his performance as Christy, while Brenda Fricker, playing Christy's mother, won Best Supporting Actress. The film is set in working-class Dublin of the 1940s and 1950s, where poverty and disease were endemic. Christy's large family has no heating and survives on a miserable diet. The pub in the film is an exclusively male space, in a society in which gender roles are strictly segregated. The man goes out to work to earn a living for the family – if he can get a job – and spends much of his spare time in the pub with other men. The Gravediggers in Glasnevin (also known as Kavanagh's) was used for the drinking scenes. This expenditure on alcohol hurts the family by reducing the household budget. When women are shown communicating with friends and neighbours, it is invariably in the street. Christy's father, played by Ray McAnally, is no different from the other men in the film. He is more comfortable talking in the pub than he is at home with his wife. The final scene of the film takes place in the local pub after the death of Christy's father. His family mourns the death in time-honoured fashion by getting drunk and singing loudly. Some of the other patrons take exception to this and a fight breaks out, instigated by Christy. He kicks a pint out of the hand of one of the drinkers to defend his father's honour.

Mulligan's of Poolbeg Street was used in the 1991 film *Hear My Song*, a biographical treatment of Irish tenor Josef Locke. The late Michael Dwyer, long-time chief film critic of *The Irish Times*, described the way the pub was used in the film: 'When the film moves from Liverpool to Dublin, one of the first shots of the city is outside Mulligan's pub as a priest in soutane walks by. This, we can assume, is an establishing shot in the same way as a red bus tells us we're in London or a shot of the Eiffel tower tells us we are in Paris.'

In the 2007 film *Garage,* directed by Lenny Abrahamson and starring Pat Shortt, Josie, the main character played by Shortt, works in a local garage. It is the centre of his otherwise lonely existence. In the pub, the locals 'take a rise' out of him about the future plans for the garage. They tell him he has no financial stake in the business and his 'five-year plan' is indicative of his delusional personality. Ultimately, they suggest, the garage will be sold for apartments by the owner. They point out the lack of investment in the premises as a sign Josie's future is endangered. The pub may be viewed as a place where cruel 'slagging', a form of bullying and verbal violence, takes place, yet it is the only place Josie can think of going. The film is a devastating study of the cruelty that can occur in an all-male environment like the pub in small-town Ireland where there are few other social outlets. In *Garage*, the pub is a lonely place, dimly lit, with only a handful of patrons. It is also the location for childish bullying of the town fool. In comparison to the graphic violence in many Hollywood depictions of the Irish pub, its portrayal by an Irish director conveys the subtleties of real-life suffering.

Television Advertising

The 1977 'Island' advertisement for Guinness is perhaps the most iconic piece of footage in the entire history of Irish television advertising. More commonly remembered as the *'Tá siad ag teacht'* advertisement – translated from Irish as 'they are coming' – it occupies a singular place in the visual cultural history and public imagination of Ireland. Broadcast at a time when most Irish people only had access to domestic television, it has acquired the patina of a popular myth and invariably makes any list of most-remembered advertisements.

An idealised version of pubs and Ireland is a consistent theme in alcohol advertising in Ireland. The 1966 'Shipyard' advertisement featured a man drinking Guinness on screen for the first time in Irish television advertising. Here, the pub is portrayed as a home from home after the labourer has put in a hard day's work. The romanticised version of the pub is also transferred to Irish pubs overseas. The 2003 advertisement 'The Quarrel' featured the Irish actor and Hollywood heart-throb Michael Fassbender going to New York to seek out his brother to rectify an unspecified argument. He goes automatically to an Irish pub where he finds his brother in the company of a beautiful woman. It is his home from home. The 1980s' 'Sally O'Brien and the way she might look at you' advertisement for Harp lager counterpointed the harsh life of an Irish emigrant in the Middle East to the vibrant atmosphere of an Irish pub. It told of the beautiful women you could meet there. Controversy arose when it was found that Sally was played by a British actress Vicki Michelle (who would later find fame as the waitress Yvette Carte Blanche in the BBC hit comedy 'Allo, 'Allo). Even the then Taoiseach Charles Haughey was exercised by this subterfuge. It turned out Vicki's grandmother was from Cork and all was forgiven. She even went on a successful tour of Irish pubs, and Sally O'Brien lookalike competitions were held up and down the country. Murphy's stout created the memorable 'Samurai' advertisement in the early 1990s. The exotic visitors were no surprise to the people drinking in a quiet bar: the Irish pub is open to everyone. There were many other Irish advertisements set in pubs. In the Beamish advertisements featuring the 'sound man, Brendan' from the early 1960s, the protagonist demonstrated his soundness by changing to Beamish from another product. The Bass 'blind tasting' advertisements from the 1970s introduced the phrase 'ah, that's Bass' to indicate something is the real thing. The customer is able to identify the ale from two others in a pub with no women and is lauded for his ability to do so by his drinking buddies. In all, the image and themes are consistent. The Irish pub is, above all else, a place of conviviality and fun. Everybody has someone to talk to, drinks moderately and enjoys the famous atmosphere.

Soap Operas

Television soap operas generally feature a pub as the centre of the social network. It is a convenient way to bring characters together. In 'Drinking and Drunkenness in *Crossroads* and *Coronation Street*', Rob King suggests drinking is portrayed as 'a predominantly convivial, collective, integrative activity'. It is, he writes, 'rooted in the pub as an arena of sociability and associated with the resolution of social conflict'. According to his research, 14 per cent of screen time on British soap operas showed actors socialising in the pub. This compared to 10 per cent in American soap operas and 6 per cent in Australian ones. The Rover's Return in *Coronation Street,* The Queen Vic in *EastEnders* and The Woolpack in *Emmerdale* are all frequently on Irish television screens. *EastEnders* is arguably the most strife-ridden soap on British television. The Queen Vic has been the scene of three extra-marital impregnations, two criminal raids, two murders and a fire that burned it to the ground. A study by Adrian Furnham and his colleagues at the University of Oxford calculated that 87 per cent of all the British soap operas mentioned alcohol, and 69 per cent of the drinks shown were alcoholic. Pubs are disproportionately used to introduce new characters, and alcohol consumption is overwhelmingly portrayed as sociable, with only occasional references made to problem drinking. The Northern Ireland politician Martin McGuinness – no stranger to controversy – was so incensed by the portrayal of drinking and alcohol in soap operas that he raised the issue in the Northern Ireland parliament in 2008: 'I'm not a fan of *EastEnders* or *Coronation Street*, but my wife and children watch the programmes and I am absolutely appalled at the level of concentration around the pub and the drunkenness that is quite clear for everybody to see – and all that before the nine o'clock watershed, when children are watching . . . I regard that as irresponsible broadcasting.' He received responses from ITV and RTÉ. ITV broadcasts *Coronation Street* to the Irish public. '*Coronation Street* has been set around the Rover's Return for 40 years now, and is a high-quality drama with a massive following in Ireland. Its popularity is across all age groups and there would be uproar if it was taken off the schedule. We receive no complaints about its content and it fully complies with pre-watershed regulation.'

RTÉ gave a lengthy response to McGuinness concerning *Fair City*: 'Almost every soap has a pub in it because it is a very convenient device in a practical sense to get people together indoors. It means you can shoot in any weather and any light because people can meet otherwise than on the street, which is subject to problems with weather and light.

All soaps are regarded as pre-watershed and they are designed to be shown for family viewing. Most producers actually minimise the amount of serious drinking in pubs.' The author took a swipe at politicians: 'My experience of politicians is that they watch very little television. They are almost the worst people for commenting on it. They tend to watch news and current affairs late at night. *Fair City* has a pub, it also has a coffee bar, but we limit the amount of pub scenes and alcohol consumed.'

Ireland has had, and continues to have, its fair share of fictional pubs. *Tolka Row*, Ireland's very first television soap opera, ran from January 1964 to May 1968. The pub set was directly modelled on Mulligan's pub on Poolbeg Street. McCoy's in the Dublin-based soap *Fair City* is the location for much of the drama in fictional Carrigstown. The Molly Malone in the now defunct *Glenroe* was generally a place of gentle ribaldry; the programme was criticised in some quarters for its lack of analysis of serious issues affecting Irish society. Tigh Thadhg in the Irish-language soap *Ros na Rún* is always central to the action. While it seems natural to some nations to see series set in pubs, this is not universally the case. In an interview in 2016, Stephen, a Londoner who has lived in Germany for twenty-five years, spoke of the cultural differences between Britain and Germany. *Lindenstrasse*, a popular soap opera on the Dar Erste television channel, bears an uncanny resemblance to *Coronation Street* and has been running since 1985. Here, the centre of the community is a Greek restaurant. According to Stephen, a soap opera set in a pub in Germany 'would look very strange indeed'.

Literature

There is a long tradition in Irish theatre of plays set in pubs. One of the most brilliant is Tom Murphy's *Conversations on a Homecoming*. Michael returns to Galway from America, where he emigrated in search of work and a better life. Set in a small west of Ireland pub in the 1970s, old friends gather to meet the recent arrival. He talks up his life in the States while denigrating the country he left behind. Tom, Michael's friend since childhood, soon picks holes in his story, and is quick to suggest he has in fact come back for good, despite being unable to admit it publicly. While Michael reminds us that success in America is by no means guaranteed, this Irish town is also the site of fading promise. A photo of JFK above the bar recalls the excitement that surrounded President Kennedy's visit to Ireland in 1963, but there is nothing glamorous about the pub in which it now hangs, with its shabby wallpaper and poor partition. The decline of the local pub is a symptom of the decline of the wider geo-graphical area. The possibility that a pub may have to close is a warning about the future viability of a whole community, an argument used to great effect by the various bodies and voices representing rural publicans down through the years. As Michael notes, the venue has gone downhill, and even J. J., the charismatic man who once rallied local youth in the 1960s, is now sick and nowhere to be seen. Missus, the landlady, has little to say except 'Yaaa', emblematic of the tedium permeating the locality.

Another of Murphy's plays, *A Whistle in the Dark*, ends with a fight in a pub in Coventry among the Carney brothers, Irish emigrants on a hiding to nothing. It was Murphy's first full-length play, and was described by one eminent theatre critic as 'arguably the most uninhibited display of brutality that the London stage has ever witnessed'. Murphy once described Ireland as a 'huge tank . . . and we're at the bottom, splashing around all week in their Friday night vomit, clawing at the sides all around'. That he chose to set the pivotal scene of his first play in a pub is indicative of the centrality of the pub to the Irish emigrant community.

In Conor McPherson's *The Weir*, the action opens in a rural Irish pub with Brendan, the publican, and Jack, a car mechanic and garage owner. They discuss their respective days and are soon joined by Jim. The three then discuss Valerie, a pretty young woman from Dublin who has just rented an old house in the area. Finbar, a businessman, arrives with Valerie, and the play revolves around reminiscences of their shared youth. After a few drinks, the group begins telling stories of the supernatural, related to their own experience and that of other locals. After each man – with the exception of Brendan – has told a story, Valerie tells her own – the reason why she has left Dublin. Her story is sad and shocks the men. The weir of the title is a nearby hydroelectric dam briefly mentioned when Finbar describes the locality to Valerie. The pub, in a state of terminal decline, is a place of malaise and wistfulness, a miniature version of the static wider society.

The second act of Sean O'Casey's masterful *The Plough and the Stars* is set in a pub among the Dublin tenements. Originally written as a one-act play called *The Cooing of Doves*, it is a tour de force laced with the colourful language and acerbic humour of the locals. Their pointless pontificating is counterpointed by a rabble-rousing speech by the

Irish patriot Pádraig Pearse taking place outside. Characters move from inside the pub to listen to the speech for a while, and subsequently return to their conversations. They are more interested in personal dissipation than the proposed freedom of their country. Sean O'Casey was very particular in his stage directions for the pub:

> A commodious public house at the corner of the street in which the meeting is being addressed from Platform No. 1; it is the south corner of the public house that is visible to the audience. The counter, beginning at Back about one-fourth of the width of the space shown, comes across two thirds of the length of the stage, and, taking a circular sweep, passes out of sight to Left. On the counter are beer-pulls, glasses and a carafe. The other three fourths of the Back is occupied by a tall, wide, two-paned window. Beside this window at the Right is a small, box-like, panelled snug. Next to the snug is a double swing door, the entrance to that particular end of the house. Farther on is a shelf on which customers may rest their drinks. Underneath the window is a cushioned seat. Behind the counter at Back can be seen the shelves running the whole length of the counter. On these shelves can be seen the end (or the beginning) of rows of bottles.

O'Casey was criticised for showing a tricolour in a pub during the original run in the Abbey Theatre, but replied that he had seen it in one himself: 'I have seen the Green, White and Gold in strange places. I have seen it painted on a lavatory in the The Gloucester Diamond; it has been flown from some of the worst slums in Dublin; I've seen it thrust from the window of a shebeen in The Digs.'

In *Trial*, O'Casey sets three of the ten scenes in Barney Kiernan's pub on Little Britain Street, frequented by members of the legal profession. This time, the cries and protests from the nearby Four Courts of the supporters of an accused man can be heard from inside the pub. The customers voice their sympathy for Robert Kelly, the condemned man, accused of murdering Constable Talbot but later acquitted. The pub functions as the forum where the public can voice their thoughts on the legal case – effectively a trial by the citizenry.

Barney Kiernan's was also the location for the Cyclops episode in Joyce's *Ulysses*. Leopold Bloom, a Jew, is taunted with racial remarks by the 'Citizen', a character loosely based on Michael Cusack, the founder of the Gaelic Athletic Association. He is presented as an archetypal nationalist extremist. It is the afternoon of the Ascot Gold Cup horse race and the Citizen is loudly announcing racist and anti-Semitic sentiments. Bloom does not respond to the jibes until he is leaving the pub: 'Jesus was a Jew. Your saviour was a Jew.' The Citizen loses his temper: 'By Jesus, I'll brain that bloody Jew man for using the Holy Name. By Jesus, I'll crucify him, so I will. Give me that biscuit box there. Where is he till I murder him.' Passers-by stop to watch the scene, and drinkers spill out from the bar. Bloom leaves in a horse-drawn cab. On this occasion, the pub is portrayed as a place of intolerance and small-mindedness.

W. F. Casey's 1908 play *The Man who Missed the Tide* was the first play staged in the Abbey Theatre to feature a Dublin pub. The pub is presented as a place of rest and solitude. *The Dreamers* (1915) by Lennox Robinson tells the story of Irish patriot Robert Emmet, and The White Bull on Thomas Street in Dublin is featured in both acts. In the first, Emmet learns his message to the leadership of his Wicklow co-conspirators has failed to get through. This means his effort at rebellion will most likely prove a failure, but he voices his commitment to the cause. In the second act, a group of his supporters have backed out of the uprising in favour of going drinking. It is the refuge of cowards and windbags – a theme echoing the works of O'Casey.

John Millington Synge set *The Playboy of the Western World* in a run-down shebeen in rural Mayo. William Butler Yeats told Synge that if he wanted to see the real Ireland, he should go to the west. Synge went to the Aran Islands in search of authentic Gaelic culture. He was particularly impressed by the simplicity of life, and the closeness to nature: 'The absence of the heavy boot of Europe has preserved in these people the agile walk of the wild animal, while the general simplicity of their lives has given them many other points of physical perfection. Their way of life has never been acted on by anything much more artificial than the nests and burrows of the creatures that live round them.' To him, they are aristocratic, having 'the refinement of old societies' blended with 'the qualities of the wild animal'. He did not like the publican, however. In a letter to Stephen McKenna in 1905, he wrote of 'the groggy-patriot-publican-general shop-man who is married to the priest's half-sister and is second cousin once-removed of the dispensary doctor' whom he found 'horrible and awful'.

Synge was occasionally frustrated with the locals' drinking habits. One day, he had arranged to go out on a boat trip, but the fishermen had not fixed a leak in the currach or looked at an oar that was losing a thole pin. When they embarked, they could only travel at 'an absurd pace' because of the damage. The men were drunk and Synge was not impressed: 'The men were unusually voluble, pointing out things to me that I had already seen and stopping now and then to make me notice the oily smell of mackerel that was rising from the waves.' He avoided the pub during his stay, but the ferry was delayed leaving Kilronan Pier one stormy morning and the passengers had to wait in the nearby pub:

> The kitchen was filled with men sitting closely on long forms ranged in lines at each side of the fire. A wild-looking but beautiful girl was kneeling on the hearth talking loudly to the men, and a few natives of Inishmaan were hanging about the door, miserably drunk. At the end of the kitchen the bar was arranged, with a sort of alcove beside it, where some older men were playing cards. Overhead there were the open rafters, filled with turf and tobacco smoke.

This pub was the 'haunt so much dreaded by the women of the other islands, where the men linger with their money till they go out at last with reeling steps and are lost in the sound'. Men sat, evening after evening, drinking 'bad whiskey and porter, and talking with endless repetition of fishing, and kelp, and of the sorrows of purgatory'.

The pub in *The Playboy of the Western World* is a place of paralysis until Christy Mahon comes along to tell the 'fools of Mayo' he has murdered his father. It is emblematic of the decay and poverty in the surrounding area. In his stage directions, Synge decrees the pub should be 'rough and untidy' and the only contents a 'sort of a counter' with 'shelves, holding many bottles and jugs'. There are empty barrels near the counter. At the back, there is a bench and table and another shelf with more jugs. There is an open fire. Pegeen, 'a wild looking but fine girl', is writing at the table. The pub is as wild and elemental as the people.

In Joseph Sheridan Le Fanu's *The Cock and Anchor* (1845), the pub is an equally elemental space. Like the late-nineteenth-century pubs in the Irish-American tenements of lower Manhattan, the pub is a den of iniquity, illegal gambling and blood sports. The protagonist visited a pub called The Old Saint Columkil, which was 'a sort of low sporting tavern frequented chiefly by horse jockies, cock-fighters and dog-fanciers; it had its cock-pits and its badger baits and an unpretending little "hell" of its own; and, in short was deficient of none of the attractions most potent in alluring such company as it was designed to receive'. As well as the 'thick fumes of tobacco' and 'the reek of spirits', the air carried the 'heavy steams of the hot dainties which ministered to the refined palates' of the tavern.

According to Sean O'Casey, if James Joyce had not chosen to live abroad, he too would have been seduced by the pub and there would have been no *Ulysses* or *Finnegans Wake*. In his later days, Joyce always had alcohol by his side from seven o'clock onwards. He was fond of champagne – which he called 'electricity' – and Jameson Irish Whiskey. He claimed Jameson reminded him of Dublin because it was the only Irish whiskey made from the 'unfiltered water of the Liffey, mud and all'. His brother Stanislaus mentioned

Joyce's interest in alcohol in his autobiography: 'In emulation of Falstaff and the poets of the Mermaid Inn, my brother began drinking Saki, which to my astonishment he found in the Bodega in Dame Street, but soon he declined upon Guinness' porter. He was talkative in his cups, and his natural speaking voice, a pleasant tenor, seemed to be keyed up a few tones higher. I hated to see him glossy-eyed and slobbery-mouthed, and I usually told him so heatedly, either on the spot or the morning after.'

In his introduction to *Joyce's Ulysses Notesheets in the British Museum*, Phillip Herring suggested the difficulty of reading Joyce's handwriting may have been a result of insobriety. In his later life, Joyce tried to hide his drinking from his wife, Nora, and often went to nearby cafes to have Pernod before dinner. In his self-coined word, Joyce may have written 'alcoherently'. Some of his most brilliant con-flations are used in his descriptions of drinking and the pub. In *Finnegans Wake*, his renowned verbal dexterity produced some great synonyms for drunkenness: 'mouldystoned', 'alebrilled' – from the Italian *brillo*, meaning tipsy – 'frother-nity' and 'absintheminded'. Typical pub talk is 'softtongues palkytalk', 'moltapuke on voltapuke' and 'chithouse chat'. The pub is both a 'gulpstroom' and a 'saloom'. Joyce was not a very good drinker, according to Richard Ellmann: 'His capacity for alcohol was small, and he was prone to drunken collapses.'

In *Dubliners*, his celebrated collection of interlinked short stories, James Joyce mentioned twelve pubs: Egan's of Abbey Street, Mulligan's of Poolbeg Street, O'Neill's of Suffolk Street, the bar of the Burlington Hotel, The Scotch House on Burgh Quay, Davy Byrne's on Duke Street, Dan

Burke's of Baggot Street, The Bridge Inn in Chapelizod, Kavanagh's of Parnell Street, McCauley's of Dorset Street, Corless' of Andrew Street and a fictional bar called The Black Eagle. When his friend Padraic Colum read through the proofs, he asked Joyce if the whole book was only about pubs. After the stories were submitted to the publisher Maunsel and Company, they demanded alterations and deletions. The manager, George Roberts, was warned by his legal advisers that some of the Dublin publicans might object to the name of their establishment appearing in print. Joyce wrote to his brother Stanislaus about the issue: 'Public houses are mentioned in four stories out of fifteen. In three of these stories the names are fictitious. In the fourth, the names are real because the persons walked from place to place. Nothing happens in the public houses. People drink.' Joyce offered to rent a car and go with Roberts to the publicans to gauge their concern, but Roberts was not interested. Joyce argued that the publicans would be glad of the advertisement, and added that by removing their names, 'the selling value of the book in Dublin would go down'. Eventually, *Dubliners* was published by Grant Richards of London.

Dublin, Joyce said, was 'the centre of paralysis' and there is a sense in his writing that the pub is Dublin in microcosm. It is a place of blather and drivel, a hiding place from the real world. Joyce makes particular use of the snug as a place of refuge. In his short story 'Counterpoints', the protagonist, Thomas Farrington, disappointed with his job as a clerk, goes to the 'dark snug of O'Neill's' in the middle of the day to escape the boredom. He drinks five glasses of porter every afternoon before 'skulking home' to his wife

and son. In the title story, 'Dubliners', Mr Casey is in the
Chapelizod Bridge Pub. In this place of paralysis, the
atmosphere is muted:

> The proprietor served him obsequiously but did not
> venture to talk. There were five of six working-men
> in the shop discussing the value of a gentleman's
> estate in County Kildare. They drank at intervals
> from their huge pint tumblers and smoked, spitting
> often on the floor and sometimes dragging the
> sawdust over their spits with their heavy boots. Mr
> Duffy sat on his stool and gazed at them, without
> seeing or hearing them. After a while they went out
> and he called for another punch. He sat a long time
> over it. The shop was very quiet. The proprietor
> sprawled on the counter reading the *Herald* and
> yawning. Now and again a tram was heard swishing
> along the lonely road outside.

In Joyce's novel *A Portrait of the Artist as a Young Man*,
Stephen Dedalus is critical of 'publicans and pawnbrokers
who live on the miseries of the people'. On the way to the
graveyard to bury his sister, the funeral party stops at a pub
and everybody is invited in. It is the first time Stephen has a
pint in front of his father, a rite of passage for the Irish male.
As a youngster, Stephen becomes aware of the role of the pub
in the lives of his elders: 'Trudging along the road or standing
in some grimy wayside public house his elders spoke constantly of the subjects nearest their hearts, of Irish politics, of
Munster and of the legends of their own family, to all of
which Stephen lent an avid ear.' In the same paragraph, Joyce

wrote one of his most famous lines, describing the nascent future Stephen perceives after listening to the pub talk: 'The hour when he too would take part in the life of that world seemed drawing near and in secret he began to make ready for the great part which he felt awaited him the nature of which he only dimly apprehended.'

Over the course of *Ulysses*, the reader gets a glimpse of the pub in the morning, from a funeral procession, at lunchtime, at dinnertime, between meals, in a maternity hospital, at closing time and even after hours, in the form of Bella Cohen's bordello. The bordello was an all-night drinking den, common at the time and the bane of both the licensed publican and the police. One episode finds Bloom 'blind to the world up in a shebeen in Bride Street after closing time, fornicating with two shawls and a bully on guard, drinking porter out of teacups.'

Finnegans Wake – Joyce's final work – is dense, allusive and, many would say, impenetrable. One straightforward reference is to the Mullingar House Inn in the Dublin suburb of Chapelizod, run by the impressive-sounding Humphrey Chimpden Earwicker. These days, there is a James Joyce burger on the menu and a plaque commemorating the writer outside the door.

W. B. Yeats is purported to have visited only one pub and not to have liked it. However, he was not averse to using the pub to promote his poetry. On April 2 1937, BBC Radio broadcast a segment by Yeats called 'In the Poet's Pub'. He started by mentioning the 'intolerable monotony' when five or six poems are read after one another and proposed a solution – perform them as if in a pub. He had seen 'folk singers who sing without accompaniment . . . with tricks to break the monotony and rest the mind'. This, he suggested, might work well on the radio: 'Why not fill up the space between poem and poem with musical notes and so enable the mind to free itself from one group of ideas, while preparing for another group, and yet keep it receptive and dreaming.' He told his listeners 'there are such pubs in Dublin and I suppose elsewhere', and asked them to imagine themselves in such an environment, 'among poets, musicians, farmers, and labourers'. Despite his avowed dislike of the pub, he was happy to suggest it as a suitable environment to listen to his poetry. He provided an example from popular verse so listeners could understand his thoughts more clearly:

> The fact that we are in a pub reminds somebody of Belloc's poem, beginning 'Do you know an inn, Miranda', and then somebody recites the first and more vigorous part of Chesteron's 'Rolling English Drunkard', and then, because everybody in the inn except me is very English and we are all a little drunk, somebody recites De La Mare's 'Three Jolly Farmers' as patter. Patter is singing or speaking very quickly with very marked time, an art known to all old actors in my youth. We are all delighted, and at every pause we want to pound the table with our tankards. As, however, a tankard must be both heard and seen, the BBC has substituted the rolling of a drum.

He championed the place where men of different classes and creeds come together as a place to enjoy poetry. In a subsequent broadcast, 'In the Poet's Parlour', he distanced himself from his previous position: 'When we were in the Poet's Pub I asked you to listen to poems written for everybody, but now you will listen, or so I hope, to poems written for poets, and that is why we are in the Poet's Parlour.' Those present were his intimate friends and fellow students. Here there were 'two or three beautiful ladies, four or five poets, a couple of musicians', and all were 'devoted to poetry'. These poems were too good for the common man in the pub, and were suited to a more refined ear. Here there were beautiful women, absent from the male space of the pub.

The Lost Man Booker Prize, given to acknowledge overlooked books from 1970 that were not eligible for the Man Booker Prize due to a rules alteration that year, was awarded in 2010 to James Gordon Farrell's *Troubles*. Farrell, a Liverpool writer of Irish descent, sadly drowned off the coast of west Cork in 1979 at the age of forty-four, when he was swept from a ledge while angling. *Troubles* tells the story of an English Major, Brendan Archer, who in 1919 goes to County Wexford to meet the woman he believes he may be engaged to marry. From the crumbling Majestic Hotel in the fictional town of Kilnalough, he watches Ireland's fight for independence from Britain. It is an excellent evocation of the complex socio-political landscape of the fragmenting country. The occupants of the hotel, a group of old women and the owner, Edward Spenser, are the last vestiges of the Anglo-Protestant class in the area. As the novel progresses, social and economic relationships break down, mirrored by the gradual decay of the hotel. In an early part of the book, Farrell uses the pub as a place to highlight the religious and cultural divides between the occupants of the Big House and the local Catholics. It is centred on the Soloheadbeg ambush

HAVE YE NO HOMES TO GO TO?

in which two policemen were murdered, regarded as the first act of the Irish War of Independence. Spenser, apoplectic when he hears of the attack, decides to go to the local pub to fly the Union Jack. A number of the old women agree to accompany him. Ripon, Spenser's son, recounts the incident to the Major:

> By the time we arrived, of course, everyone, including me, was practically fainting with terror . . . Byrne's pub isn't such a bad place, though nobody, mind you, would think of going there unless for the purpose of harassing the natives, nobody from the Majestic anyway. A bit ramshackle perhaps, with its thatched roof and stone walls . . . Dark, low ceiling, shabby, sawdust on the floor, chairs and tables all wooden, a bit of stench coming from the old *ghuslkhana*, a long mirror over the bar badly in need of silvering . . . a calendar or something with one of those frightfully gruesome Sacred Hearts on it.

They had expected fighting: 'In fact everything was quite peaceful. Surprising number of people there, sitting around or leaning on the bar, men for the most part . . . A couple of haggard and blowsy women at one table, some men playing cards at another, an old crone by the fire with a big glass of porter beside her.' Spenser started singing 'God Save the Queen', expecting a hostile response but, to his surprise, the natives joined in. After a round of applause he and his associates left, defeated. Here, the pub is the haunt of the poorer working-class Irish, an alien environment for the Anglo-Irish Protestant Ascendancy.

The pub has been variously represented in Irish literature. Writers have shaped the space to their own imagination and to fulfil myriad narrative devices. Overwhelmingly, however, it has been used as a shared public space that is a reflection of the native culture.

Smuggling Craic:

Exporting the Irish Pub

'Outdoors might be Lagos or Lima but, in the heads
of the clientele, this is Connemara in 1953 and each
of them is Brendan Behan.' – *Jon Kelly, BBC News
Magazine, 22 May 2014*

Economist and journalist David McWilliams invented the
Irish Pub Index in 2004. The idea came to him when he
was listening to Irish builders in a Moscow bar speaking of
their plans to open pubs. McWilliams thought the prosperity
of countries in Eastern Europe, and beyond, could be
measured by the number of Irish pubs opening. When he
returned to Ireland, he contacted Guinness, crunched the
numbers and saw an immediate correlation. The greatest
number of Irish pubs per capita was in Luxembourg – the
wealthiest country in the European Union. Kiev had the

lowest number of Irish pubs per head in January 2014 – a time of political crisis and economic uncertainty. McWilliams is adamant that his model is predictive and can indicate marketplaces that will implode or boom.

In the 2008 Irish film *Dick Dickman PI,* a private detective is tasked with investigating the recent disappearance of a number of Irish traditional musicians. At the very end of the film, police stop a Russian gang at the port of Rosslare, County Wexford, as they are about to board a ship. They open a packing crate, inside of which a group of traditional Irish musicians are playing. The triumphant detective delivered the punchline: 'They're smuggling craic.' Just as crack can be exported, so can 'craic', by building Irish pubs overseas. The word 'crack' has been used in the north of England and lowland Scotland to mean 'story', 'conversation' or 'news' for centuries. It originally came from the Middle English 'crak' – meaning loud or bragging talk – and came to Ireland through the settlement of Ulster Scots. It was borrowed into the Irish language and became Gaelicised to 'craic', and is now universally seen as an Irish expression of fun and enjoyment in good company.

The early 1990s saw an explosion in the construction of Irish pubs worldwide. Guinness – now owned by Diageo – initiated the Irish Pub Concept in 1992. Witnessing the spread of Irish pubs on the European mainland, they codified their own vision of the perfect Irish pub. They observed how, whenever an Irish pub opened, sales of Guinness spiked in the surrounding geographical area. Other bars started to stock Guinness to compete with the new arrival. The Irish soccer team played in the World Cup in Italy in 1990. Their huge numbers of supporters could not always get tickets for the matches, and instead went looking for pubs where they could watch the action. There was not much pub culture in Italy, and the few bars were hopelessly overcrowded by both the Irish and the locals. The situation gave encouragement to some entrepreneurs to get in on the act and so the Irish pub revolution began in Italy. There are now over 200 Irish pubs in the country. According to the Irish Pub Concept website, an Irish pub is 'always well designed, always buzzing, always cheerful, always welcoming and always serving great Guinness along with great home-cooked food'. There is a similarity we will recognise between many of these pubs: 'decorative millwork, warm lighting, ornate back bars . . . all effortlessly deliver the same sense of premium comfort, ambience and timeless conviviality'. This is something other types of restaurants and bars cannot capture, 'a concept which was hip and contemporary to its consumers in 1910 and remains equally relevant in our modern era of social engagement and connectivity'.

The golden rule is authenticity. 'Authentic Irish decor' is essential because 'bad replicas or poorly executed design are a precursor of poor financial performance'. Food, too, must be 'authentic'; the customer wants to taste 'authentic Irish food, not local variants of Irish recipes'. The Irish Pub Concept also offers strong advice on alcohol: 'Offering premium import Irish beers and spirits, and particularly offering fresh, perfectly poured Guinness, is critical. Consumers find the mystique of Guinness attractive and aspirational and they also appreciate the ceremony around the pouring of the beer.'

After outlining the necessity of playing authentic traditional and contemporary Irish music on a good sound system, with live bands 'to drive a younger late-night demographic', the guidelines move on to employees. Irish employees in key positions will further promote authenticity, but employees do not have to be Irish because 'with good training, management can lead them to understand and appreciate Irish traditions and behaviours'. As long as the employees understand the 'warmth, informality and conviviality of Irish pubs', there should be no problems.

At the start of the Irish Pub Concept programme, Guinness put advisory teams in place to assist investors and operators, and recommended vendor companies with the knowledge and technical ability to bring these ideas to fruition. After widespread success in Europe, the programme was rolled out in the United States and Canada, where the name changed slightly to the Guinness Irish Pub Concept (GIPC). They claim 2,000 enterprises were opened in Europe and approximately 800 in North America between 1992 and 2000 as a result of the programme. An 'Irish Pub Operator from New Jersey' who opened a premises using the programme's system bears testament to the formula on the website: 'People will travel for an Irish pub. We have people who drive from more than an hour away to visit our pub. First, there is the Irish history and culture that is intriguing and fun, and the music, the ambience, Irish fare, pub grub and imported spirits highlighted by Guinness create an eating and drinking establishment of entertainment and comfort. An Irish pub done right gives people a place to escape their normal daily routine and stresses.'

It is important, according to GIPC, to distinguish between 'Irish pubs that genuinely transport Irish culture, hospitality and tradition' and pubs 'with Irish names or Irish memorabilia hanging on the walls that deliver nothing other than a generic, sterile bar experience'. The Irish Pub Concept claims to take the pub experience to a whole new level of excellence 'by combining stunningly accurate interior design with great food, drink, music . . . Guests are immersed in another world of warmth, conversation, laughter and fun . . . what the Irish call "the craic".' The Irish Pub Concept purports to be a 'bullet-proof' vehicle for financial success. The level of authenticity achieved apparently makes consumers feel they are in a premium environment and therefore can indulge themselves. From this feeling comes the 'natural prompt to switch from domestic beers to import beers, from rye and bourbon to premium and single-malt whiskies'. Annually, this can translate into tens of thousands of dollars of 'incremental revenue and profit', and in a 'maelstrom of casual-dining competition and in a world of homogenous roadhouse food, the Irish Pub Concept emerges as probably one of the hottest trends in the industry . . . it also delivers one of the strongest bottom-lines in the industry and a minimal need for capital reinvestment'. It 'defies standard industry assumptions', we are assured, 'thriving successfully in towns of 25,000 people, and performing equally well in urban and suburban locations . . . the authenticity of the Irish Pub stands up to scrutiny – the deeper you dig, the more attractive it becomes'.

The Irish Pub Company (IPC) was established by Mel McNally in 1991 and has designed in excess of 2,000 Irish pubs and built over 700 outlets in fifty-three countries. It offers a choice of five models: the 'country', a cottage-like room with stone floors and wooden beams; the 'shop', intended to resemble a spirit grocer (a pub that doubles as a hardware shop or grocery); the 'brewery', with cobbled floors and upturned tables; and the 'Victorian', an ornate interior fashioned after Dublin's grander hostelries. They later introduced the 'Celtic', with 'Gaelic-style' swirls and patterns carved into wood. More recently, they have expanded into gastropubs, 'venues for sophisticates and those aspiring to "have arrived"'. The IPC has designed bars from the Fadó in Annapolis to The Temple Hill in Russia. The concept has been so successful that the company brought it all back home. It has designed over forty pubs in Ireland, including the Inn at Dromoland Castle and The Leopardstown Inn in Dublin. The pinnacle of their work is to be seen at the Nine Fine Irishmen pub in the MGM Grand Hotel, Las Vegas. Named for the leaders of an unsuccessful nationalist uprising in 1848, it is a replica Dublin pub sent from Ireland. It claims to be the biggest Irish pub in the world, and is described in *Frommer's Guide* as 'one of the most upbeat, high-energy and friendly bars you'll find anywhere, with pretty servers with exposed bellies and wearing short kilts'.

The IPC does not control the entire market. Quigley's Irish pub in Naperville, a prosperous western suburb of Chicago, sought the help of the company Love Irish Pubs, and recounts its success on its website: '"Craic" is a Gaelic term that describes the feeling you should get in an Irish Pub – fun, good conversation, good music and food, and great people. To insure that Quigley's Irish Pub would have great craic, we had the pub designed, built, and shipped over from Ireland . . . The antique fireplace and bookcases in the smoking room have been brought over from Dublin along with original Irish prints, which accent the walls.'

Gemmell, Griffin & Dunbar Ltd (GGD) claims to be the longest-established creator of Guinness-Approved Irish Bars. Its first creation was Murphy's Bleachers in Chicago. GGD promises to build a pub 'with all the charm of a green and distinct Ireland'. They recommend a large front window and a nineteen-hour day. The 'Trinity' is their flagship model; others include 'Country Cottage', 'Victorian Irish' and 'Country Shop' models. In recent times, GGD have added the 'Snug' model, which can be installed as an Irish corner in any pub.

The building of Irish pubs is a profitable worldwide industry. The tropes and signifiers have become globalised, commodified and commercialised. Rare Irish Stuff is a Dublin-based company specialising in the sale of 'unique Irish memorabilia and pub decor'. It sells phone boxes, pictures and furniture. A James Joyce Irish Pub Award retails for €295. These awards were presented to pubs in Ireland on Bloomsday 2000, and state: 'This pub has been awarded the James Joyce Award for being an authentic Dublin pub. This establishment remains an outstanding example of the tradition which Joyce immortalised in his works and is an authentic Irish pub which retains a genuineness of atmosphere, friendliness and presence of good company.' Bloomsday Publications originally presented the award to pubs including The Brazen Head and O'Neill's in Dublin, Johnnie Fox's in Glencullen, County Dublin, and Celtic Crossings in Chicago. If a pub is willing to pay the price, it will have an award 'which immediately adds a prestigious reputation to any establishment'.

At the Irish Pubs Global Conference in Dublin in 2015, there was no shortage of advice on naming pubs. A name that is easy to shorten is particularly recommended. P. J. O'Hanlon's will become P. J.'s in time, creating a sense of familiarity and camaraderie. The IPC recommends the addition of '& Sons' to a family name to create a sense of longevity and continuity. The message is consistent; use Irish surnames or words, but make sure they are easily pronounceable in the locality.

The Irish Network Japan lists sixty Irish pubs in the greater Tokyo area. While it seems plausible that you will get a fair version of an Irish pub in The Dubliners, The Galway or Brennan's, The Red Tug, Cafe Lamp and the Blue Dolphin sound less authentic. The Gnome, Man in the Moon, Public Arrows and M Bar K all claim to be Irish pubs. Saint John's Wood Irish pub is in Sapporo, capital of the northern island of Hokkaido. It does not serve Guinness but haggis is on the menu and mint julep is the speciality drink.

In February 2015, *The Irish Times* asked its readers, as part of its Generation Emigration project, to nominate a favourite Irish pub abroad. There were over 1,500 submissions from forty-one countries. The tagline for the competition was simple: 'The best Irish pubs abroad are not simply boozers. They're also unofficial community centres for our emigrant population, social outlets for Irish people far from home, and the focus of sporting and cultural activities for the diaspora.' Readers were asked to consider 'the ambassadorial role of the pub; its authenticity, social responsibility, modernity or tradition'. When *The Irish Times* had assessed the 'craic' and other factors, a shortlist of ten pubs was drawn up: The Auld Shillelagh, London; Bubbles O'Leary, Kampala, Uganda; The Drunken Poet, Melbourne,

Australia; Finn McCool's, New Orleans; Healy Mac's, Kuala Lumpur, Malaysia; The Irish, New York; Irish Pub Koblenz, Koblenz, Germany; The Irish Times, Vancouver Island, Canada; The James Joyce, Prague, Czech Republic; and the Wild Rover in Cusco, Peru. Healy Mac's, one of a chain of seven owned by Liam Healy, an emigrant from Belmullet, County Mayo, was the overall winner, with particular commendation given to its food, promotion of Irish sports abroad and 'its welcome for people of all nations'. *The Irish Times* published a photograph of the winning pub; a green Volkswagen Beetle, decorated with white shamrocks and dancing leprechauns holding pints of beer, is parked under the huge neon lights of the front entrance in Changat, Kuala Lumpur. The Malaysian chain of seven pubs is hugely successful, and even opened a new outlet in Breaffy House Hotel outside Castlebar in County Mayo in April 2015.

The Bubbles O'Leary pub won the award for 'best backstory'. It was moved from Drogheda, County Louth, in its entirety by owner Nigel Sutton. When Mulligan's Linen Mill pub closed, he bought the interior fittings and front door, shipped them to Kampala and named his newly reconstructed establishment after a friend's former teacher. This relocation of an Irish pub was not a first. As far back as 1973, the bar from Jury's Hotel on Dame Street – then located where the Central Bank is now – was exported to Zurich by a group of Dublin businessmen. The award for the most authentic Irish pub overseas went to The Auld Shillelagh in London, located on Church Street in Stoke Newington since 1991.

Irish pubs, or pubs that claim to be Irish, are everywhere. There are two in Ushuaia, Argentina, the southernmost city in the world, where the climate is subpolar and temperatures can dip as low as minus 28 degrees Celsius. There is yak on the menu in the Irish pub in Namche Bazaar in Nepal, which claims to be the highest pub in the world, at an altitude of 3,440 metres (11,286 ft). So, too, does The Dubliner in La Paz, Bolivia. When Lonely Planet compiled its list of the best Irish pubs in the world, it included the Grand Khaan in Ulaanbaatar, Mongolia; Ryan's Irish Bar in Accra, Ghana; Delaney's in Hong Kong; Flannery's Irish Geo Pub in Santiago, Chile; The Celtic Cross and Dubliner in Reykjavik, Iceland; Shenannigans in Darwin, Australia; The Dublin Irish Pub in Seoul, South Korea and the James Joyce in Athens, Greece.

Bon Appétit magazine compiled a list of the most far-flung Irish pubs in the world, providing the distance from St James's Gate, the home of Guinness in Dublin. Gili Trawangan, a small island off the coast of Lombok in the Indonesian archipelago, is home to the beachside Tír na nÓg – which translates from Irish as 'the land of the young' – and is all of 12,890 km (8,010 miles) away. Dunedin on the South Island of New Zealand is the furthest you can travel from Dublin to visit an Irish bar. Not alone is the Bog Irish Bar 19,168 km (11,911 miles) from Dublin, it also serves Guinness on tap.

The budget airfare website Cheapflights.com compiled a list of the oldest Irish pubs outside Ireland. The Tipperary in Fleet Street, London, established in 1700, was the first pub outside Ireland to sell bottled and draught Guinness. McSorley's Old Alehouse in the East Village area of Manhattan was established in 1854 (although there is some conflicting evidence about this – see p. 207). Patrick's of Pratt Street, Baltimore, dates back to 1863, while The

Mercantile in the Rocks area of Sydney, Australia, was built in 1914. The Fiddler's Elbow was opened in Rome in 1976, while the well-known Kitty O'Shea's in Paris dates from 1986.

There is widespread vilification of theme pubs. David Quantock describes them as the 'sick product of a brewer's idea of West world' in *Grumpy Old Men: A Manual for the British Malcontent*, while Jonathan Glancey, in an article in the *Independent*, calls them 'hideous constructions, banal beyond all belief'. In *The Gift of the Gab! The Irish Conversation Guide* Tadhg Hayes terms them 'kitsch bastardised versions of the real thing'. Nicholas Lezard, writing in *The Observer*, goes even further: 'Theme pubs are rubbish. Let me explain in brutally simple terms. I do not go into theme pubs because I am not a moron. Does that sound snobbish? I do not give a damn if it does.' The Rumjacks, a self-styled Celtic Punk band from Sydney, released 'An Irish Pub Song' on their 2010 album *Gangs of New Holland*, parodying the Irish pub industry in Australia:

> A hurling stick and a shinty ball,
> The bric, the brac, the craic and all,
> Let's call it an Irish pub,
> Caffreys, Harp, Kilkenny on tap,
> The Guinness pie & that cabbage crap,
> The ideal wannabee Paddy trap,
> We'll call it an Irish pub.

The history of bar culture in Australia draws from the same wellspring as Ireland. It was shaped by British and Irish settlers, and predicated on conviviality and male bonding. In

1887, Harold Finch Hatton, a British peer who spent twelve years working as a gold miner in Queensland, wrote:

> All through Australia, in every class, it is not considered good form for a man to drink by himself. Very few even of the most hopeless drunkards ever do so. The consequence is that when a man feels inclined to drink, he immediately looks out for someone to drink with . . . At whatever hour of the day a man meets another whom he has not seen for say twelve hours, etiquette requires that he shall incontinently invite him to come and drink. This is a custom that pervades every class in the colony.

In mining areas, the pub was often the first building constructed and became the centre of the entire settlement. The history of gender separation in the pub is even more pronounced in Australia than in Ireland. It persisted into the 1970s and only began to break down after women's rights activists began to publicly challenge the convention. In January 1973, a group of feminist activists staged a protest against the rule in the public bar of the Hotel Manly in Sydney. When they entered and ordered drinks, they were refused service by the publican, who claimed the hotel had no suitable toilets. The women chained themselves to a railing around the bar. The event gained significant media attention and caused the hotel industry considerable embarrassment. Within a few years, this long-standing sexist convention had disappeared in most urban areas, and was eventually outlawed by state and federal anti-discrimination law. On the other hand, there is a long history of women working in Australian pubs and it is said the term 'barmaid' originated there. However, as in Ireland, temperance campaigners were quick to label these women as immoral and given to prostitution. These were 'loose women' who enticed the weak male to come in and squander money.

There has been criticism of the drinking culture and associated behaviour of young Irish people in Australia in recent years. The Working Holiday Visa allows single Irish people between the ages of eighteen and thirty to spend a year in Australia. In theory, the participant must work for no longer than six months. It has proven outstandingly popular. In May 2014, an Irishman was found guilty of causing $500,000 worth of damage to a hotel in Melbourne and fined $10,000. 'Drunk Paddy in 500k Worth of Damages' ran a headline in the Australian newspaper *The Age*. Two years previously, the same newspaper ran an article about boxer Katie Taylor's Olympic win over Britain's Natasha Jones, with the headline 'Punch Drunk: Ireland Intoxicated as Taylor Swings Towards Boxing Gold'. Noel White, the Irish Ambassador to Australia, rushed to the defence of the Irish in Australia: 'It should come as no surprise that the media coverage of court proceedings . . . has provoked strong reaction within the Irish community and, in the process, drawn attention to the impact of language used in relation to ethnic groups and nationalities. The reaction has been . . . dismay at the casually offensive language.' He was aware, he wrote, of the persistent stereotype of the 'fighting, drinking, dissolute Irish', which is less evident these days but not entirely eradicated; 'when it does occur, its impact is not diminished by familiarity.' An anonymous letter sent to a number of Australian newspapers disagreed with the ambassador: 'Please travel to Darwin and speak with your fellow Irish backpackers who fuel alcohol-related violence, drunkenness and are generally a rude, unpleasant and grubby cohort. Weekend incidents in the Mitchell Street area are dominated by Irish and your reputation as congenial, happy-go-lucky and friendly people is fast becoming one of arrogant, drunken criminals.' A Sydney taxi driver concurred: 'Frankly, Ambassador White, that headline that you're so offended and aggrieved by has actually treated you and your people quite charitably. In my long and harrowing experience, the Irish of the eastern suburbs of Sydney were easily the most obnoxious, unruly, loutish and wretched passengers a driver would ever encounter.'

In January 2011, Australia's Channel 9 broadcast secretly filmed footage, which the presenter of the programme, *A Current Affair*, told the audience would disgust them, saying it featured uncouth 'guests in our country' who were making life a misery for local residents outside a 'notoriously rough' pub in Sydney's Bondi Junction. The report did not say Irish immigrants were the cause of the violence, but an interviewee said 'many of them are Irish', while another man said he doubted the would get away with such behaviour 'in County Kerry or wherever the hell they're from'. The report featured Irish traditional music in the background, and several shots of Irish flags flying over the Cock 'n' Bull, the Irish pub outside of which much of the violence took place. In one scene, the narrator said 'One small glance can set off a mass brawl,' while two inebriated men were shown on screen, rolling on the ground, with a few others looking on. When a reporter interviewed the local police chief, he admitted noise is an issue, but said the area was not 'viewed as a trouble black spot'. There had been nine assaults reported in a twelve-month period, he said, and seven of these were related to patrons being refused entry for being intoxicated. The interviewer countered that they had seen more than nine assaults in one week on their hidden camera, but failed to show any. Anthony Sharwood, an Australian journalist, caused outrage after he wrote 'Irish pubs are for people who love dodging vomit and flying fists.' He described typical Irish pubs as 'old-school dives which are as dark and dingy as the Guinness beer they serve'. He also referred to antisocial behaviour in Irish pubs, and claimed they are some of the most dangerous bars in Sydney. In his article, he describes two very distinct 'types' of Irish pub: 'Either you've got a miserable, stinking booze den as cold and dank and filthy as a sewer, or you've got an upmarket place full of plastic people and faux-memorabilia. Either way, you lose.' He referred to the 'problems' Irish pubs face from the 'raucously drunk backpackers who travel halfway round the world to behave even worse than they do in Cork and Dublin'. It is estimated that 22,000 young Irish people live in the greater Bondi area. Irish drinking is public and visible; the pub culture moves with the people, and the visibility continues.

The Irish pub has spread to virtually every corner of the world. It is a global commodity and has been copied, reinterpreted and reinvented. It runs the gamut from the gargantuan Nine Fine Irishmen pub in Las Vegas to the tiny Fanny Irish Pub in Madrid. Nothing has stopped the smuggling of craic.

Last Orders:

The Pub in Ireland Today

In his anthropological study of the west of Ireland, *Inishkillane*, Hugh Brody wrote of the bar as both the home of the farmer and the object of desire of the tourist: 'The society of the bar is a society of people who have chosen, for better or worse, a future on the land. In summer this society is vitalised by tourists but the vitalisation derives from the need for reassurance this group so profoundly feels precisely because they have a farming life. In coming to the countryside the tourist can be seen to affirm his liking for the entire fabric of Irish country life.'

Bord Fáilte and others with an agenda to sell Ireland as a tourist destination have long made use of the Irish pub. In her unpublished thesis, 'Representations of Ireland: Bord Fáilte', Catherine O'Leary notes that 'the pub seems to be the institution around which social life in Ireland revolves.

The impression is given that almost all pubs have resident folk singers and that most evenings there are traditional sessions, planned or impromptu.' The Eurovision Song Contest attracts a global audience and is an opportunity for the host country to showcase the best of what it has to offer to the tourist. Ireland hosted the competition in 1995, when it was broadcast from the then Point Depot in Dublin. It is a tradition to show members of the competing countries enjoying themselves in different parts of the host country. RTÉ showed the participants orienteering, climbing, kissing the Blarney Stone and retreating to the nearest iconic pub afterwards to chat with the locals. Featured were Hedigan's in Sligo, Langton's in Kilkenny, Tigh Neachtain and The Quays in Galway, and Matt Molloy's in Westport, County Mayo. It was, as Catherine O'Leary writes, an image of the Irish pub that implies 'no matter where they are, they always have time to stop and chat . . . before long the visitor will be chatting away like an old friend to the locals'.

According to Lonely Planet, the single most desired experience of tourists coming to Ireland is to listen to Irish music in a traditional pub. Drinking a pint of Guinness in a pub is the third most sought-after experience in the same survey. According to 'The Contribution of the Drinks Industry to Irish Tourism' by Tony Foley of Dublin City University, 80 per cent of international visitors to Ireland said their desire to experience an Irish pub brought them here, while 83 per cent revealed listening to Irish music in a pub was their number one wish. Fionn Davenport wrote in Lonely Planet's *Dublin* guide that 'the pub is a meeting place for friends and strangers alike, a place to mark a moment and pass the time, a forum for discourse and a temple for silent contemplation.

It is where Dubliners are at their friendliest best – and at their drunken and belligerent worst.'

In 1807, Isaac Weld stayed the night at a pub in the coastal village of Crookhaven in County Cork, where he was served 'salt-fish potatoes and whiskey, the common fare of the country'. He was happy with his meal. However, travellers to Ireland have not always been so pleased with the culinary offerings in pubs. Eric Newby, the British travel writer, spent time cycling around Ireland in 1986 with his wife. In *Round Ireland in Low Gear*, he recalls stopping in Sixmilebridge in County Clare, and notes there were seven pubs in the village, only one of which served any type of food. They thought this extraordinary, but as they proceeded through Ireland they were disabused of their notions. In Rosscarbery in County Cork, they counted six pubs around a square only 90 metres (100 yards) long. They chose Nolan's Lounge, the only one serving food on Sunday afternoon. They were served 'powdered mushroom soup and damp ham sandwiches'. It was, he wrote, 'no *route des gastronomes*'.

Many pubs in Ireland now depend heavily on food sales. According to a University of York report by Drs Cabreras and Mount in 2014, 65 per cent of pubs in rural areas serve drink only. Thirty-two pubs in Ireland – twenty-five of them in the Republic – are recommended in the 2016 *Michelin Eating Out in Pubs* guide. For many pubs, the reality has been either to start serving food or to close the doors. In an interview, Colm Cronin of Cronin's Sheebeen pub in Westport, County Mayo – one of those recommended – said over 50 per cent of his business is now food. While he wishes his pub were more of a drinking venue, the reality is that the older people in the area who patronise the pub are gradually dying out and are not being replaced by younger customers.

The decline in the number of pubs in Ireland, particularly in rural areas, has never been far away from the glare of the media. In 1991, there were 10,500 pub licence holders and 300 off-licences, employing an estimated 33,000 full-time and 15,000 part-time staff. In 2002, 9,896 licences were issued; by 2009, the figure stood at 9,082. In 2002, there were 808 off-licences; this had increased to 1,770 by 2009. Wine licences increased from 2,023 to 3,705 during the same period. Pub licences dropped by 959 between 2007 and 2012. One third of all pubs in Leitrim and Longford have closed. There are around 7,500 pubs in Ireland today. The furore over the decline in the number of pubs must be viewed through the prism of historic oversupply. Compare these numbers to other countries: the combined population of New York and California is close to 56 million. In 2011, there were 6,556 pubs – or bars and saloons – between the two. The population of Ireland is just over 4.5 million.

In 2010, Attitudes and Behaviour – Ireland's largest independently owned research company – published 'Quantum Change in Irish Drinks Culture'. The study analysed drinking patterns in Ireland between 2002 and 2010. In 2002, two out of every three Irish adults went to the pub to drink alcohol at least once a month. This had halved by 2010. The decline was even more marked among people who went to the pub more often. During the same period, the number of people who drank at home rose significantly. The share of alcohol sales achieved by licensed premises fell from 64 per cent to 46 per cent over the eight-year period.

A central finding of the report was the huge increase in the level of pre-drinking (or 'prinking') – drinking at home before going out later. These trends have continued unabated.

As part of the 2005 Intoxicating Liquor Act, the Government proposed to introduce a new type of licence. It was to be called a café-bar licence and would require the owner to serve food and alcoholic and non-alcoholic drinks all day long. It was envisaged as a bar along continental lines, where the emphasis would not be primarily on alcohol. The then Minister for Justice, Michael McDowell, justified his position: 'I want to repeat what I have said many times on the subject; we need a cultural shift in this country in our approach to alcohol consumption, a shift towards moderate social consumption patterns and away from the binge drinking that so often results in alcohol-related damage.' The proposed licence would cost less than the traditional pub licence and would be confined to premises smaller than 130 metres (427 ft) squared. The customer would not be allowed to drink standing up, and no alcohol could be brought outside the premises. The bill failed. Over seventy parliamentarians were involved in the collation of a 252-page submission outlining the opposition of publicans and the Vintners Federation of Ireland to the proposed legislation. Gordon Holmes, the chairperson of the Liquor Licensing Commission, believed self-interest and the influence of publicans brought down the proposal: 'I would hope that sectoral interest would not overrule public interest. In this case, I think it has.' Opposition was particularly strong from politicians representing rural constituencies, none more so than Mary Coughlan, who represented far-flung County Donegal in the north-west of the country, where there was a pub for every 270 people. The introduction of this new licence would introduce unfair competition and devalue the cost of a traditional pub licence, she argued. Her party – Fianna Fáil – claimed to be impartial, but the presence of six publicans on their benches added little strength to that argument. The Junior Minister in charge of alcohol policy at the time was Sean Furlong, a publican. Another trenchant critic of the proposal, John McGuinness, owned a building in which his brother ran a pub. Eddie Bohan, a Fianna Fáil Senator at the time, had previously been President of the Vintners Federation of Ireland and Chairperson of the Licensed Vintners Association. However, it was not just the politicians and publicans who objected to the proposals. Many health specialists and anti-alcohol groups argued it would be detrimental to set up even more outlets where alcohol could be purchased. They might look and feel European, but this would be no guarantee that Irish people would drink in a moderate fashion, they argued. Others pointed out there were already too many drinking establishments to police and the addition of more would overstretch scarce resources. Ultimately, a compromise was reached. Restaurants in Ireland had previously only been allowed to serve wine, but now they would be allowed to serve all types of alcohol. The Vintners Federation was appeased. Minister McDowell believed he had been 'ganged up on'.

On 17 June 2005, Philip Donnelly from St Albans in Hertfordshire, England, wrote to The Irish Times referring to the phenomenon of superpubs: 'The slobbering greed of publicans has seen the rise of the booze-barn, a multi-storey money factory serving alcohol-flavoured swill to the clueless, against a backdrop of foreign football and pornographic music videos . . . anybody over the age of 25 who would willingly endure more than five minutes in one of these obnoxious gin mills needs to have their head examined, as conversation consists of sporadic yelling and most of their pint ends up jostled onto their shoes.' According to the *Oxford English Dictionary*, a superpub is a 'very large public house' usually 'situated in a town centre and frequently containing a dance floor or stage'. Catherine Pepinster of the *Independent* writes that they are defined by large windows, through which you can see the patrons. Paul Moody and Robin Turner in *The Search for the Perfect Pub* claim the first British superpubs – what they call 'enormodromes' – were located in the city of St Albans in Hertfordshire, which is also where the Campaign for Real Ale (CAMRA) was started.

When superpubs came to Dublin, they were a radical departure and were designed differently. Pub design offers interesting cross-cultural comparisons. In general, permissive societies, those in which alcohol is traditionally an accepted, unremarkable and morally neutral element of life, will have visible drinking places, with large windows and open spaces. There is nothing to hide from because the consumption of alcohol does not engender moral opprobrium. Even when the climate does not allow permanent outdoor tables in such cultures, a glassed-in pavement section is common. Such drinking places often extend physically into the environment, overlapping and merging with the everyday world. In societies like Ireland and Scandinavia, with an ambiguous and uneasy relationship with alcohol and where drinking is a moral issue for some people, drinking places are more likely to be enclosed with solid walls and doors, frosted windows and substantial screens or partitions, ensuring the activities of customers are concealed and contained. The older the pub in Ireland, the more nooks and crannies it seems to have. There are often clear front windows but with stained-glass panels erected directly behind them, to a height of half the window, obscuring the inside but allowing some light through. There are also many pubs with tiny windows, through which little natural light penetrates. These physical features may in part reflect the equivocal status of drinking places in societies. The prevailing climate must also be considered.

The era of superpubs in Ireland was ushered in by the arrival in Dublin in the late 1990s of Zanzibar and Pravda, both of which are now closed. Zanzibar, developed by the O'Dwyer brothers, cost more than £3 million and had a North African theme, while the Russian-themed Pravda was created by the Thomas Reid Group. Zanzibar opened in June 1997 and accommodated up to 1,200 people. Pravda was another sprawling hostelry, decorated with colourful communist-style murals. At the time the two superpubs opened, Frank Fell, chief executive of the Licensed Vintners Association, welcomed them: 'It would be a phenomenon happening in most of the larger cities throughout Europe and they mark a considerable departure from the traditional idea of an Irish pub.' Declan Martin, economic director of the Dublin Chamber of Commerce, said the designing of premises to accommodate more people was inevitable, 'given the increase in business generally and the rise in population and number of visitors . . . it makes pretty basic business sense to think big'. Such places, he said, brought variety to the pub scene, and their design-conscious interiors made a change from 'the Formica tables and the leatherette seats of the past'. Dublin was booming during the late 1990s: 'Anyone who is not doing well in the pub business is doing something seriously wrong . . . you want to keep up with the trends and give them the best and the newest.' Some industry sources at the time argued that traditional pubs would always be able to function and that themed pubs had a narrowly defined life cycle. They were right in both cases.

Some of the many reasons cited for the decline of the pub in Ireland, particularly rural ones, include: the smoking ban introduced in 2004, the cost of alcohol in discount retail outlets, the economy, the increasing popularity of eating out, drink-driving legislation, tighter controls on licensing laws, the increasing cost of rates and supplies, swingeing taxation on alcohol sold in pubs, greater use of social media and technology, a regression of social capital and sense of a wider community in society, an increasing range of home entertainment, and the penchant of younger people for 'prinking'. Rural politicians and publicans bemoan the loneliness of the isolated bachelor who can no longer go to town and have a few pints because he is afraid of the fascist drink-driving laws. Michael Healy-Rae represents south Kerry in the Dáil. In 2013, he started a campaign to allow people living in rural areas to have a few pints and drive home. The idea originally came from his brother Danny Healy-Rae, who proposed a motion to Kerry County Council that was passed by five votes to three. There were seven abstentions and twelve absentees. Healy-Rae and three other councillors who supported the motion were publicans. He described the rural dwellers as 'living in isolated rural areas where there's no public transport of any kind, and they end up at home looking at the four walls, night in and night out, because they don't want to take the risk of losing their [driving] licence'. He lamented the impact of this unfortunate situation: 'All the wisdom and all the wit and all the culture that they had, the music and the singing, that's all being lost to the younger generation because these older people might as well be living in Japan and Jerusalem because the younger generation don't see them at all anymore.'

The proposal garnered international media attention. Healy-Rae was interviewed by a German television crew, who sympathised with his pleas because the same thing was happening in parts of rural Germany. The Spiegel channel broadcast the documentary *Drink and Drive* in 2013 to an audience of two million. One scene showed a pensioner called 'Francie' drinking and singing in a pub. 'Francie', the narrator says, 'with his thick grey sideburns and green hat, looks exactly as you would imagine a real Irishman to look. He has always driven to the pub . . . how else could he get home?' But gone are the days when you can drive home after a few pints, we are reminded, even in rural areas with no buses and taxis. 'A man must be allowed to drink a few pints. He has a right to it. And, by God, after two or three or four pints you should still be allowed on the road,' says Francie as he takes a long drink. Later, as he gets into his car, we can hear him say, under his breath, that he will set his collie dog on the police if they stop him on his way home. In the next scene, Dan O'Connell is drinking at home. He is too afraid to go for a few pints. His house is dirty; one shot shows a filthy fridge with nothing in it except for cans and bottles of lager. Another scene shows a minibus, with the driver incongruously holding a pint of beer in his hand. The bus is to take people to and from the pub, obviating the need to drink and drive. To achieve some balance, the final section shows local politician John Brassil addressing a council meeting and describing the proposal as 'ludicrous'.

On Spiegel's website, Danny Healy-Rae is described as the man 'fighting for more merriness', and as 'a member of parliament who annoyed urban Irish politicians like a polter-geist from the country for decades'. This may be a reference to Healy-Rae's father, the late Jackie Healy-Rae. Michael Healy-Rae brought the proposal to the national parliament, where he asked the Minister for Transport to introduce legislation to allow Gardaí to issue permits to 'persons living in rural isolated areas to allow them to drive home from their nearest pub, after having two or three drinks, on little-used roads, driving at very low speeds'. This would, he said, 'greatly benefit people living alone looking at four walls and restore some bit of social activity in local pubs and may also help prevent depression and suicide'. His request was politely dismissed by Minister Leo Varadkar – a qualified medical doctor – who said he understood the issue but 'for the State to encourage the consumption of alcohol as a remedy for complex health issues would be irresponsible in the extreme. Indeed, alcohol is a factor in a large number of suicides. Issues relating to the health of rural communities require a multifaceted approach by Government.'

The tensions between the Government and publicans surrounding alcohol legislation are revisited each year as Good Friday approaches. To many, the law against the sale of alcohol on that day is anachronistic and a reminder of a failed theocratic state. Others see it as a lost business opportunity. Bishop Alphonsus Cullinan of Waterford and Lismore told Siobhán Maguire of *The Sunday Times* of the significance of the ban for those who observe Good Friday as a holy day:

> Some will object and say that this day is only for Catholics and other Christians and only for practising ones at that. Therefore they claim the ban discriminates against those of other religions or none. If that is the case then to be consistent we would have to get rid of the public celebration of all Christian feast days which affect the public calendar: Christmas, Easter and St Patrick's Day. They have no significance otherwise, even though they have been commandeered by commercialism to a great extent. Protestors against the ban on the sale of alcohol in pubs and shops on Good Friday cannot have it both ways. They cannot object to the ban adversely affecting their trade because they greatly benefit from other religious feasts in terms of increased trade.

Padraig Cribben of the Vintners Federation of Ireland estimates the loss to the exchequer in taxes to be €6 million, while Adrian Cummins of the Restaurant Association of Ireland claims reversing the ban would be worth €25 million to the industry: 'Aside from the laws showing a nineteenth-century image of Ireland to incoming tourists, many restaurants decide to close their doors on Good Friday.'

In 2010, a court case threw an international spotlight on Good Friday drinking. The Celtic League Rugby Union scheduled a match between Munster and Leinster at Thomond Park in Limerick on Good Friday. The Vintners Federation was up in arms. It estimated €10 million would go a-begging. After a court case widely dubbed 'The Good Friday Disagreement', the publicans were successful and for the first time since 1927 people were allowed to consume alcohol on licensed premises in Ireland on Good Friday. Surprisingly, this temporary legislation did not result in a relaxation of the law and thus far was a once-off derogation. The case highlighted divergent viewpoints. Brother Shawn O'Connor, head of the Franciscan Friary in Moyross, Limerick, a group lauded for its work in a severely disadvantaged community, took a dim view of the legal decision:

> I heard someone quoted this week who said that rugby is more important than religion – that's just ridiculous and it's a shame. If you identify yourself as a Catholic then you should be nowhere near Thomond Park or a pub on that day . . . this is like something out of the Old Testament. If you're going against God and making a public stand about it then you are serving Mammon over God. I don't care how much money you pull in, it will backfire on you on a spiritual level.

Politicians of various hues exercised their verbal dexterity. Senator Joe O'Toole wanted the law changed: 'Everyone's a winner. Free will prevails; the Church-State separation is maintained. We render to Munster the things that are Munster's and to God the things that are God's. We save jobs. The economy gains.' Ivana Bacik, Independent Senator for the National University of Ireland, agreed: 'Let those of us who don't believe that Good Friday is a particularly special day choose to do what we want to do in pubs and clubs.' Senator Donie Cassidy, Fianna Fáil stalwart, regretted the lack of respect for 'the crucifixion of the Good Lord'. On 25 March 2010, Judge Tom O'Donnell – while recognising the potential for 'controversy in several quarters' – granted Limerick publicans an exemption from the State ban on opening on Good Friday. Because the stadium was allowed to serve alcohol, it would have been absurd, he contended, not to let pubs in the vicinity trade. Publicans in Limerick were granted legal permission to trade between 6.30 p.m. and 11.30 p.m.

Ray Oldenburg outlined the many benefits of the pub as a 'third place': continuity, enhanced sense of place, accrual of social capital and the reinforcement of a collective identity. Third places are public locations outside of home and work that are host to regular, voluntary, informal and happily anticipated gatherings of individuals. This is the idealised place where, as in the American sitcom *Cheers*, 'everybody knows your name'. Oldenburg suggested that third places work like 'sorting places': 'People find that they very much like certain persons and dislike others. They find people with similar interests and they find people whose interests aren't similar but are interesting nonetheless. Third places often serve to bring together for the first time people who will create other forms of association later on.' Oldenburg issues a note of caution when considering the functions of the third place: 'The fundamental motivation for this type of belonging is neither personal advantage nor civic duty. The basic motivation, that which draws people back time and again, is fun.' At a further point, he notes 'when the good citizens of a community find places to spend pleasurable hours with each other for no specific or obvious purpose, there is purpose to such association'. Oldenburg wrote of 'the solidarity of kin or friendship groups . . . the acceptance of the individual as a man among men, as an equal in his own right . . . drinking together is a manifestation of the equality and solidarity of town and country folk, of the guest and host, the politician and his constituents, the seller and the buyer.' For Oldenburg, a third place should offer informality, inclusiveness, novelty, diversity and a neutral space where young and old can interact, a forum for political and intellectual discourse and, if possible, a degree of social care for its patrons.

The pub in Ireland has been successful in fulfilling these criteria in the past, but it has seen a decline. A website called The Disappearing Irish Pub relates the story of The Rushes Inn in County Laois, which has literally become a dump. Situated on the N78 road, now bypassed by the M9 motorway, the pub has been abandoned:

> The old car park is covered in rubbish. Black refuse bags and household waste are strewn across the entire area . . . weeds are waist-high . . . The porch of the pub has already collapsed, and the burnt-out shell is about to cave in. Gone are the lovely shrubs and flowers, the carefully kept frontage and well-painted façade. Plaster is coming off the walls and the windows are sadly now all gone. The TV aerials on the roof are gone, but the 'Nature Channel' seems to be getting great reception; the chimneys

that used to draw smoke from the generous open fires within are now a nursery for trees and other plants. The interior is a burnt and charred shell; rubbish, fallen rafters and masonry have turned a once warm and welcoming hostelry into a death trap.

According to the website, this is 'not only a shame but also a tragedy, as there has been a tavern or inn on this route for many centuries'. It lists the reasons: 'a combination of drink-driving laws, lower traffic (due to motorway), the recession, emigration and changing drinking habits (more people deciding to drink at home) have all contributed to its demise. The sad fact is that this is happening all around the country . . . as much a symbol of our changing society as it is a consequence of recession.'

Some people have started to take action in their local area against the disappearance of the pub. In 2008, Patsy Brogan and his Bog Hotel near Frosses in the Bluestack Mountains in Donegal were constantly in the news. He was invariably photographed with his 28-year-old Polish assistant Daria Weiske. The bar, built in a shed adjoining Brogan's cottage, achieved notoriety when a young man was driven in a collapsed state to the emergency room in Letterkenny General Hospital after a night spent drinking there. Brogan was not charged because it could not be proven that he was charging for alcohol. 'My house is a *céilí* house and people are welcome to come and have a bit of craic and a wee drink if they want; sure there's no harm in that,' he said.

In April 2015, *Sligo Today* was invited to Lackagh, near Drumfin, County Sligo, by Eugene Mulligan and Eugene

Quigley, to visit their shebeen. The journalists found four customers sitting at a makeshift counter. There was a white box for voluntary donations. One of the men commented that 'the prices in the pubs are too expensive, so this is far better. You can sit with friends, have a little fun. There are no expensive taxi fares as we all live close by.' Every Friday, the guests chip in to a fund used to buy stock from a legitimate source. The amount each person contributes is whatever they feel is fair for the drinks they consume throughout the week. The entire operation, they say, is non-profit.

Community-owned pubs have become increasingly common in England. They are run on a cooperative basis; one share, one vote. The Pub is the Hub organisation supports communities through the process of setting up a pub. Established in 2001, it guides a group through the legalities, and liaises with drink-supply companies and other stakeholders. In its brochure, the organisation emphasises the challenges involved. Slightly over 50 per cent of the ventures do not reach fruition or do not survive. A 'Community Right to Bid' clause was included in the 2012 Localism Act in Great Britain. Communities can 'stop the clock' on the sale of valuable local assets and amenities like the post office, village shop or pub, giving the community time to bid on them in the interests of the locals. Voluntary and community councils have a right to nominate what they consider 'Assets of Community Value'. This can freeze the sale for six months. The community must express a wish to purchase the business within six weeks of it going on sale. If this is agreed, they can then invoke the 'stop the clock' rule. The White Horse at Upton in the Norfolk Broads is one of the many case studies presented on the Pub is the Hub website. It is the sole pub in the village and was due to close in 2012, with the retirement of the landlord. The villagers established a Community Interest Company and issued £120,000 worth of shares. The pub has been completely refurbished and the community has added a restaurant, a family-friendly garden and a marquee for special events. They also included a multifunction suite where information technology classes for older people are held and free Internet access is available. A prescription collection service, a walking group, an arts-and-crafts session and a meals-on-wheels service for the elderly and disabled all operate from the pub. With only 700 residents in the community, they also managed to open a shop in a barn adjacent to the pub. The business opened in April 2015 and is thriving. The benefits are obvious: employment for locals, an improved quality of life for the community and an enhanced sense of community spirit. On 23 March 2015, the first Community Pubs Day was held in Great Britain and a range of measures to make it easier to open a pub were announced. Speaking at The Ivy House pub in Southwark, Communities Minister Stephen Williams said, 'Our pub protections mean that communities can use community rights to keep the amber nectar flowing. We're now also extending funding to the community shares unit so that local groups have a round on us and access advice and guidance they need to buy their treasured asset and prevent developers calling time on their much-loved local.'

The Support Your Local campaign was launched in Dublin in early 2015. Its policy document states:

The hospitality industry operates at the heart of every community across Ireland and is the focal point of towns and villages across the country. It is a vital part of our tourism infrastructure and supports local producers and local jobs right across Ireland. In recent years this task has not been an easy one, with over 1,500 pubs closed since 2007 . . . However, there is an important role that can be fulfilled by the local pub, in particular in combating isolation in rural areas. The local pub can offer communities a place to convene and share experiences. It has the capacity to become a cornerstone for rural life, offering those living in isolated areas a central meeting point, a welcoming local amenity.

In late 2015, Delaney's Pub on Aungier Street in Dublin closed for renovations and reopened as Bow Lane cocktail bar. The excellent *Come Here To Me* (*CHTM*) blog lamented the demise of the old bar. It was, they argued, one of the last of a certain type of bar in the inner city serving the local community: 'An anachronistic institution for this part of town, it was a pub that did not attempt to compete for the business of tourists or anyone else. By no means was it an unwelcoming bar, but it was certainly a local bar for local people with a sizeable number of patrons coming from the nearby York Street flats. It was a pub that offered cheap pints, a Lotto Draw for the local football club on Mondays, karaoke on Tuesdays and bingo on Wednesdays.' The advertising blurb for the new establishment described it as 'an authentic, late-night cocktail bar that appeals to a cross-section of Dublin society from the gritty underclass of sophisticates to creatives and the party set. Bow Lane has areas that satisfy a want for exclusivity and other areas that create a space for typical Dublin social intercourse.' The locals did not sound like the target market. *CMTM* was not mourning the loss of a spectacular premises: 'This was not an extraordinary pub that could boast the best pint of Guinness in the city or a remarkable Victorian interior, but it was a genuine neighbourhood bar in a part of town that has very few left. Its closing down and redevelopment (almost) overnight into an expensive cocktail bar should not go unnoticed.' It was the sad loss of a small third place for the locals of Dublin's inner city.

Cocktail bars are not new. In 1932, *The Irish Times* denounced the cocktail, warning readers: 'It is supposed by the many to induce an appetite and to stimulate intelligent conversation; in fact, it absorbs the pancreatic juices and encourages cheap wit.' At the annual meeting of the Irish Association for the Prevention of Intemperance in 1936, it was noted that 'appalling revelations have been made in the press lately about cocktail and sherry parties even among business girls in their own apartments'. At the meeting, held in Bewley's on Grafton Street in Dublin, calls were made for 'the discontinuance of cocktails and the elimination of drinking clubs', as well as 'the elimination of drinking at public dances'. Later in 1937, *The Irish Times* reported the belief of a doctor from Clare Mental Hospital that 'now that women have taken with avidity to tobacco and cocktails, one can visualise the most appalling results for the human race at a not far distant date'. At the 1938 centenary celebrations in honour of Father Mathew in Dublin's Mansion House, the Bishop of Kilmore warned against the dangers of cocktails:

I am told of a danger, not from the good old glass of whiskey, but rather from a new thing I have heard of called the cocktail, and I am told it is not workmen you will see going after cocktails, but people who have some claim to education and better positions in life than the workmen, and that these people are falling more or less into the cocktail fashion. I have not seen it with my own eyes, but I have heard stories, which, if they are true, make me very sorry. If what I have been told is true, we should get busy about it, and open the eyes of fathers and mothers to it.

Madigan's of North Earl Street sold cocktails in the early 1960s. Five shillings purchased a Singapore Sling, an Alexander or Frank's Special. Gin Slings, Moscow Mules and High Balls were available for a shilling less. The garish orange menu did not provide the customer with a break-down of the ingredients, but the front cover was interesting. It featured a pencil drawing of Nelson's Pillar – a statue of Lord Horatio Nelson on O'Connell Street, later blown up by Irish Republicans in 1966 – with a cartoon bubble emanating from his mouth containing the words 'for a topping cocktail'. The bar has outlived the statue – Madigan's is still open for business. Contemporary Dublin offers a plethora of cocktail bars: The Blind Pig, The Vintage Club, The Liquor Rooms, Pygmalion and Lost Society are among the better known and marketed. The Vintage Cocktail Club in Crown Alley is reckoned by many cognoscenti to be the top of the pile. Behind an unassuming black door, it can only be entered after ringing a bell and will, fans say, transport you to an era of prohibition. Cocktail drinking is a popular urban pursuit, especially so among females. Only time will tell if these establishments continue to proliferate, pushing more traditional pubs aside.

In recent years, craft beer pubs have mushroomed in urban Ireland – particularly in Dublin. Galway Bay Brewery alone owns six pubs in Dublin, as well as two in its home city. Tasting trays now allow patrons to sample a selection of beers. The Beer Market in Dublin has numbered taps. The board above the bar tells you what is in each tap, what price it is, what type of glass it comes in, and the percentage of alcohol in the beer. The pub has employed this system because the beers are on swift rotation and can change throughout the night. When one keg finishes, a different beer is tapped. L. Mulligan Grocer, the much-praised gastropub in Stoneybatter, Dublin, has even garnered praise in *The New York Times* for its selection of craft beers and whiskeys. The author, David Farley, particularly recommended Brú Dubh, 'a dry Irish stout with hints of caramel'. Two years earlier, Rosie Schaap visited L. Mulligan for the same publication and wished she could take some of the available beers home to the United States. She found Belfast Blonde 'faintly sweet, a little lemony and diabolically easy to drink'. She noted Galway Hooker was 'just hoppy enough, not astringently so' and pointed out that it was 'named after a boat, not a prostitute'. The craft beer phenomenon is a long way removed from the 'pint of plain' advocated by Flann O'Brien in his poem 'The Workman's Friend', in which he famously suggests Guinness as a cure for any ailment:

When things go wrong and will not come right,
Though you do the best you can,
When life looks black as the hour of night -
A pint of plain is your only man.

When money's tight and hard to get
And your horse has also ran,
When all you have is a heap of debt -
A pint of plain is your only man.

When health is bad and your heart feels strange,
And your face is pale and wan,
When doctors say you need a change,
A pint of plain is your only man.

When food is scarce and your larder bare
And no rashers grease your pan,
When hunger grows as your meals are rare -
A pint of plain is your only man.

In time of trouble and lousey strife,
You have still got a darlint plan
You still can turn to a brighter life –
A pint of plain is your only man.

Innovation in the pub industry seems constant. In 2014, Noreen O'Sullivan, owner of Rocky O'Sullivan's bar in Nenagh, County Tipperary, was elected the first female president of the VFI. In her acceptance speech, she referred to the crucial role of women in Irish pubs, but warned, 'symbolism alone will not address the issues we face as an industry'. She highlighted the role of the pub in the Irish economy. In Tipperary, at the time of her speech, there were 4,385 jobs in pubs, generating a payroll of over €100 million. She finished with a challenge to the members: 'The Irish pub has a future worth fighting for. The pub of tomorrow will be very different to the pub of today. Publicans must focus on changed offerings with an increased emphasis on events. Constant evolution and innovation will ensure survival.'

Bibliography

Anbinder, Tyler, *Five Points: The Nineteenth Century New York Neighbourhood that Invented Tap Dance, Stole Elections and Became the World's Most Notorious Slum* (New York, The Free Press, 2002)

Archdeacon, Thomas, *Becoming American* (New York, The Free Press, 1983)

Ardagh, John, *Ireland and the Irish* (London, Hamish Hamilton, 1994)

Arensberg, Conrad, *The Irish Countryman: An Anthropological Study* (New York, Natural History Press, 1937)

Arensberg, Conrad and Sol Kimball, *Family and Community in Ireland* (Camden, Harvard University Press, 1940)

Armorey, Thomas, *The Life of John Bunkle* (London, S. Prowett, 1825)

Baillie, Brian, 'Ireland Sober Is Ireland Free: The Confluence of Nationalism and Alcohol in the Traumatic, Repetitive and Ritualistic Response to the Famine in James Joyce's *Ulysses*' (Unpublished thesis, 2005)

Bales, R. F, 'Cultural Differences in Rates of Alcoholism', *Quarterly Journal of Alcohol Studies* (1946)

Bales, R. F., 'Attitudes Towards Drinking in the Irish Culture' in Pittman and Snyders (eds), *Society, Culture and Drinking Patterns* (New York, John Wiley, 1962)

Barich, Bill, *A Pint Of Plain: Tradition, Change and the Fate of the Irish Pub* (London, Bloomsbury, 2009)

Barr, Andrew, *Drink: A Social History* (London, Pimlico, 1998)

Barratt, James, R., *The Irish Way: Becoming American in the Multiethnic City* (New York, Penguin, 2013)

Binchy, D. A. (ed.), 'Críth Gablach', *Mediaeval and Modern Irish Series 11* (Dublin, Dublin Institute for Advanced Studies, 1941)

Blake, Liam and David Pritchard, *The Irish Pub* (Bray, Real Ireland Design, 1997)

Blamires, Harry, *New Bloomsday Book: A Guide Through Ulysses* (New York, Routledge, 1999)

Blessing, Patrick, J., *The Irish in America* (The Catholic University of America Press, Washington, 1992)

Blocker, Jack S. et al., *Alcohol and Temperance in Modern Society: An International Encyclopaedia* (ABC Clio, California, 2003)

Bloom, Harold (ed.), 'Introduction', *Sean O'Casey* (New York, Chelsea House Publishers, 1987)

Bohan, C., 'Calls for Ireland to Follow as Scotland Pushes Ahead with Minimum Alcohol Price' (*TheJournal.ie*, 2014)

Boland, Rosita, *Sea Legs: Hitch Hiking the Coast of Ireland Alone* (Dublin, New Island, 1992)

Boyd, Ernest, *A Literary History of Ireland* (Dublin, Allen Figgis, 1968)

Broderick, John, *London Irish* (London, Barrie and Jenkins Ltd, 1994)

Brody, Hugh, *Inishkillane: Change and Decline in the West of Ireland* (London, Allan Lane, 1973)

Brown, Peter, *Man Walks into a Bar: A Sociable History of Beer* (London, Pan Books, 2004)

Brown, S. and A. Patterson, 'Knick-Knack Paddy-Whack, Give a Pub a Theme' in *Journal of Marketing Management* (2013)

Brown, Stephen, 'Marketing for Muggles: Harry Potter and the Retro Revolution', *Journal of Marketing Management* (2001)

Brown, Terence, *Ireland: A Social and Cultural History, 1922–2002* (London, Harper and Perennial, 2004)

Brown, Thomas, N., *Irish American Nationalism* (New York, J. P. Lippincott Co., 1996)

Browner, Frances, *Coming Home* (Dublin, Original Writing Company, 2008)

Burnett, J., *Liquid Pleasure: A Social History of Drinks in Modern Britain* (London, Routledge, 1999)

Butler, Shane, *Alcohol, Drugs, and Health Promotion in Modern Ireland* (Dublin, Institute of Public Administration, 2002)

Byrne, Anne, Ricca Edmondson and Tony Varley, *Arensberg and Kimball and Anthropological Research in Ireland: Introduction to the Third Edition*, Conrad Arensberg and Solo Kimball, *Family and Community in Ireland* (Galway: CLASP, 2001)

Byrne, Niall J., *The Great Parchment Book of Waterford* (The Irish Manuscript Commission, 2008)

Byrne, S., *Costs to Society of Problem Alcohol Use in Ireland* (Dublin, Health Service Executive, 2010)

Cabras, Ignazio and Michael Mount, *The Role of Pubs in Creating Economic Development and Social Wellbeing in Rural Ireland* (York, University of York Press, 2014)

Cameron, Charles, *How the Poor Lived in Dublin: Reminiscences of Sir Charles Cameron* (Dublin, CB, 1913)

Carleton, William, *Traits and Stories of the Irish Peasantry* (Dublin, Curry, 1830)

Caruth, Cathy, *Trauma: Explorations in Memory* (Baltimore, Johns Hopkins University Press, 1994)

Caruth, Cathy, *Unclaimed Experience: Trauma, Narrative and History* (Baltimore, Johns Hopkins University Press, 1996)

Casey, William F., *The Man who Missed the Tide: A Play in Three Acts* (Dublin, Corrigan and Wilson, 1909)

Cassidy, Constance, *Cassidy on the Licensing Laws* (Dublin, Clarius Press, 2010)

Cassidy, Tanya, *Alcohol in Ireland: The Irish Solution* (PhD Dissertation, Department of Sociology, University of Chicago, 1997)

Cassidy, Tanya, 'Irish Drinking Worlds: A Sociocultural Reinterpretation Of Ambivalence', *International Journal of Sociology and Social Policy* (1996)

Cassidy, Tanya, 'Just Two Will Do' in M. Peillon and E. Slater (eds), *Encounters with Modern Ireland; A Sociological Chronicle, 1995–1996* (Dublin, Institute of Public Administration, 1998)

Cassidy, Tanya, 'Sober for the Sake of the Children: A Discussion of Alcohol Use Among Irish Women' in M. Leonard and A. Byrne (eds) *Women in Ireland: A Sociological Profile* (Belfast, Beyond the Pale, 1997)

Cavan, Sheri, *Liquor License: An Ethnography of Bar Behavior* (Chicago, Aldine, 1966)

Charast, Michelle A., *Emerald Pub to Silver Saloon: Building an Irish Saloon Culture in the American Mining West* (Brown University Providence Rhode Island, Browne Digital Repository, 2012)

Christiansen, B. and J. Teahan, 'Cross Cultural Comparisons of Irish and American Adolescent Drinking Practices and Beliefs', *Journal of Studies of Alcohol,* 48, 6 (1987)

Clarke, P., *The English Alehouse: A Social History, 1200–1850* (London, Longman, 1983)

Clinard, M., 'The Public Drinking House and Society' in Pittman, C. and C. Synder (eds) *Society, Culture and Drinking Patterns* (London, John Wiley, 1962)

Clinch, P., Convery, F. and B. Walsh., *After the Celtic Tiger: Challenges Ahead* (Dublin, O'Brien Press, 2002)

Clissmann, Anne, *Flann O' Brien: A Critical Introduction to His Writings* (Dublin, Gill & Macmillan, 1975)

Coffey, Michael and Terry Golway, *The Irish in America* (New York, Hyperion, 1997)

Collins, Glenn, 'The Few, The Proud: The Pubs that Still Resist the Pull of the Television Screen', *The New York Times* (7 March, 2009)

Connell, K. H., *Irish Peasant Society* (Oxford, Clarendon Press, 1968)

Connery, Donald S., *The Irish* (New York, Simon and Schuster, 1968)

Connolly, Linda, *The Irish Women's Movement: From Revolution to Devolution* (Dublin, The Lilliput Press, 2002)

Coogan, T. P., *Ireland: A Personal View* (London, Phaeton, 1975)

Coogan, T. P., *Ireland since the Rising* (New York, Praegar, 1966)

Coogan, T. P., *Wherever the Green is Worn: The Story of the Irish Diaspora* (London, Arrow Books, 2002)

Corcoran, Mary and Perry Share, *Belongings: Shaping Identity in Modern Ireland* (Dublin, Institute of Public Administration, 2008)

Corkery, Daniel, *Synge and Anglo Irish Literature* (Cork, Mercier Press, 1966)

Corkery, Donald, *The Irish* (London, Eyre and Spottiswoode, 1968)

Corkery, Tom, *Tom Corkery's Dublin* (Dublin, Anvil Books, 1980)

Costello, Peter, *Dublin's Literary pubs* (Dublin, A&A Farmer, 1998)

Costello, Peter, *James Joyce: The Years of Growth, 1882–1915* (Ann Arbor, University of Michigan Press, 1992)

Cowley, Ultan, *The Men Who Built Britain: A History of the Irish Navvy* (Dublin, Wolfhound Press, 2001)

Cronin, Anthony, *Dead as Doornails* (Dublin, Lilliput Press, 1999)

Cronin, Anthony, *No Laughing Matter: The Life and Times of Flann O'Brien* (London, Grafton Press, 1989)

Cullen, Louis, *An Economic History of Ireland* (London, B. T. Batsford, 1972)

Curtin, C. & C. Ryan, 'Clubs, Pubs and Private Houses in a Clare Town' in C. Curtin and T. Wilson (eds) *Ireland from Below* (Galway, Galway University Press, 1989)

Daly, E. D., 'The Struggle Between the State and the Drunkard', *Statistical and Social Inquiry Society of Ireland* (1897)

Danaher, Kevin, *The Year in Ireland* (Dublin and Cork, Mercier Press, 1972)

Davis, Ben, *The Traditional English pub: A Way of Drinking* (London, The Architectural Press, 1981)

Davis, Graham, *The Irish in Britain 1815–1914* (Dublin, Gill & Macmillan, 1991)

Davies, Jim, *The Book of Guinness Advertising* (London, Guinness Publishing Ltd, 1998)

De Bovet, Marie Anne, *Three Months in Ireland* (London, Chapman and Hall, 1891)

Dickinson, P. L., *The Dublin of Yesterday* (London, Methuen, 1929)

Donegan, Lawrence, *No News at Throat Lake* (New York, Atria Books, 2000)

Dudgeon, Jeff, 'Mapping 100 years of Belfast Gay Life', *The Vacuum* (Belfast, Factotum, 2004)

Dunlop, John, 'Philosophy of Artificial and Compulsory Drinking Usage in Great Britain and Ireland', *Society and Politics in England, 1780– 1960* (London, Houlston and Stoneman, 1839)

Dunne, Catherine, *An Unconsidered People: The Irish in London* (Dublin, New Island Books, 2003)

Durkheim, Emile, *Suicide* (Chicago, Free Press, 1951)

Dwyer, June, 'A Drop Taken: The Role of Drinking in the Fiction and Drama of the Irish Literary Revival', *Contemporary Drug Problems* (1986)

Eagleton, Terry, *Crazy John and the Bishop and other Essays on Irish culture* (Cork, Cork University Press, 1998)

Eagleton, Terry, *The Truth about the Irish* (London, St Martin's Griffin, 2001)

Eames, Alan D., *The Secret Life of Beer: Legends, Lore and Little-Known Facts* (North Adams, MA, Storey Publishing, 2004)

Ellmann, Richard, *James Joyce* (Oxford, Oxford University Press, 1982)

Ellmann, Richard, *Yeats: The Man and the Masks* (London, W. L. Norton and Company, 1970)

Estyn Evans, E., *Irish Folkways* (London, Routledge and Keegan Paul, 1957)

Estyn Evans, E., *Irish Heritage: The Landscape, the People and their Work* (Dundalk, Dungalgan Press, 1943)

Fallon, Brian, *An Age of Innocence: Irish Culture 1930–1960* (Dublin: Gill & Macmillan, 1999)

Fallows, Marjorie, *Irish Americans: Identity and Assimilation* (Englewood Cliffs, NJ, Prentice-Hall, 1979)

Fanning, Charles, *The Irish Voice in America* (Kentucky, The University of Kentucky Printing Press, 1990)

Feeney, John, *John Charles McQuaid: The Man and the Mask* (Cork, Mercier Press, 1974)

Fennell, Desmond, *The State of the Nation: Ireland since the Sixties* (Dublin, Ward River Press, 1983)

Fennell, James, and Turtle Bunbury, *The Irish Pub* (New York, Thames & Hudson, 2008)

Ferriter, Diarmuid, *A Nation of Extremes: The Pioneers in Twentieth-Century Ireland* (Dublin, Irish Academic Press, 1999)

Fiske, John, *Introduction to Communications Studies* (London, Routledge, 1982)

Fiske, John, *Television Culture* (London, Methuen, 1987)

Fitzpatrick, David, *Irish Emigration, 1801–1921* (Dublin, Economic and Social History Society of Ireland, 1990)

Flavin, Susan, *Consumption and Culture in Sixteenth-Century Ireland: Saffrons, Stockings and Silk* (London, Boydell and Brewer, 2014)

Foley, Tony, *The Contribution of the Drinks Industry to Irish Tourism* (Drinks Industry Group of Ireland, 2013)

Forbes, Dr John, *Memorandums Made in Ireland in the Autumn of 1852* (London, Smith, Ellis & Company, 1853)

Foster, John Wilson, *Fictions of the Irish Literary Revival* (Dublin, Gill & Macmillan and Syracuse University Press, 1987)

Foster, R. F., *Modern Ireland, 1600–1972* (London, Allen Lane, 1988)

Gefou-Madianou, D. (ed.), *Alcohol, Gender and Culture* (London, Routledge, 1992)

Gibbons, Luke, *The Quiet Man* (Cork, Cork University Press, 2002)

Gibbons, Luke, *Transformations in Irish Culture* (Cork, Cork University Press, 1996)

Gifford, Don, *Joyce Annotated: Notes for Dubliners and A Portrait of the Artist as a Young Man* (Berkeley, University of California Press, 1967)

Gilley, S., 'English Attitudes to the Irish in Britain, 1780–1900', in Colin Holmes (ed.), *Immigrants and Minorities in British Society* (London, George Allen & Unwin, 1978)

Ginna, Robert Emmett, *The Irish Way: A Walk Through Ireland's Past and Present* (New York, Random House, 2003)

Graham, Brian, *In Search of Ireland: A Cultural Geography* (London, Routledge, 1997)

Grantham, Bill, 'Craic in a Box: Commodifying and Exporting the Irish Pub' in *Journal of Media and Cultural Studies*, 23, 2, (2009)

Gray, B. and K. Inan, *Irish Drinking: Breaking the Silence* (Alcohol Concern, 1990)

Gray, Tony, *Mr Smyllie, Sir* (Dublin, Gill & Macmillan, 1994)

Grebe, J. W. and Mark Morgan, 'The Irish and Alcohol: A Classic Case of Ambivalence' in *The Irish Journal of Psychology*, 15, 2-3 (1994)

Greenslade, L., M. Pearson, and M. Madden, 'A Good Man's Fault: Alcohol and the Irish People at Home and Abroad' in *Alcohol and Alcoholism*, 30, 4 (1995)

Gulliver, P. H. and Marilyn Silverman, *Merchants and Shopkeepers: A Historical Anthropology of an Irish Market Town, 1200–1991* (Toronto, University of Toronto Press, 1995)

Hadley, Charles, *An Inquiry into the Influence of Spirituous Liquors* (Dublin, Richard Milligan and Sons Ltd, 1830)

Hall, Samuel Carter and Anna Maria Hall, *Ireland: Its Scenery and Character* (London, Jeremiah How, 1843)

Hancock, W. N., *On the Statistics of Crime Arising from or Connected with Drunkenness, as Indicating the Importance of Increasing the Punishment of Habitual Drunkards and of Those who Seriously Injure their Children by what they Spend on Drink* (Economic Science and Statistics of the British Association, 1877)

Hansard's Parliamentary Debates (available online)

Harris, Rosemary, *Prejudice and Tolerance in Ulster: A Study of Neighbours and 'Strangers' in a Border Community* (Manchester, Manchester University Press, 1972)

Harrington, J. P., *The English Travel Writer in Ireland: Accounts of Ireland and the Irish through Five Centuries* (Dublin, Wolfhound Press, 1991)

Harrison, L. R., 'Consumption and Harm: Drinking Patterns of the Irish, the Irish in England and the English' in *The Journal of Alcohol and Alcoholism*, 28, 6 (1993)

Hatton, Harold Finch, *Advance Australia: An Account of Eight Ye**
Work, Wandering and Amusement in Queensland, New South Wa
and Victoria (London, W. H. Allen, 1886)

Haughton, James, *On the Connexion between Intemperance and Crim*
(Dublin, Dublin Statistical Society, 1849)

Haughton, James, *On the Intimate Connection Between Ignoranc*
Intemperance and Crime (The Dublin Statistical Society, 1851)

Haughton, James, *On the Necessity for Prompt Measures for th**
Suppression of Intemperance and Drunkenness (Statistical and Social
Inquiry Society of Ireland, 1857)

Haughton, James, *Some Facts which Support the Idea that the Desire for*
Alcoholic Stimulants Is not only Transmitted by Hereditary Descent,
but that it Is also Felt with Increasing Force from Generation to
Generation, thus Tends to Deteriorate the Human Race (Statistical and
Social Inquiry Society of Ireland, 1858)

Haughton, James, *Statistics of Crime* (The Dublin Statistical Society, 1850)

Haughton, James, *The Use of Alcoholic Liquors – Economically, Socially*
and Morally Wrong (Transactions of the Dublin Statistical Society,
1849)

Hayden, Tom, *Irish on the Inside: In Search of the Soul of Irish America*
(New York, Verso, 2001)

Healy, John, *No One Shouted Stop* (Achill, House of Healy, 1988)

Herring, Philip, *Joyce's Ulysses Note Sheets in the British Museum*
(Chicago, University of Chicago Press, 1974)

Hey, Valerie, *Patriarchy and Pub Culture* (London, Tavistock Publications,
1986)

Holmes, Gordon A., *Commission on Liquor Licensing: Final Report*
(Ireland, Department of Justice, Equality and Law Reform, 2003)

Hughes, Tadhg, *The Gift of the Gab: The Irish Conversation Guide*
(Dublin, O'Brien Press, 2012)

Igoe, Vivienne, *A Literary Guide to Dublin* (London, Methuen, 1994)

Inglis, Tom, 'Pleasure pursuits' in M. Corcoran & M. Peillon (eds) *Ireland*
Unbound: A Turn of the Century Chronicle (Dublin, Institute of Public
Administration, 2002)

Johnson, James, *A Tour of Ireland with Meditations and Reflections* (London, S. Highley, 1884)

Joyce, James, *A Portrait of the Artist as a Young Man* (New York, B. W. Huebsch, 1916)

Joyce, James, *Dubliners* (London, Grant Richards, 1914)

Joyce, James, *Finnegans Wake* (London, Faber and Faber, 1939)

Joyce, James, *Ulysses* (Paris, Shakespeare and Company, 1922)

Kavanagh, Patrick, *The Complete Poems* (Newbridge, The Goldsmith Press Limited, 1984)

Kavanagh, Peter, *Patrick Kavanagh: A Life Chronicle* (New York, The Peter Kavanagh Hand Press, 2010)

Kavanagh, Peter, *Sacred Keeper: A Biography of Patrick Kavanagh* (The Curragh, Ireland, 1979)

Kearns, Kevin, *Dublin Pub Life and Lore: An Oral History* (Dublin, Gill & Macmillan, 1996)

Kearns, Kevin, *Dublin Tenement Life* (Dublin, Gill & Macmillan, 1996)

Kearns, Kevin, *Streets Broad and Narrow: Images of Vanishing Dublin* (Dublin, Gill & Macmillan, 2000)

Kelly-Holmes, Helen, '"Strong words softly spoken": Advertising and the Intertextual Construction of Irishness' in Jonathon Smith and Ulrick Hanna Meinhoff, *Intertextuality and the Media: From Genre to Everyday Life* (Manchester, Manchester University Press, 2000)

Kennedy, Douglas, 'Where the Grass is Always Greener', *The Sunday Times* (10 November 1996)

Kennedy, Robert E., *The Irish, Emigration, Marriage and Fertility* (Berkeley and Los Angeles, University of California Press, 1973)

Kerrigan, C., *Father Matthew and the Temperance Movement* (Cork, Cork University Press, 1992)

Kiberd, Declan, *Inventing Ireland: The Literature of the Modern Nation* (London, Jonathan Cape, 1995)

Kiely, Benedict, *Drink to the Bird: A Memoir* (London, Methuen, 1974)

Kiely, Dr Jim, *Strategic Task Force on Alcohol: Second Report* (Ireland, Health Promotion Unit, Department of Health and Children, 2004)

King, R., 'Drinking and Drunkenness in *Crossroads* and *Coronation Street*' in J. Cook and M. Lewington (eds) *Images of Alcoholism* (London, British Film Institute, 1979)

Knupfer, Genevieve, Robin Room, 'Drinking Patterns and Attitudes of Irish, Jewish and White Protestant American Men' in *Quarterly Journal of Studies on Alcohol* (1967)

Larkin, Emmet, *James Larkin: Irish Labour Leader, 1876–1947* (London, Routledge & Kegan Paul, 1968)

Lawson, William, 'Licensing and Public House Reform in Ireland', *Statistical and Social Enquiry Society of Ireland*, 6 (1902)

Le Fanu, Joseph Sheridan, *The Cock and Anchor Dublin* (William Curry Junior and Company, 1845)

Lee, J. J., *Ireland, 1912–1985* (Cambridge University Press, 1989)

Lee, J. J., *The Modernisation of Irish society, 1848–1918* (Dublin, Gill & Macmillan, 1973)

Leitch, Maurice, *Liberty Lad* (Belfast, Blackstaff Press, 1985)

Lender, Mark Edward and James Kirby Martin, *Drinking in America: A History* (Ney York, The Free Press, 1982)

Lewis, G. C., *Observations on the Habits of the Labouring Classes of Ireland* (Dublin, Milken and Son, 1836)

Lindberg, Richard, *The Gambler King of Clark Street: Michael C. McDonald and the Rise of Chicago's Democratic Machine*, Elmer H Johnson & Carol Holmes Johnson Series in Criminology (Southern Illinois University Press, 2009)

Lyons, F. S. L., *Ireland Since the Famine* (London, Fontana Press, 1971)

Lyons, J. B., *Oliver St John Gogarty: The Man of Many Talents* (Dublin, 1980)

Lyons, J. B. 'The Drinking Days of Joyce and Lowry' in *The Malcolm Lowry Review* (1992)

Mac Amhlaigh, Donall, *An Irish Navvy: The Diary of an Exile* (London, Keegan Paul, 1964)

McBride, Joseph, *Searching for John Forde* (London, Faber and Faber, 2003)

McCarthy, Pete, *McCarthy's Bar* (London, Hodder and Stoughton, 2000)

McCormack, W. J., *Blackwell Companion to Modern Irish Culture* (Oxford, Blackwell Publishers Ltd, 1999)

Mac Donald, Michael Patrick, *All Souls: Growing Up in Boston's Irish Ghetto* (London, Little Browne, 2000)

McGowan, Philip, 'The Intemperate Irish in American Reform Literature' in *Irish Journal of American Studies,* 4 (1995)

McManus, Seamus, *The Story of the Irish People: A Popular History of Ireland* (Dublin, Irish Publishing Company, 1921)

McNabb, P., 'Social Structure' in J. Newman (ed.) *The Limerick Rural Survey 1958–1964* (Tipperary, Muintir na Tíre, 1967)

McNee, Gerald, *In the Footsteps of the Quiet Man* (Edinburgh, Mainstream, 1990)

McPherson, Conor, *The Weir* (London, Nick Hearne, 1998)

McRedmond, Louis (ed.), *Modern Irish Lives: Dictionary of 20th-Century Biography* (Dublin, Gill & Macmillan, 1998)

Madden, Aodhan, *Fear and Loathing in Dublin* (Dublin, Liberties Press, 2009)

Malcolm, Elizabeth, *Ireland Sober, Ireland Free: Drink and Temperance in Nineteenth Century Ireland* (Syracuse, Syracuse University Press, 1986)

Malcolm, Elizabeth, 'The Rise of the Pub: A Study in the Disciplining of Popular Culture' in *Irish Popular Culture 1650–1850* (Dublin, Irish Academic Press, 1998)

Malone, Aubrey, *Historic Pubs of Dublin* (Dublin, New Island Books, 2001)

Mass Observation, *The Pub and the People: A Worktown Study* (London, Gollancz, 1943)

Massie, Sonja, *The Complete Idiot's Guide to Irish History and Culture* (Indianapolis, Alpha Books, 1999)

Messenger, John Cowan, *Inis Beag: Isle of Ireland* (United States, Waveland Press, 1983)

Messenger, John Cowan, *Inis Beag Revisited: The Anthropologist as Observant Participator* (Salem, Wisconsin: Sheffield, 1989)

Messenger, John Cowan, 'Sex and Repression in an Irish Folk Community' in Donald S. Marshall and Robert C. Suggs (eds), *Human Sexual Behavior: Variations in the Ethnographic Spectrum* (New York, Basic Books, 1971)

Miller, Karen, *Emigrants and Exiles: Ireland and the Irish exodus to North America* (New York, Oxford Publications, 1985)

Molloy, Cian, *The Story of the Irish pub* (Dublin, Liffey Press, 2002)

Monaghan, David, *Jaywalking with the Irish* (Lonely Planet Travel Literature, 2004)

Mooney, Jennifer, *Irish Stereotypes in Vaudeville 1865* (New York, Palgrave and Macmillan, 2015)

Moore, George, *A Drama in Muslin: A Realistic Novel* (Vizetelly and Company, 1886)

Morewood, Samuel, *An Essay on the Inventions and Customs of Both Ancients and Moderns in the Use of Inebriating Liquor* (London, A. and R. Spottiswoode, 1824)

Morewood, Samuel, *A Philosophical and Statistical History of the Inventions and Customs of Ancient and Modern Nations in the Manufacture and Use of Inebriating Liquors; with the Present Practice of Distillation in all its Varieties: Together with an Extensive Illustration of the Consumption and Effects of Opium, and other Stimulants Used in the East, as Substitutes for Wine and Spirits* (Dublin, W. Curry and W. Carson, 1838)

Morris, Desmond, *Pub Watching with Desmond Morris* (London, Sutton Press, 1993)

Moryson, Fynes, *An Itinerary, Written by Fynes Moryson, Gent, First in the Latine Tongue, and then Translated by him into English: Containing his ten Yeeres Travell through the Twelve Dominions of Germany, Bohmerland, Sweitzerland, Netherland, Denmarke, Poland, Italy, Turky, France, England, Scotland, and Ireland* (London, J. Beale, 1617)

Muhlin, G. L. 'Ethnic Differences in Alcohol Misuse: A Striking Reaffirmation', *Journal of Alcohol Studies*, 46 (1985)

Muir R., *Public Houses and Places: The Social Value of Community Public houses* (London, IPPR, 2009)

Murphy, John, *Irish Shopfronts and Pubs* (San Francisco, Chronicle Book, 1994)

Murphy, Tom, *A Whistle in the Dark* (London, Bloomsbury Methuen Drama, 1989)

Murphy, Tom, *Conversations on a Homecoming* (Dublin, Gallery Press, 1985)

Nast, Thomas 'Saint Patrick's Day . . . Rum Blood . . . The Day We Celebrate' (cartoon) in *Harpers Weekly* (New York, Harper and Brothers, 1872)

Negra, Diane, *The Irish in Us: Irishness, Performativity and Popular Culture* (Durham, Duke University Press, 2006)

Nemo, John, *Patrick Kavanagh* (Boston, Twayne, 1979)

Newby, Eric, *Round Ireland in Low Gear* (London, Collins, 1987)

Nolan, Pat, *Drinks Industry Ireland* (Dublin, Louisville Publishing Ltd, 2010)

Norris, David, *A Kick Against the Pricks* (Dublin, Transworld Ireland, 2012)

O'Brien, Darcy, *Patrick Kavanagh* (Lewisburg, Bracknell University Press)

O'Brien, Edna, *Mother Ireland* (London, Penguin Books, 1976)

O'Brien, Gareth, 'Breaking the Code of Silence: The Irish and Drink', *Irish American Magazine* (2012)

O'Casey, Sean, *The Plough and the Stars* (London, Faber and Faber, 2001)

O'Ciarain, Sean, *Farewell to Mayo* (Dublin, Brookside, 1991)

O'Connor, Barbara 'Myths and Mirrors: Tourist Images and National Identity' in B. O'Connor and Mike Cronin (eds), *Tourism in Ireland: A Critical Analysis* (Cork, Cork University Press, 1993)

O'Connor, Garry, *Sean O'Casey: A Life* (London, Hodder and Stoughton, 1988)

O'Connor, K., *The Irish in Britain* (Dublin, Torc Book, 1974)

O'Connor, Ulick, *Brendan Behan* (Dublin, Abacus Press, 1993)

O'Connor, Ulick, *Oliver St John Gogarty* (London, Mandarin Paperbacks, 1990)

O'Farrell, P., *The Irish in Australia* (Kensington, New South Wales University Press, 1987)

O'Gorman, Andrew, *A Handbook for the Licensed Trade* (Dublin, A. O'Gorman, 1994)

Ó Gráda, Cormac, *Ireland: A New Economic History* (Oxford, Oxford University Press, 1994)

O'Hehir, Brendan and Dillon, John L., *A Classical Lexicon for Finnegans Wake* (Berkeley, University of California Press, 1977)

O'Neill, Timothy, *Life and Tradition in Rural Ireland* (London, J. M. Dent, 1977)

O'Rahilly, Thomas Francis, *Early Irish History and Mythology* (Dublin Institute for Advanced Studies, 1957)

O'Reilly, James (ed.), Larry Habegger and Sean O'Reilly, *Travelers' Tales Ireland, True Stories of Life on the Emerald Isle* (San Francisco: Travelers' Tales, Inc., 2003)

O'Sullivan, Michael, *Brendan Behan: A Life* (Dublin, Blackwater Press, 1997)

Oldenburg, Ray, *The Great Good Place: Cafés, Coffee Shops, Commumity Centres, Beauty Parlors, General Stores, Bars, Hangouts, and How They Get You through the Day* (New York, Marlowe & Co, 1997)

Oldenburg, Ray, *The Great Good Place: Our Vanishing Third Place* (New York, Marlowe, 1999)

Osborne, H., 'Prevention and Elimination of Disease, Insanity, Drunkenness, and Crime – A Suggestion', *Statistical and Social Inquiry Society of Ireland*, Vol. X (1895)

Oway, Caesar, *Sketches in Ireland, Descriptive of Interesting Portions of the Counties of Donegal, Cork, and Kerry* (Dublin, W. Curry, Jr. & Co, 1839)

Pepper, Barrie, *Irish Pubs* (Orpingtin, Kent, Eric Dobby, 1998)

Perceval, R., 'Alcohol and Alcoholism in the Republic of Ireland', *International Journal on Alcohol and Alcoholism* (1955)

Peter, Ada, *Dublin Fragments Social and Historic* (Dublin, Hodges, Figgis & Co, 1925)

Petty, William, *Political Economy of Ireland* (Cambridge University, 1691)

Phipps, William, *The Vintners Guide Compiled by William Phipps Containing Useful Information as well for the Vintner as for the Brewer, Distiller and Merchant* (Dublin, J. Bromell, 1825)

Piers, Sir Henry, *Chronological Description of the County of Westmeath* (Dublin, 1786)

Pittman, David, 'International Overview: Social and Cultural Factors in Drinking Patterns, Pathological and Non-Pathological' in D. Pittman (ed.), *Alcoholism* (New York, Harper & Row, 1967)

Pittman, David J. and Charles R. Snyder, *Society, Culture, and Drinking Patterns* (New York, John Wiley and Sons, 1962)

Pixley, William, *The Statistical Journal and Record of Useful Knowledge* (London, Cunningham and Salmen, various)

Plunkett, Horace, *Ireland in the New Century* (London, John Murray, 1905)

Powers, Madelon, *Faces Along the Bar: Lore and Order in the Working Man's Saloon, 1870–1920* (Chicago, University of Chicago Press, 1998)

Purcell, Mary, *Remembering Matt Talbot* (Dublin, Veritas, 1954)

Quantick, David, *Grumpy Old Men: A Manual for the British Malcontent* (London, Harper Collins, 2000)

Quilligan, Colm, *Dublin Literary Pubs and the Writers they Served* (Dublin, Writers Island, 2008)

Quinn, Antoinette, *Patrick Kavanagh: A Biography* (Dublin, Gill & Macmillan, 2003)

Quinn, J. F., *Father Mathew's Crusade: Temperance in Nineteenth-Century Ireland and Irish America* (Amherst, University of Massachusetts Press, 2002)

Rae, Stephen, *Killers: Murders in Ireland* (Dublin, Blackwater Press, 1998)

Rees, Catherine, *Changes in Contemporary Ireland: Texts and Contexts* (Cambridge Scholars Publishing, 2014)

Rhodes, Gary, D., *Emerald Illusions, The Irish in Early American Cinema* (Dublin, Irish Academic Press, 2012)

Rich, Barnaby, *A New Description of Ireland* (London, Thomas Adams, 1610)

Rich, Barnaby, *The Irish Hubbub* (London, Matthews, 1622)

Robinson, Lennox, *The Dreamers: A Play in Three Acts* (Dublin, Maunsel and Company, 1915)

Rockette, Kevin 'The Irish Migrant and Film' in *Screening Irish America* (Dublin, Irish Academic Press, 2009)

Rockette, Kevin, Luke Gibbons and John Hill, *Cinema and Ireland* (New York, Taylor and Francis, 2014)

Room, Robin, *Alcohol and Developing Societies: A Public Health Approach* (Helsinki, Finnish Foundation for Alcohol Studies & Geneva, World Health Organization, 2002)

Ross, D., 'Suggested Practical Checks on Excessive Drinking and Habitual Drunkenness', *Statistical and Social Inquiry Society of Ireland*, 6 (1875)

Roth, Eric, and Eileen McNamara, *The Parting Glass: A Toast to the Traditional Pubs of Ireland.* (New York, Stewart, Tabori & Chang, 2006)

Russell, George, 'The Liquor Commission', *Irish Statesman* (4 April 1925)

Ryan, John, *Remembering How We Stood: Bohemian Dublin at the Mid Century* (Dublin, Gill & Macmillan, 1975)

Scarbrough, Gwen, 'New Places, Non Places and the Changing Landscape of the Irish Pub' in *Irish Sociological Chronicles*, 6 (Dublin, Institute of Public Administration, 2008)

Schlepper-Hughes, Nancy, *Saints, Scholars and Schizophrenics Mental Illness in Rural Ireland* (Berkeley, University of California Press, 2001)

Scott, Y., *A Study of Licensed Premises: A Report Commissioned by the Drinks Industry Group* (Dublin, DIG, 1994)

Select Committee on Drunkenness of the House of Commons, *Evidence on Drunkenness presented to the House of Commons* (London, 1834)

Share, Perry, *A Genuine 'Third Place'? Towards an Understanding of the Pub in Contemporary Irish Society* (30th SAI Annual Conference, Cavan, 26 April 2003)

Shea, Ann M., and Marion R. Casey, *The Irish Experience in New York City: A Select Bibliography*(New York, New York Irish History Roundt able, 1995)

Sheridan Le Fanu, Joseph, *The Cock and Anchor: Being a Chronicle of Old Dublin City* (Dublin, W. Curry, 1845)

Silva, Corrine and Roisin Ban, *The Irish Diaspora in Leeds* (Leeds, Leeds Irish Health and Homes, 2006)

SIRC (Social Issues Research Centre), *Social and Cultural Aspects of Drinking: report to the European Commission* (Oxford, SIRC, 1998)

SIRC, *The Enduring Power of the Local* (Oxford, SIRC, 2008)

Slater, Eamon, 'When the Local Goes Global' in E. Slater and M. Peillon (eds) *Memories of the Present: A Sociological Chronicle of Ireland 1997–1998* (Dublin, Institute of Public Administration, 2000)

Slater, I., *National Commercial Directory of Ireland Including, in Addition to the Trades' Lists, Alphabetical Directories of Dublin, Belfast, Cork and Limerick: To Which Are Added, Classified Directories of the Important English Towns of Manchester, Liverpool, Birmingham, West Bromwich, Leeds, Sheffield and Bristol, and in Scotland, Those of Glasgow, Paisley and Greenock* (Manchester, I. Slater, 1846)

Smith, M. A., *Leisure, the Public House and Social Control* (Centre for Leisure Studies, University of Salford, 1982)

Smith, M. A., *The Pub and the Publican* (Centre for Leisure Studies, University of Salford, 1981)

Sommerville-Large, Peter, *Dublin* (London, Hamish Hamilton, 1979)

Stivers, Richard 'Historical Meanings of Irish American Drinking' in L. Bennett and G. Ames (eds) *The American Experience of Alcohol* (New York, Plenum Press, 1985)

Stivers, Richard, *Hair of the Dog: Irish Drinking and its American Stereotype* (New York and London, Continuum, 2000)

Swift, R. and S. Gilley, *The Irish in Britain, 1815–1939* (London: Gill & Macmillan, 1989)

Synge, John Millington, *The Playboy of the Western World* (New York, Dover Publications, 1993)

Taylor, Sybil, *Ireland's Pubs: The Life and Lore of Ireland through its Finest Pubs* (Middlesex, Penguin Books, 1983)

Thom's Official Directory (Dublin, 1850–70)

Thorne, R., 'Places of Refreshment in the Nineteenth-Century City' in A. D. King (ed.), *Buildings and Society* (London, Routledge & Kegan Paul Ltd, 1980)

Tilki Mary, 'The Social Contexts of Drinking Among Irish Men in London: Evidence from a Qualitative Study' in *Drugs: Education, Prevention and Policy,* 13,3 (2006)

Tod, I. M. S., 'On the Principles on which Plans for the Curative Treatment of Habitual Drunkards Should be Based', Statistical and Social Inquiry Society of Ireland, VI (1875)

Tönnies, Ferdinand, *Gemeinschaft Und Gesellschaft* (Community and Civil Society) (J. Harris and M. Hollis, transl. Cambridge, Cambridge University Press, 1887)

Tovey, Hilary and Perry Share, *Sociology of Ireland* (Dublin, Gill & Macmillan, 2003)

Townsend, Paul A., *Father Mathew: Temperance and Irish Identity* (Dublin, Irish Academic Press, 2002)

Tracy, Honor, *Mind You, I've Said Nothing: Forays in the Irish Republic* (London, Methuen and Company Ltd, 1953)

Uris, Jill and Leon, *Ireland: A Terrible Beauty* (London, Corgi, 1976)

Ussher, Arland, *The Face and Mind of Ireland* (London, Victor Gollancz, 1949)

Wakefield, Edward Gibbon, *An Account of Ireland, Statistical and Political in Two Volumes* (London, Longman, Hurst, Rees, Orme and Brown, 1812)

Walsh, B. M. and D. Walsh, 'Drowning the Shamrock: Alcohol and Drink in Ireland in the Post-War Period' in Single et al. (eds) *Alcohol, Society and the State* (London, Palgrave Macmillan, 1981)

Walshe, John Edward, *Rakes and Ruffians: The Underworld of Georgian Dublin* (London, Rowman and Littlefield, 1979)

Waters, John, *Jiving at the Crossroads* (Belfast, Blackstaff Press, 1991)

Waters, Maureen, *The Comic Irishman* (Albany, New York, State University of New York Press, 1984)

Weld, Isaac, *Illustrations of the Scenery of Killarney and the Surrounding Country* (London, Longman, Hurst, Rees & Orme, 1807)

Whelan and Layte in Fahy, Russell and Whelan, *Best of Times? The Social Impact of the Celtic Tiger* (Dublin, Institute of Public Administration, 2007)

Whitelaw, James, *An Essay on the Population of Dublin Being the Result of an Actual Survey taken in 1798* (Dublin, Graisberry and Campbell, 1805)

Whyte, J. W., *Church and State in Modern Ireland* (Dublin, Gill & Macmillan, 1980)

William, H. A., *'Twas Only an Irishman's Dream: The Image of Ireland and the Irish in American Popular Song Lyrics, 1800–1920* (Urbana, University of Illinois Press, 1996)

Williams, Niall and Christine Breen, *O Come Ye Back Home to Ireland: Our First Year in County Clare* (New York, Soho Press, 1987)

Wilson, R. W., & Williams, G. D. 'Alcohol Use and Abuse among US Minority Groups: Results from the 1983 National Health Interview Study' in D. L. Spiegler, D. A. Tate, S. A. Aitken, and C. M. Christian (eds), *Alcohol Use Among US Ethnic Minorities* (Rockville, US Department of Health and Human Services, 1989)

Wilson, Thomas, *Drinking Cultures: Alcohol and Identity* (Oxford, Berg Publishers, 2005)

Wilson, Thomas M. and Hastings Donnan, *The Anthropology of Ireland* (Oxford: Berg, 2006)

Woodham-Smith, Cecil, *The Great Hunger* (New York, Harper & Row, 1963)

Woods, James and Nicola J. Adams, *Liquor Licencing Laws in Ireland* (Self-published, 2011)

Young, Henry, *A Short Essay on the Grievous Crime of Drunkenness* (Dublin, 1823)